Black and Not Baptist

BLACK AND NOT BAPTIST

Nonbelief and Freethought in the Black Community

Donald R. Barbera

iUniverse, Inc.
New York Lincoln Shanghai

Black and Not Baptist
Nonbelief and Freethought in the Black Community

All Rights Reserved © 2003 by Donald R Barbera

No part of this book may be reproduced or transmitted in any form or by any means, graphic, electronic, or mechanical, including photocopying, recording, taping, or by any information storage retrieval system, without the written permission of the publisher.

iUniverse, Inc.

For information address:
iUniverse, Inc.
2021 Pine Lake Road, Suite 100
Lincoln, NE 68512
www.iuniverse.com

ISBN: 0-595-28789-1

Printed in the United States of America

Contents

Thank You xi
Preface: Nonbelief and Skepticism In The Black Community 1
    Getting Started 3
    Organization 9
    A Word On Polls 10
    Explanation of Terms 11

RELIGION AND THE BLACK COMMUNITY

Chapter 1:   Race and Religion 17
    The Black Monolith 17
    The Negro Thought Police 19
    Where is the Variety of Thought? 20
    Religion Is Serious Business 21
    Changing Times 21
    Tolerance and Forbearance 22
    A Different Perspective 24

Chapter 2:   The Black Church 26
    The Black Church Today 27
    New Way of Counting 28
    Lying for the Church 28

    Culture and Decline 29

    Non Religious Growing 30

    American Individualism 31

    Females Dominate United States Religion 33

    End of Days 34

    The Church as Entertainment 34

    Social Aspects of Church 37

Chapter 3:   Understanding Black Religion 39

    Slave Christianity 40

    Diversity of Slave Religion 41

    Christianity and Africa 42

    The Bible and Slavery 45

    Islam and Slavery 46

Chapter 4:   Black Belief 47

    Belief in God 48

    The Bible 49

    Education and Religion 51

Chapter 5:   Sleeping with Extraterrestrials 52

    At Home With Superstition 53

    Paranormal is Almost Normal 53

    Psychics for the Community 56

    Psychic Surgeons and Faith Healers 58

    The Power of Prayer? 58

    Faith Healers 59

    After All These Years 61

The Religious Landscape

Chapter 6:   Global Religious Estimates 65

    Religious Splits and Rifts 66
Chapter 7:   Religion in the United States 68
    Common Ground 68
    The Short End of the Stick 69
    Religious Shift 71

BELIEF & BEHAVIOR

Chapter 8:   Actions Speak Louder Than Words 75
    Who's Fooling Whom? 76
    Crime 76
    Was It Good for Us? 78
    Rape 83
    Prostitution 84
    Pornography 85
    Strip Clubs Growing in Popularity 87
    Spousal Abuse and Child Abuse 88
    Drug Abuse 89
    Alcohol Abuse 89
    Degrading Music 90
    Smoking 91
    Gambling 91
    White Collar Crime 94
Chapter 9:   No One is Immune 98
    Fleecing the Flock 100
    Prosperity Preaching 101
    Show Me the Money? 103
    Sexual Impropriety 104

GOING AGAINST THE GRAIN

Chapter 10: Black Nonbelievers 109
- Why Do Blacks Become Atheists or Agnostics 109
- Who, Why and Where 110
- Family Life 111
- Traditional God 112
- Suffering and Pain 114
- Morals and Ethics 115
- Intellect 116
- Women and the Black Church 116
- God and Children 117
- Afterlife 118
- Fundamentalism 118
- Black Reaction 119
- Intolerance 120
- Religion 120
- The Black Church 121
- Breaking Away 123
- The Importance of Coming Out 127

Chapter 11: The Infidels 128
- Reginald Finley 128
- Frances Parker 131
- Naima Washington 133

Chapter 12: Other Black Atheists 137
- Glenn Ellison Jr. 137
- Chris Felton 138
- Eddie Daniel Glover 140
- Sid Davis 141

Charles Cooke 145

　　J. R. Ector 147

　　Kareem Lane 149

　　Omari Christian 150

　　Eugene Globe 151

　　Wayne Evans 152

　　John Rogers 152

Chapter 13: Atheist Essays, Letters and Conversations 153

　　Are Black People Too Religious? by Patrick Inniss 153

　　We Are Condemned by Frances Parker 156

　　African-American Atheism and the Appeal to Culture by Frances Parker 157

　　Divine Paternal Absence? by Adrian Archer 160

　　The Last Unfavorable Minority by Chaka Ferguson 161

　　Atheists and Agnostics—Any Difference? 2001, a Discussion from the Black Freethinkers website 163

　　The Crisis of the Religious Black Intellectual by Norm R. Allen, Jr. 166

IS IT TIME TO REEVALUATE THE ROLE OF RELIGION?

Chapter 14:　September 11, 2001 171

Chapter 15:　Conclusion—They Do Protest Too Much 174

　　On Ignorance 178

　　How Much Intolerance? 184

　　No Protection for Nonbelievers 185

　　Danger in Religion? 186

　　Compromising Health 188

　　Morality Without God 190

　　Concerns 192

　　Calling Religion to Task 194

Chapter 16: Alternatives and Options 199
    Universalist Unitarians 199
    Humanism 201
    African Americans for Humanism 203
    Humanism and Atheism 204

Appendix: History of Black Nonbelief and Skepticism, etc. 205
Atheists, Freethinkers, Nonbelievers, Skeptics, Etc. 207
About the Author 231
Endnotes 233

Thank You

Many people helped me with this project. Some helped by just taking the time to talk with me. Some helped by volunteering their assistance and actually putting me in contact with other people. Some helped in pointing out historical references and sources for freethought and nonbelief, while others helped by encouraging me to continue.

First, I would like to thank Frances Parker, Naima Washington and Reginald Finley for their willingness to become the "three" Black atheists and for their patience, input and knowledge. Frances is a fellow writer and the author of Bad Faith, a brief novel that examines nonbelief and religious conflict. Frances also contributed two essays that appear in Chapter 13: Atheist Essays, Letters and Conversations. Billed as America's most dangerous Black atheist, Reginald is the host of a popular Internet talk show, The Infidel Guy, which regularly features interviews with a variety of freethinkers, intellects and academics. He is controversial, thoughtful and unafraid. Naima is a special person who is unafraid to speak her mind or share her knowledge. She resides in New York City and is a feminist, humanist, activist and an avid Flo Kennedy fan.

Special thanks also go to Norm Allen Jr. who helped get me started on my search and provided invaluable feedback and information that helped get this project rolling. Norm is the author of *African-American Humanism: An Anthology*. His most recent book is The *Black Humanist Experience: An Alternative to Religion*. Special thanks also go to Dr. Anthony Pinn for answering an "out of the blue" correspondence and for his candor and inspiration to keep going. Dr. Pinn is the author of *Why Lord? Suffering and Evil in Black Theology* and the recently published, *Varieties of African American Religious Experience*. Thanks to Bonnie Lange, editor of the Truth Seeker, who surprised me with a personal call and extended conversation. Thanks also to Warren Allen Smith whose work provided much information that I needed and whose correspondence were both helpful and enlightening, as well as, entertaining and informative. Thanks to syndicated columnist Dr. Charles W. Faulkner for his insight and cooperation. A special salute to all of my Internet friends at the Black Freethinkers web site, who all contributed, encouraged and helped me keep a fresh perspective, http://groups.yahoo.com/group/Black_freethinkers. Thanks to all of the following people who if they did not contribute directly to this effort, directed me to someone who could help or provided information or encouragement: Judith Hayes, Dr. Corey Washington, Michael Werner, John Hattan, Carol Smith (editor, Humanist Quest of Milwaukee), James Underdown, (Executive Director, Center for Inquiry-West, The West Coast's Home of Science and Reason), Bobbie Kirkhart, Thomas Flemming (Historian), John Gentry (Ex-Christian Organization), Ralph Dumain, Margaret Downey, Steven Mahone (Board of Directors, Freethinkers of Colorado Springs), Reed Esau (Celebrity Atheist List), Susan Sackett (President, HSGP), Kel Crum, Steve Landale (Interim Minister, All Souls Church, Unitarian Universalist, New London, CT), Jimmy Dunne (President of Humanists of Houston), David Bodner, Dr. Yehudi Webster, Steve Yothment (AFS VP, Editor of Atlanta Freethought News), Rev. Adele Smith-Penniman, Dorothy L. Weir, Rev. Art McDonald (Allegheny UU Church, Pittsburgh), John Buehrens, Eric Krieg, Richard C. Carrier, Bill Schultz, Will Frank, Shana Goodwin, Rev. Gordon Clay Bailey, Jan Sacowicz and Hasani Kudura.

Last and certainly not least, I thank my wife of 20 years, Deedee. Through the rewrites, revisions and reviews, she stayed close and more importantly—understanding. She is my worst critic and my strongest supporter and I thank her for being both.

Don R. Barbera

Preface:

Nonbelief and Skepticism In The Black Community

If the concept of God has any validity or use, it can only be to make us larger, freer, and more loving. If God cannot do this, then it is time we got rid of him—James Baldwin, The Fire Next Time (1963)

God has been replaced, as he has all over the West, with respectability and air conditioning—Imamu Amiri Baraka, "What Does Non-Violence Mean?" Home, 1966

Preface:

Nonbelief and Skepticism in the Black Community

"In religion and politics, people's beliefs and convictions are in almost every case gotten at second-hand, and without examination."

—Mark Twain

Any writing about religion in the Black community is a complex undertaking and this book holds no illusions of even scratching the surface of Black nonbelief much less of being an exhaustive study of it. In many ways, it is nothing more than an expansion of my curiosity about a taboo subject—atheism. The main purpose of this book is to show that nonbelief exists in the United States Black community and to introduce the reader to these people, including their opinions and thoughts on a variety of subjects. Because my research uncovered such a variety of philosophies and lifestyles, a portion of this book will focus on the current religious climate in both the Black and white communities, including an examination of the overall effectiveness of religion in changing behavior.

GETTING STARTED

I thought this book would write itself. The topic is controversial, unusual and about a rarely discussed subject in the Black community—nonbelief. Why write a book about Black nonbelievers? Because, contrary to popular stereotypes in both the Black and white communities—they exist.

Maya Angelou once said in a speech, "I know people that swear there are more than 50 million Black people in the Baptist church. And there are only three Black atheists in the whole world."[1] Even though spoken in jest, on the surface it appears her comment is not far off the mark. That comment stirred my curiosity enough for me to consider looking into it.

When my uncle Syl died two summers ago, my consideration grew even more when I found out that he was an atheist. Uncle Syl was many things during his lifetime including a musician, actor, artist and poet. I remember him having a small part in the movie *Carmen Jones* starring Harry Belafonte and Dorothy Dandridge. Both he and my Aunt Dominica were always open to the outrageous ideas of their hyperactive nephew. I remember the lemon tree in their back yard in Watts, the tetherball pole where my cousin Tina whipped my ass regularly while my cousin Olive looked on and laughed at my incompetence, but I have no memories of Uncle Sylvester's atheism.

I realize now that there was probably good reason why I didn't know. My mother attended a Catholic boarding school and her mother was a devoted Catholic. My father also came from a staunch Catholic background. Considering those roots, it is little wonder I didn't know. What I didn't know then is that most atheists don't advertise. Still, my Uncle Syl's atheism intrigued me and I began to wonder how many other Black men and women were out there living otherwise normal lives—without religion or God. As a freethinker and former print journalist, my instincts came alive immediately and I started to consider how I could find these people who live free of traditional religion, which if you are Black, means Christianity.

I know a few Black Catholics, as most of my family is Catholic. I know the number of Black Catholics in this country is small in comparison to the number of Black Baptists. I certainly knew plenty of Baptists growing up, as it seemed to be the most popular denomination in my neighborhood and town. African Methodist Episcopalians, Muslims, Holiness and even Lutheran's were also familiar to me, but I knew of no Black atheists—at least not any that were alive. I was familiar with the atheists of the Harlem Renaissance, but I didn't know of one present-day Black atheist. So, I set out to find the "three Black atheists" of the jest.

Researching the Subject

Although, this started as a search for three Black atheists—it turned into an expedition into various religious beliefs including an enlightening history of freethought, humanism and atheism in the Black community. The first thing I did as I prepared for the writing of this book was to begin to research atheism as a subject. Entering the world of atheism is an immersion in logical arguments, theories of reason and the rules of evidence. It is a world where nothing is sacred and everything is open to question.

Researching Black belief patterns was both predictable and enlightening. It was predictable in that my findings told me what I already knew and that is that most Blacks are highly religious, have little doubt that God exists and that the Baptist denomination is the most popular among Blacks in the United States. It was also enlightening to find out about Black humanists and that sub-Saharan Africa is predominantly Christian and Catholic, even though it is Christianity with a tribal twist.

I knew there were Black atheists in the United States and I knew there had to be more than three. It seemed they would be easy to find in this age of high-speed communications and the Internet. I was wrong. When I started, if there were any Black atheist out there, none of them hung out shingles announcing it and as a member of a historically oppressed class, I certainly understood. It is tough enough being a Black person in the United States without calling additional attention to one's self by announcing such an unpopular stance, but I figured that at the very least I would be able to find three Black atheists. Unfortunately, for me, most Black nonbelievers stay submerged in an ocean of Black Christianity and give no clue to their existence or whereabouts.

I started my research on the Internet and I immediately found a host of atheist and agonistic web sites but none with any visible Black connections. I found an article on the Harlem Renaissance, but the article did me little good because all the Black atheists, freethinkers or humanists the article mentioned are dead. I continued my search on the web using "mega" and "meta" search-engines, but I kept finding the same articles, until I stumbled across the American Atheist home page.

One web search led me to an article by the late John G. Jackson that gave an overview of prominent atheists and freethinkers of the Harlem Renaissance, including A. Phillip Randolph, Hubert Harrison and others. I thought it would go quickly since I had found a starting point, but once again, I was wrong. However, the related web links featured a tie to *The Secular Humanist* home page. I did not know what I would find on that link, but I was hoping that it would provide some direction. It did. The link to the Secular Humanist Home page put me in contact with Norm Allen Jr., Executive Director of the African Americans for Humanism organization and author of *African American Humanism: An Anthology*. He is also the editor of *The African American Humanist Newsletter*.

Based in Buffalo, New York, *The African American Humanist Newsletter* publishes articles relating to humanist activities, the separation of church and state and a variety of essays and articles relating to humanism and free thought. It resulted in my subscribing to the newsletter and familiarizing myself with African American humanism. After I read Mr. Allen's book, I decided to start corresponding with him and it was through that correspondence that the name of Dr. Anthony Pinn came up. Dr. Pinn is an associate professor of theology at McAlester College of Minnesota.

Searching the web, I found a variety of Dr. Pinn's essays and several books written by him including, *Lord Why? So Much Suffering* and *African American Beliefs*. It was easy to see he held a different view of religion in the Black community and he had published several books chronicling his studies. I read both of his books and was at once enlightened and intrigued. Both Mr. Allen and Dr. Pinn believe the individual is the ultimate master of their fate and put little confidence in traditional religious belief.

I also started to correspond with Dr. Pinn on a variety of subjects relating to religious belief in the United States and in the Black community in particular. Both Dr. Pinn and Mr. Allen are Black, humanists and atheists, but I didn't count them in my search simply because they were the first two I found and they are not typical of the average Black atheist as both are writers and well known in the humanist and freethought community.

Though I continued my correspondence with Dr. Pinn and Mr. Allen, my search continued without much success although my knowledge was growing, as were the number of Blacks I knew who had a differing point of view. While I was not finding many people, I was finding plenty of information about humanism, freethought, agnosticism, atheism and alternate types of belief apart from Christianity. This not only helped give me some understanding of the topics but it also helped me prepare questions for when I did find these invisible people—the three Black atheists.

My luck changed when I began examining databases. There are literally thousands of databases available on the Internet and my first search produced a list of more than 100 Black agnostics and atheists. I was excited for about 30 seconds because it dawned on me that I would need to contact each one of them and judging from the few I'd met, I realized how closely guarded they are and knew they probably would not appreciate the intrusion.

My initial goal was to contact 1,000 people with the minimal hope of getting at least 50 replies. A form e-mail requesting help in my research went to each of 1,000+persons identifying themselves as Black atheists, humanists or agnostics. I received 76 replies from my first try, which far exceeded my hopes. Unfortunately, 60 of them essentially said, "lose this address" which I did, but my second try produced better results. I received 117 replies from which I sorted until I had 30 left. There was no specific criterion for my selection of that number.

I eliminated responses from respondents under 18 although I captured and logged their comments. I did not think a 13-year-old had lived long enough to be sure, knowing from experience how volatile and subject to change the teen years are even for those who can be sure, it was also a legal consideration. I received replies from respondents of African descent in several countries including Great Britain, Canada, the Netherlands and even Brazil. I also eliminated these but kept the information. My only selection criterion was to make sure the respondents were between 20 and 60 which was also an arbitrary choice, and that they represented a wide range of geography and gender. My survey was in no way scientific nor was it intended to be. It was simply a way to collect opinions on a variety of subjects and to capture the voices of a diverse group that few believe exists in the "Black community."

Because of the large number of records in each database I searched, my inquiries were necessarily limited. For instance, my primary source had over 1.6 million records. From those records, I counted a total of 751 Black agnostics and 264 Black atheists, which accounted for less than 1 percent of the total records. Of the agnostics, there were 429 males and 322 females. Among the atheists, there were 166 males and 98 females. Although I searched seven other databases, the results remained consistent. Within the primary database, approximately 40,000 people claimed "none" as a religious preference, which represents approximately 4.5 percent of the total. Ages for atheists and agnostics ranged from 13 years old to 81. However, 55 percent of atheists were under 30. Interestingly many of those claiming "none" didn't know they were actually Christian.

Delving into the world of nonbelief and doubt of Christian religious tradition is akin to walking through a minefield wearing a blindfold and is much more dangerous because the opportunity for offending or affronting "believers" increases as one moves deeper into the field. Judging from the responses I received, my delving into this area was not always welcome and certainly not understood. Many of those who contacted me thought that to even seek another point of view was blasphemous. Many thought that I would certainly be condemned to eternal damnation if not struck down on the spot. Others thought that I was only misguided and would "give up this nonsense" of finding nonbelievers in the Black community. These replies came from those Blacks who had mistakenly identified themselves agnostics or atheists.

Research on the Web

Doing research on the Internet is interesting but often imprecise. The World Wide Web presents an abundance of information and misinformation and it is often difficult to tell one from the other. Some information comes from known sources such as the Gallup Poll, the federal government and well-respected colleges and universities. However, there is just as much "unsure" data on the web that comes from unidentified sources with personal agendas and/or hidden agendas. There are sites on-line that are excellent sources like university libraries and the Library of Congress or a collection of news magazines like *Time* and *Newsweek*. In addition, there are private organizations such as the Secular Humanist organization, the Atheist Alliance, The Adherents, *Britannica*, the Gale Group, *The World Almanac* and the US Census reports. Most of the sources are free. There are also paid sources, but paying for information is no guarantee of its authenticity. The value of using the Internet include speed, convenience and the ability to do complicated on-lines searches to gather data located hundreds or even thousands of miles away. Of course, the main drawback is there is no way to verify information without doing more research, which usually requires a trip to the library.

When it comes to dealing with people, using the Internet makes the job even more complex. Privacy is a vital concern on the Internet. Individuals try to protect their privacy from unscrupulous web surfers in order to avoid unwanted contact and possible fraud. Making the task even more difficult is the rightful refusal of some people to be categorized by religion, race or any other classification. Further complicating the issue is the anonymity of the web. Contacts from unknown people are often unwanted, unwelcome, and make it difficult to make contact with individuals on a personal basis. The Internet thrives because aliases and pseudonyms are a way to ensure anonymity. Individuals often have numerous alternate identities and communicate only under those names. People often pretend to be what they are not. They change gender, age, race and religion. Democrats become alias Republicans to skew polls and give misleading information.

Whites become Black to eavesdrop or even participate in Black discussion groups. Telephone numbers, addresses and real names are jealously guarded.

Using the Internet

Why did I use the Internet? I used the Internet because it is available and I wanted to test its effectiveness as a viable information source. Of course, nothing beats face-to-face meetings, telephone conversations and real letters, which I also used, but the Internet was the prime vehicle for a large portion of this information which was supplemented by books, magazines, newspapers, conversations and letters. The majority of the information I present here is available on the Internet along with much more. Obviously, large research documents and out-of-print items still require that one become friends with a librarian or in this case several librarians.

ORGANIZATION

This book is broken into six sections in order to break up the material and divide the topics into individual subjects without breaking the content of the book. Each section addresses some element of belief or nonbelief in the world community and in the Black community in particular, including attitudes toward nonbelievers, current belief patterns and finally, belief and behavior.

Section One: *Nonbelief and Skepticism in the Black Community* outlines how this book came about and the research that went into putting it together. In addition, it contains a brief explanation of the terms used throughout the book, as well as an explanation of how polls and surveys were used for my research. It will also give the reader an idea of how difficult it is to find Black nonbelievers, but also how few people, especially in the Black community, believe they exist.

Section Two: *Religion and the Black Community* looks at a brief history of the Black church, how it developed and its current state within the Black community, including a comparative analysis of Black and white belief. It also looks at cultural church differences and the effect they have on attendance.

Section Three: *The Religious Landscape* provides information about the number of religious adherents on a global basis and then examines the religious terrain in the United States, including the current religious climate in the country.

Section Four: *Belief and Behavior* is a candid statistical look at how belief and behavior are very much at odds in the United States. It will look at aberrant, criminal and destructive behavior that reveals that as much as Americans claim Christianity their actions don't exemplify the Christian ethic.

Section Five: *Going Against the Grain* starts with a look at contemporary atheist, agnostics and a variety of religious skeptics, including their idea opinions and essays. It introduces the reader to Black atheists, agnostics and humanist revealing who these people are and what they really believe.

Section Six: *Is It Time to Reevaluate the Role of Religion* starts an examination of the role of religion in the world and in the Black community in particular, including a candid look at the September 11, 2001 terrorist attack and reaction to it. Finally, the book closes out with a brief history of Black nonbelief and skepticism that is followed by an appendix containing an alphabetical list of atheists, agnostics, freethinkers, humanists, skeptics and more.

There are five kinds of lies: lies, damned lies, statistics, politicians quoting statistics and novelists quoting politicians on statistics.

—Stephen K. Tagg

A Word On Polls

Although, I have tried to be as accurate as possible, religion is in a constant state of flux and numbers change almost daily as people drop in and out of religion. Dealing with statistics is part science and part sleight of hand, especially when using small sets of data to extrapolate tendencies that will be applied to a larger group. The 2000 United States presidential race is a good example of what can happen when sample groups are used to predict real group behavior, but for the most part, most polls have a high degree of accuracy.

I have used information from a variety of sources including polls, studies and surveys. It should be clearly understood that social scientists know that people often answer questions the way they "think" they are supposed to answer, rather than as they really feel. Poll data on religious matters are notoriously unreliable, as participants often describe themselves inaccurately trying to make themselves or their religions "look good." "Unfortunately, there's a well-known tendency for individuals in self-report surveys to exaggerate what they perceive to be socially desirable behavior," says Mark Chaves of the University of Arizona.[2]

Responses to questions can also be influenced by an array of factors including data collection techniques or even how a particular question is worded or asked. Because religion is increasingly tied to citizenship and patriotism, as well as individual character, people tend to answer questions in a way that puts them in a positive light, while downplaying any negative interpretations. For instance, seventeen percent of Americans claim to tithe 10 to 13 percent of their earnings, but polls have consistently shown that the actual number who actually tithes is closer to 3 percent. These figures show how widely polls and reality can vary.[3] Also, polls and surveys are conducted using a limited sampling of usually a thousand people and even though the margin for error in these polls is small, they represent predictions based on sampling.

Explanation of Terms

I have chosen the word "nonbeliever" because of the negativism associated with the word atheist or those "without a belief in God or gods." I dislike using the term "nonbeliever" because it seems like a politically correct waffle word designed not to offend believers and nonbelievers alike. Still, for the purposes of this writing the term "nonbeliever" will be used to indicate those who do not believe in the traditional God of Christianity, Islam or Judaism. My use of the terms "nonbelievers" and "freethinkers" covers a wide range of categories including rationalists, atheists, agnostics, humanists, deists, pantheists, naturalists and Unitarian Universalists who all share some of the same traits with the most common being skepticism concerning religion.

Religion can also be a confusing term. The term "religion" can include a variety of ethical, moral and philosophical values and practices, but for this writing the term "religion" will be used to denote a system of beliefs and values based on the concept of a god or supernatural being. In the broad definition of the term "religion," a variety of entities could fit the term including political parties and businesses in that they have definite philosophies, codes of ethics and practices, but without a belief in a god they can't be considered religious groups in the accepted sense of the word.

In keeping with American writing tradition, throughout this book I refer to God in capital letters. In addition, I refer to God as "He" simply because that has also been traditional. Any reference to the concept of other "gods" is in lowercase letters. When speaking of the "Black community," I am speaking of those people of African descent living throughout the world including geographic locations from as near as the Caribbean Islands and Canada to as far away as mainland Africa and Australia. I am quite aware that we all are descendants of Africa in some fashion and that race is largely a social construct, but for the purposes of this writing when using the terms "Black community" or "Black", I am referring to those who historically have also been known as "colored", Negroes and Blacks in "traditional" record keeping around the globe. Although, the majority of the book refers specifically to African Americans, others of African lineage including those living in Canada, Great Britain, Latin America and Africa will be mentioned to demonstrate the breadth of Christianity and other religious beliefs in the Black community at large.

I will speak of atheists, agnostics, humanists, deists, rationalists, pantheist and various subgroups. Although my focus will primarily fall upon nonbelief and skepticism within the Black community, for purposes of diversity and education from the standpoint of exposing the reader to a variety of ideas, opinions and studies, I will include some small discussion of these other groups.

Since I started writing this book, some major things have happened in the world and in my life. On September 11, 2001, Islamic terrorists crashed two passenger jets into the World Trade Center twin towers killing more than 3,000 people, destroying both buildings and several around it. That same day another part of the same terrorist cell crashed another hijacked airliner into the Pentagon killing more than 190 people. Forty-five people died when a fourth highjacked airliner crashed in a field in Pennsylvania after the passengers overcame the highjackers. The death toll of that one day surpassed even the December 7, 1941 Japanese surprise attack on Pearl Harbor, which killed 2,400 and plunged the United States into World War II.

Another side of human behavior jumped into the headlines a few months later as the Catholic Church came under heavy fire for its role in hiding sexual abuse in the church. It seemed like every day another priest fell to charges of pedophilia, rape or sexual abuse while charges of "cover-up" and collusion battered the Catholic Church. As the Catholic Church sagged beneath the weight of the scandal, other incidents of sexual misconduct in other denominations slipped to the inside pages and escaped most eyes.

Business behavior grabbed headlines in mid-2002 with the multi-billion dollar bankruptcy of the Enron Corporation brought about by accounting improprieties and fraud. Thousands of employees lost their retirement benefits because of shady deals and questionable accounting practices by "Big Eight" accounting firm Arthur Andersen, which shredded incriminating papers trying to avoid prosecution. At the same time, Xerox, Tyco and other companies came under the spotlight for the same behaviors. Telecommunications giant WorldCom filed for bankruptcy after "misstating its earnings" by a more than $1 billion dollars which it later revised another billion or two. The number of companies caught cheating seemed to grow each day as more fraud, shady dealing and outright cheating became known.

On March 20, 2003, after much saber rattling following the September 11, 2001 World Trade Center terrorist attack, the United States declared war on Iraq. Less than two months later, the war was over as US troops marched into Baghdad toppling the regime of Saddam Hussein both literally and figuratively.

However, the biggest thing that happened to me during that time was the diagnosis of my father with Lou Gehrig's disease, his coming to live with me, and his death seven months later. We all have to deal with the death of a loved one eventually, but few people sit through the process. At 82, my father was in good health except for Lou Gehrig's disease, which usually attacks at a younger age. A retired physician, his mind was still sharp and he had lost little of his diagnostic skills, a fact that was not lost on my family and me as he provided daily accounts of the disease's progress whether we wanted to know or not. He was also a devout Catholic and partook of the sacraments until the hour of his death. That entire event stands out not only because of my loss but also because of the things I learned. How does all of this tie into nonbelief and skepticism in the Black community? It doesn't, at least not directly. Obviously, numerous people of African descent were affected by the news events of the past 18 months, but it is only how those events relate to human behavior that it is linked to this book.

It will become clear as we pass through the halls of nonbelief, freethought and humanism that these concepts are clearly not in line with Black mainstream thinking, but represent an extreme minority point of view. However, it is a view that is rising rapidly as rates of education and upward mobility continue to rise across the United States and people are less inclined to take things at face value and are seeking better and more meaningful answers.

In the Black community there is an unspoken rule to never air dirty laundry in public, and for years the inner workings of the Black community stayed hidden beneath a veil of dark silence, but with integration came a mingling of the races and consequently few secrets remain. Now, there is one less. Not only do Black nonbelievers exist, they walk unnoticed among the "true-believers" along with a host of other religious skeptics, doubters and freethinkers. How many? No one knows for sure, but judging from the contacts I made developing this book, although nonbelief may be a minority position in the Black community, it is not rare—just hidden.

Religion and the Black Community

That night I was escorted to the front row and placed on the mourners' bench with all the other young sinners, who had not yet been brought to Jesus.... Finally all the young people had gone to the altar and been saved, but one boy and me.... Finally Westley said to me in a whisper: "I'm tired o' sitting here. Let's get up and be saved." So he got up and was saved.... I kept waiting serenely for Jesus, waiting, waiting— but he didn't come. I wanted to see him, but nothing happened to me. Nothing! I wanted something to happen to me; but nothing happened...So I decided that maybe to save further trouble, I'd better lie, too, and say that Jesus had come, and get up and be saved.... That night...I cried.... [My aunt] woke up and told my uncle I was crying because the Holy Ghost had come into my life, and I had seen Jesus. But I was really crying because I couldn't bear to tell her that I had lied, that I had deceived everybody in the church, that I hadn't seen Jesus, and that now I didn't believe there was a Jesus any more, since he didn't come to help me. —Langston Hughes, contrasting how he was simultaneously "saved" and "lost" in a single event, in "Not Without Laughter."

Chapter 1

▼

Race and Religion

"He is less remote from the truth who believes nothing, than he who believes what is wrong."

—*Thomas Jefferson*

Few noted Denzel Washington's pointed remarks at the NAACP 2000 Image Awards after he accepted an award for his work as Ruben "Hurricane" Carter in the hit movie *The Hurricane*. Mr. Washington remarked that "over here, we thank God..." His remark was prompted by what many Blacks felt was a noticeable lack of thanks or deference to God at the Academy Awards a few nights earlier. No one seemed to notice a few years later when milestone Black actor and director Sydney Poitier received the Academy's Lifetime Achievement Award and spent five minutes thanking all the people who helped make his career without once mentioning God. Poitier's remarks are an exception whereas Mr. Washington's remarks were more typical although indicative of his deep religious belief and personal commitment. However, his comment also revealed how the Black community is often viewed as a single group where all are connected by the same experiences, same motivations and even the same beliefs.

The Black Monolith

Commonness of skin color often leads to convenient assumptions about the Black community that are not only incorrect, but also help to perpetuate stereo types. Within the Black community, ones 'Blackness' is often not based on ones blood connections but instead upon ones loyalty to popular group thought. This form of tribalism turns the Black community into a monolithic presence that can thwart progress by painting individuals into a Black corner where only opinions supportive of the status quo are allowed. Today it seems that Blackness is more a series of popular stances espoused by popular figures rather than a state of mind or of being. This method of thinking owes itself to old stereotypes, failure to think outside the box and a susceptibility to group thought. For a variety of reasons too complex to discuss here and that are outside the scope of this writing, the culture of Blackness does not reward individualism outside "accepted" group norms.

The idea of groupthink seems especially prevalent in the Black community where anyone who goes against the "party line" is subject to immediate criticism as an Uncle Tom, Oreo or even traitor rather than being viewed as an independent thinker. Stepping across these hidden and undrawn lines carry real consequences as the sometimes bitter debates between Black liberals and conservatives demonstrate.

Race and racism turn any discussion of stereotypes into a sensitive subject in the Black community. Nevertheless, many Blacks would be surprised to know that they use many of the same stereotypes to characterize each other that would be considered offensive if used by whites. Blacks use these stereotypes in an almost unconscious manner to establish standards of behavior for other Blacks. At first glance this setting of standards seems relatively harmless, but when it is considered that to hold individuals to a single standard of behavior restricts all and may be even more harmful, for it makes artificial barriers with the decisive factor based on looking the same—then it is not so harmless.

That any Black man or woman is able to think beyond the moment, express complex ideas beyond sports and sex may come as a surprise to many Americans, especially many African Americans. Many people of African descent can't dance, sing or play dominos and they may also be affluent, Republican and have never tasted a chittlin' in their life, but that doesn't make them any less Black. Neither are all Black folks afraid of the dark, criminally oriented, dope doers or Baptist, but these are the stereotypes many Blacks accept without question. Not all Blacks are Christians; neither are they all Democrats and poor, nor do they all live in the ghetto and aspire to be rappers or sports stars. Clearly, this is true, but it may be a surprise to just as many outside the Black community as well as to many within it.

Religion and politics are two topics of conversation that most avoid, but in this case, they are appropriate to use as examples. To many in the Black community, a Black Republican is out of place, for it is assumed that all Blacks are Democrats. Of course, it is not true, but the fact remains that a Black Republican is thought of as an anomaly in the Black community. The same can be said of Black nonbelievers.

THE NEGRO THOUGHT POLICE

Not long ago a commentary appeared in the now defunct *Emerge Magazine*[4] that talked about the Negro Thought Police who were described as the self-appointed gatekeepers of "correct" Black thinking and action. It was an interesting commentary claiming that one does not easily go against the grain in the Black community without risking serious consequences and penalties, including being expelled from Blackness. Who makes the rules? Who determines the essential formula? No one knows for sure, but if one should happen to go against the grain of popular Black thought, they will undoubtedly meet the Negro Thought Police. Curiously, it is a form of Orwellian thought policing that only comes to the surface after the fact and apparently is only detectable by the self-appointed commissioners of the Negro Thought Police.

Recently, the Rev Jesse Jackson and the Rev. Al Sharpton picked up their "NTP" badges to bring a hot spotlight on the hit movie *Barbershop*. Apparently, the Rev. Jackson and Rev. Sharpton were offended by the movie's cantankerous elder statesman, "Eddie," played by Cedric the Entertainer. "Eddie" declared that Martin Luther King Day should be celebrated with a romp under the sheets in tribute to Rev. King's womanizing ways and that Rosa Parks did nothing more than get off her tired feet. The Right Reverends rushed to condemn the public flaying of the sainted Civil Rights icons and called for the offending scene to be removed from the movie. This is just a recent instance when popular entertainment has come under negative scrutiny from others who feel they are the defenders of Blackness. The same thing happened with the movie *The Color Purple*. The movie, which had an almost all Black cast, was nominated for 13 Academy Awards, but it won none after the NAACP denounced it as portraying Black men in a bad light.

Part of the same group that decides who is Black, also decides other modes of Black behavior and belief including the opinions on affirmative action, vouchers, political parties, religion, music, proper speech and who one can hang out with.

At one time, group thinking helped serve the Black community by protecting us from outsiders, but the Black community has become a metaphor for a group that is no longer physically isolated and live daily in a variety of circumstances that cannot be so easily pigeon-holed.

WHERE IS THE VARIETY OF THOUGHT?

Scholars and writers such as Cornell West and Derrick Bell could be considered as examples of those who espouse the majority position of African America and are by far more popular than any dissenting voices. Nevertheless, there is the loyal opposition that regularly breaks lockstep with general or mainstream Black thinkers. People like Shelby Steele and John McWhorter regularly step into the breach and voice differing opinions despite the risk of excommunication from the community. Obviously, there are many more on all sides of the issues and there is a lively, if sometimes hostile, dialogue taking place.

However, in the realm of religion, it appears there is no loyal opposition but rather an overwhelming majority all tuned to the same station, singing the same hymn and chorus. Black theological scholarship includes the aforementioned Cornell West, as well as noted scholars such as Albert Cleage and James Cone. Although there are differences in their viewpoints, all seem to stay well within the realm of accepted Black thought concerning Christianity. By making Christianity the only page in the book it seems that Black theologians have severely limited their point of view and by default made Christianity the conformist belief of Black men and women while almost ignoring Islam, Hinduism, Judaism, atheism, humanism or tribal African religions.

> *"...The dilemma faced by Black religious intellectuals is that they advocate solutions to problems which were largely created or exacerbated by religion...These thinkers cannot be sufficiently critical of religion because they are very dependent upon it. They are therefore condemned to be limited in their perception and understanding of the problems they seek to solve."*
> —Norm R. Allen, Jr., The Crisis of the Religious Black Intellectual

RELIGION IS SERIOUS BUSINESS

Comedian Richard Pryor tested the limits of Black tolerance more than once with unveiled remarks about religion. On an early Richard Pryor album, the comedian explained that the reason the notorious blood-sucking vampire, Dracula, cringes before the crucifix is because "Dracula's afraid of bullshit."[5] That crack didn't play well in many parts of the Black community and with good reason. Christianity is taken seriously in the Black community where even the mention of God or Jesus can draw a round of applause even at seemingly incongruous events such as rap concerts and comedy shows. It makes no difference, in the Black community—Jesus is not for joking.

It is no wonder that skepticism and nonbelief are viewed as outside the realm of blackness in the Black community. Nonbelief and freethought are often viewed as "white" things or as foreign to the Black community. The reasons for this are both complex and simple. They are complex because of how Black people came to this country, how they were treated and because only now are we beginning to understand how more than 400 years of physical and mental incarceration can affect a people. Yet, it is simple because to consider another perspective only requires the ability to think.

CHANGING TIMES

The late George Schuyler made the observation in 1932 that, "On the horizon loom a growing number of iconoclasts and atheists, young Black [sic] men and women who can read, think, and ask questions, and who impertinently demand to know why Negroes should serve a God who permits them to be lynched, Jim-crowed and disenfranchised...There are hundreds of these sorts in every community. Coupled with those who have left the church completely and the vast number who are on the rolls but never attend, they make for a formidable and increasing majority."[6]

Although nearly 70 years have passed since Schuyler made that statement, time has proved him right in many aspects as now nearly 32 percent of the American Black community is considered "unchurched."[1][7] Regardless of convenient

---

1. "Unchurched" refers to people who have not attended church within the past six months other than for special occasions such as Christmas, Easter, weddings or funerals.

excuses or even beliefs such as "I don't need to be in church to worship God" or "I have my own way of worshipping God, "the facts are clear that the "unchurched" follow their own counsel as do most Americans and do not adhere strictly to the tenets of Christianity and therefore are at least skeptics and more than likely—pretenders. While it is clear that Blacks are not common among organized nonbelievers and freethinkers, it is significant that disbelief exists at all in the Black community.

Obviously, there is a host of other taboos and "no-no's" in the Black community, but probably the most controversial stance in the majority Black community is disbelief or disregard for a personal God. Nonbelief is atypical and consequentially nonbelievers and freethinkers in the Black community tend not to shout it out. They are invisible in a sea of Black Christianity and judging from the few I know personally, most plan to stay that way. Race and religion are volatile subjects in any community, but in the Black community, one is discussed only from a perceived majority point of view and the other is not discussed at all outside of academia. Religion is hardly a topic that promotes rational discussion under normal circumstances and in a community where a large portion of past and present Black leadership used the pulpit to launch careers, the tolerance for differing viewpoints, especially nonbelief, is exceptionally constricted.

TOLERANCE AND FORBEARANCE

The Black community has long had a history of tolerance and forbearance, but when it comes to religious skepticism or disbelief it is clear there are limits to its acceptance. In the United States, nonbelief is a minority position and within the Black community, it is a minority position within a minority. Most Blacks seem to be very serious about the God of Christianity and those who do not hold any belief keep their opinions to themselves.

Knowing that the river of the status quo is not easily rowed against is often the only protection available to the nonbeliever or freethinker in a country where 95 percent of the population claims a belief in God or "universal spirit." It is clear that any stance to the contrary will be met with at least raised eyebrows if not outright hostility, especially in the Black community. In the Black community social realities often dictate that discretion become the better part of valor where religious belief is concerned because more often than not those who reveal the truth are punished rather than praised.

For nonbelievers and freethinkers clearly there is a need to be pragmatic. Unpopular ideology can sink careers and even endanger lives and most nonbelievers realize that it is a foolish person who does not at least consider the consequences of espousing an unpopular viewpoint regardless of its truth. In a Machiavellian sense, it is much easier to succeed dressed in popular clothes giving others the comfort of their illusions or self-deceptions rather than going about in the nakedness of nature, which in this case is nonbelief.

Clearly, in the realms of politics, business and certain social situations, radical stances are neither wanted nor appreciated. There is a wealth of Black thought that is given short shrift because it goes against the grain of popular thinking which is sad, because there are many who have much to contribute, but mistrust and stereotypes keep many away. The truth is that many of Black America's most revered icons were battered and bruised by divisive rhetoric that came from within the Black community itself.

Malcolm X was not immediately welcomed into the community of the Civil Rights movement where many vilified him as a troublemaker and agitator. Neither were Black power advocates Stokley Carmichael, Huey P. Newton, or Bobby Seale because they were a new generation that wanted action—now. Even Martin Luther King Jr. met with harsh criticism when he ventured into protests against human rights abuses and the Vietnam War. Without recounting the various rifts that have taken place in the Black community, the one element that continues to surface is disapproval for those who shun the status quo.

Christianity is such a powerful force in the Black community that other stances are not generally considered, understood or tolerated. Despite a lack of opposing voices, there are those in the Black community who do not believe in Christianity, who have challenged its dogma and have not been silent in their opinions. Most apparent among them are the Muslims of the Nation of Islam. Although these Muslims make up only a small portion of non-Christians in the Black community, their presence is clearly visible.

The Nation of Islam, which once made claims that Islam is the Black man's natural religion and led by the charismatic Minister Louis Farrakhan, counts for only a small, although growing, number in the steadfastly Christian Black community. Although Islam is tolerated and accepted to some degree, it is not clearly understood, even though there are nearly 2 million followers of Islam in the Black community. Christianity is the dominant religion in the United States and especially the Black community, but it is not the only religion. It is just one of many subscribed to by Blacks around the globe.

A Different Perspective

Things have changed drastically in the last 60 years. As Blacks have moved steadily into the mainstream, the variety of Black thought, circumstance and culture has also changed. The monolithic Black community no longer exists as change has removed barriers that once afflicted all Blacks. This is not to say that problems no longer exists because a quick glance at newspaper or television news will cast dark shadows on that view as racism and bias continue to thrive in the United States. However, any comparison of 2003 with 1943 and the conditions of Blacks must be positive.

As much as some may wish to deny it, those negative sides of humanity that are apparent in all groups have come to the surface in the Black community and it must acknowledge that they were always there. We may pretend that nonbelief and skepticism are an anathema to the Black community, but there is a rich history of nonbelievers, freethinkers and humanists who contributed much to the Black community in the United States and the world.

Among them are people like A. Phillip Randolph, Lucy Parsons, Richard Wright, Joel A. Rogers and many others, who were unafraid to take on ignorance, even in the churches to which some of them belonged. Still, any hints of nonbelief or skepticism in the Black community remain virtually invisible, camouflaged by indignant denial and indistinct expressions, such as secularist, nontheist, freethinker or humanist among others which help conceal clear atheistic or agnostic connections which are certainly not conventional and clearly go against Black mainstream thinking.

Many of these nonbelievers sit next to you in the pews on Sunday. They are called "stealths." Stealths populate almost every congregation, in every church, in every city and town. What is a stealth? I had no idea they existed and had never heard the term outside of its military context until I had a telephone conversation with the Black pastor of a Universalist Unitarian Church. She explained that among many congregations there are members who are actually atheists or agnostics even though they outwardly profess a belief in God. She told me other members termed them "stealths" because they are undercover nonbelievers. From personal experience and interviews with friends and associates, I found that "stealths" exist universally and in the Black community as well. Why do these "stealths" attend church when they don't believe in God?

As a Black man the "why" seemed obvious as it is no secret in the Black community that church attendance is seen as a desirable activity that reflects well upon the individual, often giving social leverage and building reputations. It is a way of "fitting in" that usually causes few problems for the stealth. "Stealths" of this nature are often known but are accepted because of their willingness to coexist and not rock the religious boat. These stealths contribute to a growing number of nonbelievers in the Black community and although nonbelief is a minority position in the United States, it is a position that is larger than the number of adherents of both Judaism and Islam combined in the United States. Only by careful observation can we see that nonbelief and skepticism are no strangers to the Black community.

Chapter 2

The Black Church

> *"The Negro church, however, although not a shadow of what it ought to be, is the greatest asset of the race."*
>
> —*Carter G. Woodson, The Mis-Education of the Negro.* [8]

The number of predominantly Black Christian churches in the United States numbers over 50,000. Christianity and the Black community enjoy an unusual relationship that extends back to the time of slavery when the church was the only place where Blacks held any amount of power or control over their lives. The early Black church served as part psychological refuge as well as an organizing point for social and political activities.

As Christianity grew, slaves organized their own "invisible institution" inside the church and through the use of signals, passwords, and messages unnoticed or ignored by whites, they called other slaves to "hush harbors" where they mixed African rhythms, singing, and beliefs with evangelical Christianity. The church provided a spot where Blacks could speak freely of their troubles and their dreams without fear of reprisals from white slave masters, even though more often than not, "loyal" spies hid among the faithful.

Historically, the Black church has served as a major foundation of Black spiritual and community life. It has long held a position of leadership in the Black community and as a by-product; the Black community expects its churches and leaders to become involved in issues of the secular world. Because of racism, religious leadership of the Black community came by default, as there were no other channels for Blacks to deal with whites during the early days of slavery and later institutional bigotry.

The history of the Black church is filled with individual and group acts of heroism, as well as, the names of many of the Black community's greatest leaders, such as Congressman Adam Clayton Powell, Rev. Martin Luther King Jr. and a virtual "Who's Who In Black America" list ranging from the Rev. Al Sharpton to the Rev. Jesse Jackson.

The Black church continues to serve as a community gathering point to this day and is still the most stable and dominant organization in the Black community. Throughout history the Black church held a position of authority and leadership in the "Black community" providing shelter, guidance and hope for a people who had no where else to turn. Blacks adopted a foreign religion, modified it and turned it in their favor making it at once a provider of hope and salvation as well as a spoon for stirring political and social foment.

THE BLACK CHURCH TODAY

At one time Christianity was a major binding force in the Black community and still is to a large degree, but integration, upward mobility, higher education and flight from the ghetto, have rendered long established generalizations suspect and no longer provide an accurate view of reality. That is not to say that the Black church is not a viable force in the Black community, it is. It remains dedicated to social change, community outreach and the cause of humanity but its influence as a change agent for human behavior has never been apparent outside of a dedicated few, and even that small influence may be starting to wane as Black church attendance continues to drop.

Falling Attendance Rates

Church dropout rates are increasing and nonbelief is on the rise, not only in the Black community, but also all over the United States. The reasons for this decline are myriad, but paramount among them is the church's inability or refusal to adjust to the rapid changes in American society and the corresponding changes in the makeup of its congregations. The attendance drop off in Black churches corresponds with 32 percent of the Black community that is now considered "unchurched." Although it is considerably smaller than the 45 percent figure cited for the white populace of United States, it represents about 8-10 million people—mostly Black men and, that it exists at all is startling considering the "statistical" religiosity of the Black community.⁹

Although there is an increased interest in spirituality in the United States, that interest has not translated into increased church attendance and the Black community is no exception. Church attendance in the United States has been declining steadily for the past 10 years and not only are fewer people attending church, but the number of nonbelievers and freethinkers is increasing.

Results compiled in an USA Today-CNN Gallup poll found that 30 percent of American adults, including Blacks, classified themselves as spiritual, but were not interested in attending church.¹⁰ According to the Barna Research Group, church attendance today is suffering from a steady five-year decline and has dropped to its lowest levels in nearly two decades. Other researchers say the decline is most apparent in mainstream religions. Some researchers say that nearly 78 million Americans are "marginal Protestants" which is nearly 12 million more than the Barna group found. Established, mainstream denominations now worry that one-man television factions are siphoning off members and money that would otherwise go to hometown churches. Dr. Martin Marty, a Lutheran scholar, says the "ruffle-shirted, pink-tuxedoed pitchmen" are formidable rivals, and "the loser is the local church." ¹¹ The Black church has felt the pinch as a new generation of outrageous fashion peacocks siphon off local churchgoers with megachurches and with each deserting member goes their money.

New Way of Counting

Part of the decline in church attendance can be attributed to a new way of counting. For years, polling groups such as the Gallup Organization, The Barna Research Group, USA Today, CNN and others have relied on direct opinion polls that show that U.S. church attendance has remained steady at nearly 40 percent for the past thirty years, but new research shows there may be a significant gap in the numbers, as well as, a significant decline in Christian belief in the United States.

Lying for the Church

Research conducted by Stanley Presser of the University of Maryland and research assistant Linda Stinson of the U.S. Bureau of Labor Statistics indicates that many Americans have been deliberately misreporting church attendance and inflating attendance figures 25-35 percent. Interestingly, those with the most fervent belief are the ones who are most likely to inflate their reporting.[12, 13]

For years, no one thought to use actual observance of church attendance as a way to measure it. Many of the groups collecting this information are religious groups such as the Gallup Poll or Barna research, although such affiliation shouldn't make a difference in the collection of data, it apparently has, as over the years figures have remained virtually unchanged despite the changes in society. It was the unchanging church attendance figures that first alerted pollsters that something was wrong. Those unchanging attendance rates made researchers take a closer look and it appears that the investigation revealed a self-inflicted blind spot among some researchers.

Researchers say people often exaggerate to make their particular religious group look good in the polls, a phenomenon that is termed "social desirability bias." Presser found that many Americans were not at church when they claimed to be. A group of Canadian researchers also found the same thing. To gather more accurate information, researchers started observing attendance habits in real time, and found that eyewitness observation showed a marked difference from detached polls.

Other researchers also started to use actual observance of church attendance habits, which they compared against membership rolls, and they also kept diaries covering varying time periods of up to a year or longer that tracked real attendance figures. Suddenly, the 40 percent attendance rate that remained unchanged for nearly 30 years appears to be largely inflated and real attendance rates are closer to 20 percent, which is a significant decline translating to a loss in attendance of nearly 40-60 million people or more.[14]

The new study also casts doubts on the two major sources that claim to have widely measured church participation, the National Opinion Research Center and the Gallup organization.[15] There is now evidence that in the entire history of the United States the majority of Americans were never regular churchgoers despite laws which required membership in an "established" church during pre-Revolutionary times in order to own property, vote or exercise other rights.

CULTURE AND DECLINE

Even the 86 percent of the U.S. population that classify themselves as Christians must be examined closely to see where the drop in church attendance has occurred. Major differences in the "commitment" to Christianity accounts for a significant amount of the decline. Nearly 30 percent of those claiming Christianity are entirely secular in their behavior while another 29 percent are barely or marginally religious. Researchers found that only 19 percent practice their religion on a regular basis.[16] These figures also coincide with Presser's numbers.

How much influence religion ever had on American life is debatable. In an age of science and technology, more and more people are unwilling to accept answers without evidence and it is not just the general population that is looking for concrete answers, the controversial Jesus Project stirred interest after it asserted that less than 30 percent of the sayings in the Bible attributed to Jesus were actually said by him. This air of skepticism is apparent in the continuous decline in church attendance.[17]

NON RELIGIOUS GROWING

A recent CNN/USA Today/Gallup poll also showed that nearly 60 percent of Americans believe that religion "is losing its influence" on American life.[18] Researchers from the University of Michigan Institute for Social Research also believe that the importance of religion in general has been in steady decline in the Western world for some time.[19]

Approximately 33 million Americans have switched their religious preference and identifications. This switch has not only involved a change of religious loyalties but in many cases quitting religion altogether. In the last five years, most major religions showed losses in membership. The top three gainers were Evangelist Christians at 47 percent which represented an increase of 384,000 people, Non-Denominational Christians that represented an increase of 721,000 people and those claiming no religion grew by 23 percent, an increase of 6.6 million people.[20]

Because of the dominance of fundamentalist religion in the news, there is a perception that religion is growing and leaning toward the more literal and fundamental, but that is not the case. Viewing the religious landscape in the United States is in some ways akin to viewing an iceberg because what is beneath the surface is obscured by the glaze of evangelical fundamentalism, which grew in popularity during the late 80's and early 90's. However, in sharp contrast to these widely held beliefs the American Religious Identification Survey detected a "wide and possibly growing swath of secularism among Americans."[21]

Included in these numbers is the group known as "unchurched" adults which represents almost a third of the nations adults, a number that is between 60 to 65 million nationwide. Polls from Barna and Gallup both indicate that about one in two or 45 percent of whites are considered unchurched. Approximately, one out of every six unchurched adults claims to be atheist or agnostic or is affiliated with another religion such as Judaism or Islam.[22] In the Black church there is also a hint of an underlying sexual battle as less men attend church as more women join.

AMERICAN INDIVIDUALISM

Another reason for religion's decline in the United States can be attributed to the "individualism" of Americans. In the United States, people tend to think of themselves as individuals first which is in keeping with the founding traditions of this country. According to researcher George Barna, the Christian Church is struggling to influence the nation's culture because "believers think of themselves as individuals first, Americans second, and Christians third. Until that prioritization is rearranged, the Church will continue to lose influence, and Biblical principles will represent simply one more option among the numerous worldviews that Americans may choose from." [23]

That spirit of individuality went into the founding of the United States and that spirit of independence showed itself in the American Revolution, the women's suffrage movement, the Civil Rights era and the gay and feminist thrust for recognition. This air of self-reliance and concern for individual rights also colors the religious canvass where individuality and ungiving dogma often clash and increasingly religion is the loser as more and more shun church attendance preferring to set their own direction which regularly includes choosing religious standards designed to fit personal beliefs, personal standards and most of all personal convenience. What has happened is that the concept of Christianity has changed to fit the beliefs of the people who practice it.

As with most things, religion and religious belief are in a constant state of flux. Before I could finish this writing new findings from the American Religious Identification Survey show that the amount of Americans claiming Christianity has dropped from the 1990 figure of 86 percent to an all time low of 77 percent. Part of the change can be attributed to immigration and a change in the total religious make up of the United States, but the greatest increase is in the number of adults who do not claim religion at all which has more than doubled from 14.3 million in 1990 to 29.4 million in 2001.[24] There is a large nonreligious population in the United States and this includes those who attend church regularly. They are a group that is almost totally secular in outlook and amount to little more than "arm-chair" Christians as their practice of religion is limited to their interpretation of it. These unchurched or little-churched individuals help contribute to the overall decline in attendance.

Even with the overall decline, "typical" Black church attendance was almost 50 percent higher than the "typical" white church and the "typical" Sunday service is 70 percent longer than "typical" white service.[25] In addition, the Barna Research Group also says that women now make up 60 percent of the church population and that the highest attendance rates come from the population 50 and older.[26] Other research confirms these finding as there is substantial participation among older Black adults.[27] In 1988, nearly 80 percent who attended church regularly were over the age of 40. The reasons for the higher attendance rates and longer services are open to debate although clearly part of it lies in the traditions of the Black church which encompass a wide variety appealing factors such as music, fellowship and even style.

Three decades ago, E. Franklin Frazier predicted that the domination of the Black church in the Black community would decrease as Blacks became integrated into the institutions of the American community.[28] Frazier's prediction is only partly true as the church is now an essential piece of Black cultural heritage. The church continues strongly in the South where it is often the center of community affairs, but in the North where there are other diversions, it has not fared so well and Frazier's comments seem more on target.

Even where church is attended is under study as there are marked differences between rural and urban Black church attendance. Although studies are still ongoing, the implications are that although church attendance is lower in the city, those who do attend, tend to be motivated more by religious sincerity than tradition or habit. Researchers have found that attendance in urban areas represents a clear choice to do so. Motivation for rural Black church attendance is more complicated. Often, attendance in rural areas is considered "mandatory." The rural community does not offer the anonymity or privacy afforded by large urban areas and attendance becomes almost "mandatory" as non-attendance is immediately noticeable and not approved. Membership in the rural and Southern churches is nearly involuntary.

According to a 1988 Gallup poll, Black church attendance actually increased from 57 percent to 62 percent compared to 1978. However, those rates have changed. The median adult attendance per church service in 1999 was 90 people, which is slightly below the 1998 average of 95 adult attendees. The 1999 median of 90 adult attendees is down 10 percent from the 1997 average of 100 attendees, and down 12 percent from 1992 (102 adult attendees), according to the Barna Research Group.[29] Black congregations had the highest median attendance with 120.[30] Data from the National Survey of Black Americans indicates that overall Black religiosity has remained stable although there has been major defection among youth groups in urban areas and in the North while rural and Southern communities have remained staunch supporters of Christianity.[31]

FEMALES DOMINATE UNITED STATES RELIGION

Increasingly, Black churches have become female dominated as fewer and fewer Black males attend church with any regularity. In Charyn D. Sutton's book, *Pass It On: Outreach to Minority Communities*, it is pointed out that the Black church is now majority female in its membership despite mostly male leaders. Sutton claims that women over 40 now make up the backbone of the Black church.[32] As the shift continues many men in the Black community view church attendance as a "female" thing and often have a low view of the "preacher-female" relationship.

The Barna Research Group concurs, saying that women are the "backbone" of Christian churches throughout the country and that without women Christianity would have "nearly 60 percent fewer adherents." The research showed that Christian women are "more committed" and "shoulder a heavier level of burden" in making a church successful. Although women lead men in almost every category of devotion, commitment and action, the church clergy remains nearly 100 percent male.[33]

Recently, the Southern Baptist Convention voted to ban women from the pulpit, saying, "the office of pastor is limited to men, as qualified by Scripture." The 15-member Southern Baptist committee that voted unanimously to re-enforce its belief that women should not lead churches, debated the topic for a total of 10 minutes. There were two women on the committee as well as at least one Black man. With the church becoming overwhelming female, the general male membership has dropped off dramatically with men accounting for more than 50 percent of the unchurched Black population.

END OF DAYS

Now, the majority of those males who do attend church are over 50 or under 15, leaving a large age gap in an aging church population. It is significant to note that of the teenagers who do attend church most will stop attending as soon as they escape parental authority and the majority will not return until middle age when life begins to compress and near its end. Research shows that many of those who have no religious affiliation are male, young, never married, with low levels of income and education and reside outside the South.

The entire church going population of the United States is aging and makes up the majority of those who still attend church and it is no different in the Black church. Researchers have speculated one reason for this occurrence is that as people get older they become more aware that death is inevitable and hedge their bets by taking Pascal's Wager.[1] The attractiveness of Pascal's Wager becomes especially apparent as life begins to compress and near its end. This process probably starts as people become aware of their own mortality and the undeniable fact that death will occur.

It is this realization that often leads people into hope that life can be continued indefinitely and religion holds out that promise with an eternal life after death. "Everyone wants to go to heaven but no one wants to die" is an expression that his been around for decades and used to deride man's expressed religiousness but reluctance to attend the grand homecoming that awaits after death. Understanding this phenomenon gives at least one reason for an aging church population.

THE CHURCH AS ENTERTAINMENT

> *The people who are out there don't see it as entertainment, although that is in fact the way it is. These people don't go to movies; they don't go to bars and drink; they don't go to rock-and-roll concerts—but everyone has to have an emotional release. So they go to revivals and they dance around*

---

1. "It makes more sense to believe in God than to not believe. If you believe, and God exists, you will be rewarded in the afterlife. If you do not believe, and He exists, you will be punished for your disbelief. If He does not exist, you have lost nothing either way." Adrian Barnett, 1998. Blaise Pascal was a French mathematician who the popular computer programming language PASCAL was named after.

and talk in tongues. It's socially approved and that is their escape.... It was my duty to give them the best show possible. Say you've got a timid little preacher in North Carolina or somewhere. He'll bring in visiting evangelists to keep his church going. We'd come in and hit the crowd up and we were superstars. It's the charisma of the evangelist that the audience believes in and comes to see.

—Marjoe Gortner[34]

The Black protestant church is known for its soul stirring gospel music from the late Mahalia Jackson and James Cleveland to the Mississippi Mass Choir. It is known for its musical innovation, bright soloists and deep emotional tug with music that is so stirring as to induce tears, laughter and even spontaneous outbreaks of dancing. Black preachers are known for their fiery sermons and hypnotic rhythms, as well as theatrics when they deliver the Word. Working together, music and a good preacher provoke high emotion both visually and aurally. Preaching is very much a performance art in the Black church that relies on dazzling oratory, repetition, timing and audience participation to create an atmosphere conducive to manipulation and persuasion.

Entertainment plays a large role in most Black churches across the United States as well as in white churches and accounts for significant increases in attendance levels. In a book entitled *Amusing Ourselves to Death* by Neil Postman, Columbia University professor of education and special education, there is a chapter detailing television's effect on religion, and he concludes that by putting religion on television, religion becomes entertainment.

Many different methods have been employed to improve church attendance and one of the most common methods used is to combine it with something else like entertainment, which seems to be one of the most popular methods. At first this combination of religion and entertainment seems to work as more people attend and enjoy church, but what is often left unresolved is the "why" of the increase and in most cases "entertainment" stands out as the differentiator.[35] Churches have used this strategy successfully for years, the problem surfaces in distinguishing the two. How many attend for the entertainment value and how many attend for the spiritual value?

"...televangelism is the innovator of the new paradigm of church. For years now, preachers with charisma, charm and Volkswagen-sized Rolexes have taken to the airwaves (not to mention the red-light districts). They put on a show filled with energetic gospel music, religious celebrities, enthusiastic crowds, miraculous faith-healings and watered-down, feel-good messages. These sermons lack any theological content but are rich in production value and soap-opera melodrama."[36]

Black churches differ in almost every aspect from white churches, the music is different, the dress is different and the message is different even though the denominations may be the same. Music is an essential element in the Black church. It often sets the tone for the service and can be a determining factor in attendance and participation. The phenomenon is nothing new. Black revivals and retreats often are hard to tell from their secular counterparts and gospel rap concerts, praise festivals and pageants are now part of the regular offering. The Black church has always been a leader in adopting and amalgamating new things into its services, but entertainment is the most popular and most effective.

For years, churches in the Black community have differentiated themselves by the quality of the choir rather than the content of the preaching. Some would argue that the content of the preaching is improved by the quality of the music. However, observation of attendance patterns makes it clear that Black churches without quality choirs and excellent musicians lose out to the churches that have them, despite the message or the messenger. Regardless of its musical innovation and stirring preaching, the Black church is not known for its theologians or its religious scholarship. As much as Christianity has influenced the Black church and as much as the Black church has influenced Christianity in white America, its influence seems to be an influence of style rather than of substance.

Long before religion came to radio or television, it has always had an element of entertainment because in many places there was nothing else to do except go to church. The church is where people met, exchanged recipes, socialized and in effect it became an entertainment venue especially in rural communities. People looked forward to going to church because that's where they could see their friends and be entertained. Religion has skirted the edges of entertainment for years and much of Black popular music can be traced directly to the Black church and the blues which both influenced each other.

Thomas Dorsey was a blues musician and was the pianist in Ma Rainey's blues band. After the death of his wife and child, Dorsey composed *Precious Lord, Take My Hand* and never played the blues again. Still, when Thomas Dorsey came on the scene in the 30's his blues-based gospel music was decried in the church, but now it is the standard for gospel music.

Rap, jazz, rock, blues, as well as, traditional gospel are common in church today. Kirk Franklin has become rich and famous with his brand of Hip Hop gospel which is accepted into more and more churches. It is clear that when it comes to secular entertainment, the church either ignores it, attacks it, or mimics it and the Black church is known for its embrace of popular cultural entertainment.

SOCIAL ASPECTS OF CHURCH

Socializing plays a large roll in any group activity and attending church is not only a group activity in the Black community, it is a group activity that is widely approved of in the United States. Political conventions and rallies produce much the same effect as church attendance in that the amount of general socializing and business that occurs has no direct bearing on the event other than it takes place on the premises.

Any time people come together necessitates some form of social interaction and a church congregation is no different. For many, church attendance is largely a social occasion that presents a chance to visit with friends, discuss issues and even make business contacts. Sociologist Lyle Schaller is one the few who has written about this phenomenon. Schaller understands the social element involved in church attendance, as church is one place where people of similar sentiments can come together on a regular basis. Schaller believes that most people are first attracted to a particular church by pre-existing social ties to current members. [37]

The top reasons to attend church seem to be primarily social although according to the Barna research group the number one reason for attending church is the theological beliefs and doctrine of the church, but the second most important reason reported by Barna was "how much the people seem to care about each other," which is a definite social reason. Other reasons included, the quality of the sermons that are preached, how friendly the people in the church are to visitors, how much you like the pastor, and the convenience of weekend service times. [38]

People are social animals and only the most reclusive don't require some type of human contact. Just about everyone socializes to some extent in their everyday lives either through work associations, groups of like-minded friends, relatives and day-to-day interactions necessary to survive. There are also after work associations including social clubs, physical training and the nightlife. Generally, all Americans have some outlet for entertainment. For many, socialization is provided on the job, in school, entertainment venues and church. Social scientists have studied the social aspect of churches for years and have found that church attendance fulfills the same social needs as the other venues. Because many religious people shun the nightlife, dancing, drinking and even certain kinds of music, Sunday morning church services become opportunities for socializing and the preacher becomes the Master of Ceremonies, the comedian, the director and the storyteller who provides entertainment for the congregation.

Chapter 3

▼

Understanding Black Religion

"American Blacks are, by some measure the most religious people in the world."

—*George Gallup*

Considering the legacy of slavery and oppression in the United States and the sanctioning of much of it by the Christian Church and the Bible, it would seem that Christianity would be far down the list for Blacks, but just as Africans were brought to the United States against their will, acceptance of Christianity also was not a choice. This disconnect seems even more difficult to understand in the light that Black Christians were constantly told that their bondage to the white man had been decreed by God. The Rev. Thomas Bacon of Maryland preached to a congregation of slaves, "Almighty God hath been pleased to make you slaves here, and to give you nothing but Labour and Poverty in this world…If you desire Freedom, serve the Lord here, and you shall be his Freemen in Heaven hereafter." [39]

Religion and Christianity in particular, hold a curious position within the Black community. It is curious because of the way Christianity was introduced in the United States and Africa. It is also curious how a religion that has its roots in Judaism, ancient pagan ritual and European culture has been shaped into an almost new religion in the Black community.

It is clear that Christianity and Islam spread to Africa during the time of slave trade, and along the western coast of Africa, Islam had made a significant impression. Many of the slaves who came to the United States were Muslims and never converted. Islam exerted a powerful presence in Africa for several centuries before the start of the slave trade and it is estimated twenty percent of enslaved people were practicing Muslims. Catholicism had even established a presence in areas of Africa by the sixteenth century. There were other religions as well that were exported along with Islam and Catholicism. Although it is clear that Islam and Catholicism had spread to Africa during the time of slavery, most slaves worshipped the indigenous Gods of Africa before their capture and transit to the United States where slave-masters forced them into Christianity.

SLAVE CHRISTIANITY

The reason for this conversion is at once complex and convoluted, while it is also sensible and profitable from the slave masters point of view. During the period of slavery, Christianity provided hope when there was none; provided comfort when conditions were brutal and harsh and most of all provided an area of life that the slave master did not control. Slave masters explained slavery using the Bible as justification, while slaves were led to believe that they were the cursed children of Ham whose role it was to suffer and serve the white man, with their only hope coming through the acceptance of Jesus Christ as their savior and the inheritance of heaven when they died.

Most Blacks accepted the slave brand of Christianity at face value. Moreover, white missionaries persuaded Blacks that life on earth was insignificant because 'obedient servants of God could expect a reward in heaven after death.' The white interpretation of Christianity effectively divested the slaves of any concern they might have had about their freedom in the present. [40] Through teaching slaves the message of the Bible, they could be encouraged to bear their earthly burden in exchange for heavenly rewards later on—and they could be frightened into believing that disobedience to earthly masters would be perceived by God as disobedience to Him.[41]

Eventually, Christianity was adopted by the slaves who combined it with traditional African religions and turned it into something the church fathers in Rome and England never dreamed. The twin themes of love and mercy especially appealed to many of the slaves who found the message comforting in its concern for people and the promise of a better life. One of the most appealing portions of

Christianity came from the Old Testament with the story of the children of Israel. For many slaves the story of the Israelites bondage in Egypt under Pharaoh and their deliverance to the Promised Land by Moses after much suffering, paralleled their own condition as slaves. The freedom story of the Israelites brought some comfort that a better life awaited after the suffering.

Later this manner of thinking was formalized and elevated in what is commonly known as "Liberation Theology" which is a theory that turns on the bearing of "redemptive" suffering. For those who are familiar with the concepts of liberation theology and redemptive suffering this is an obvious and somewhat distorted oversimplification but it is not my intent to discuss the various views of theology in the Black community other than to mention that they exist.

Although most Africans practiced their tribal beliefs, preserving African religions in North America proved to be difficult because of the concerted effort of white owners to erase "heathen" customs. As much as slaves may have tried to maintain their native religions, the reality of slavery made it extremely difficult as entire villages were separated along with families, husbands, wives, and children. Language barriers, customs and the brutality of American system of slavery, increased this division and separation.

Though separation and language barriers were an effective means of preventing any type of cohesiveness among the slaves, the introduction of Christianity provided a vehicle to meld those tribal traditions that still existed with a foreign religion. This melding of religious cultures produced a hybrid slave religion of Christianity that incorporated the rhythms, styles and feel of traditional African religions. It was also the first thing that whites did not control and because of that, in many ways, slave religion was a form of rebellion.

DIVERSITY OF SLAVE RELIGION

Not all slaves were Christians. Many slaves were former priests and leaders of various African religions such as Yoruba and did not accept the teachings of Christianity. There were even more slaves who clearly saw the incongruity of the words of the Bible and the actions of the slave masters. These slaves remained faithful to the old beliefs of Africa or didn't believe at all. There is little known about these slaves other than a few first names and locations, but they were real and are captured in history. In Anthony Pinn's book, *Varieties of African American Religious Experience*, slave narratives of those who did not accept Christianity are outlined as well as other beliefs systems such as Voudon (Voodoo), Santeria, Condomble and the religions of the Yoruba people.

Christianity and Africa

It is difficult to generalize about Africa because of its size and because there is still much that is not known about it. One cannot write about Africa as if it were a single, homogeneous society, or fail to consider its cultural fragmentation, as well as, its diverse physical, social and economic environments. It was predicted by several major Christian organizations that by the turn of the millennium, Africa would be a predominantly Christian nation and it appears that those predictions have been on target as large portions of the African population identify themselves as Christians. In 1900, indigenous religions made up the majority of African religions in sub-Saharan Africa, but now those religions have dwindled and have largely been replaced by Christianity. In Northern Africa, Islam reigns as the dominant religion although Christianity has made some inroads as witnessed by the religious factional fighting in Ethiopia.

Although, Christianity clearly has a foothold in sub-Saharan African, it is not clear how deep its roots are in practice as many observe a mixture of tribal religions melded with Christianity. This patois is largely regional and varies from village to village, as many Africans have been reluctant to abandon the old ways entirely and instead have found new ways to incorporate tribal religion with Christianity.

The Religion of the Yoruba People

Those who follow Yoruba religion believe that through foresight, proper character, appropriate behavior, and sacrifice, ones life can be improved on earth rather than waiting for an afterlife, which is quite similar to humanist thought that holds no particular reverence for any entity but relies of self-sufficiency and living a good life now.

The religion is based on a belief in one god, the creator, along with a number of deities that represent various forces of nature. These deities are called Orishas, which is a Yoruba word. During slavery in Cuba, praise of the Orishas was often disguised as prayer to the Catholic saints who are very similar in that each saint has a specialty, such as St. Christopher who is the patron saint of travelers;

Shango is the God of lightning, thunder, fire, the drums and dance among the Orishas.

Although most Western texts mention African slaves being taught Christianity, few make mention of the religion they brought with them, and when it is mentioned African religions are often labeled as primitive and superstitious. Most African religions were more complex than whites realized at the time and actually had many similarities with Western religions including the concept of one God as well as a host of saints or lesser gods known as Orishas. In addition to the indigenous religions brought from Africa, it is also clear that just as Christianity spread from Israel as far north as Spain, Islam spread to the east and west and finally south into sub-Saharan Africa and the slaves brought to the Americas represented a blend of religious backgrounds.

Yoruba was the primary religion practiced in the area where the majority of slaves were captured by African and Arab tribes and then sold to European traders. The Bantu people populate the area now known as Nigeria, Benin and Togo where the Yoruba religion is still practiced today although it is beginning to fade as Christianity and Islam overtake it. Ironically, Yoruba is experiencing a rebirth in the United States and other places around the world as it is dying out in Africa.

Orisha worship spread to the new world through the slave trade. In order to preserve their religious traditions, the African slaves substituted Christian saints for the gods or Orishas, which allowed them to keep their religion alive beneath a thin veneer of Catholicism. African slaves brought to Brazil by the Portuguese in the 1550's never relinquished their religion, but mixed it with Catholicism, keeping its gods and rituals alive in stories and secret ceremonies. The Africans also found much in common with the religious practices of the native Brazilian Indians. [42] This hybrid religion took deep hold in African communities in Brazil and Cuba and years later following the Cuban revolution of 1959, the religion spread to Puerto Rico, Venezuela and the United States, especially New York City and Florida. Curiously, the Yoruba religion is beginning to grow in the United States just as it is being replaced by Christianity and Islam in Africa.[43]

New World Religion

Numerous texts written by pre-twentieth century white authors belittled African religion calling it nothing more than a childish and primitive ritual despite the long and complex history of African religious practices. Hollywood was particularly potent in distorting and debasing African religion on film making it seem superstitious, savage and ignorant. However, the religion that was practiced by the slaves who were brought to the United States is still practiced and is just as complex and rich as Christianity.

Santeria or Regla de Ocha as it is also known, is an indigenous form of Yoruba religion that has absorbed aspects or Roman Catholicism while maintaining Yoruba traditions. There are nearly 3 million adherents of this religion in Cuba where it was once outlawed by the Communist government. In Brazil, this hybrid religion is known as Candomble. Although Candomble and Santeria share roots in traditional Yoruba religion, Candomble has adopted some rituals and ideas from the indigenous Indians of South America while also blending in strains of Portuguese Catholicism.

Candomblé resembles the ancient Yoruban traditional religions also worshiped in Santería, and retains the Yoruban names of the Orishas. Candomblé ceremonies follow much the same pattern as those of the Santería and Voudon. Santería or Lucumi originates in West Africa in what is now Nigeria and Benin. It is the traditional religion of the Yoruba peoples there. The slave trade brought many of these people to the shores of Cuba, Brazil, Haiti, Trinidad and Puerto Rico among others. In the New World, much of the religion was hidden behind a facade of Catholicism. [44, 45]

Santeria is a broad group of religious and spiritual practices developed in Cuba based on traditional Yoruba religions and is widely spread throughout the Caribbean and South America. Santeria has been influenced by other African ethnic groups and even European Christianity. It is difficult to determine worldwide numbers of Santerians because the religion goes by different names in different regions. According to recent estimates, there are nearly 800,000 Santerians in the United States. Although "Santeria" is commonly used in comparative religion/academic literature, it is becoming increasingly accepted among practitioners of the Western Yoruba/Orisha religious tradition. There are Brazilian, Haitian, and other Caribbean forms of religion that are closely related to Santeria because of their common roots. Candomble and Umbanda in Brazil and Voudon in Haiti overlap somewhat with Santeria.

Voudon or Voodoo as it is commonly known also originated from the same area in Africa as Yoruba. Hollywood moviemakers during the mid 1900's gave Americans, including African Americans, a distorted image of Voodoo, concentrating on voodoo dolls and zombies, but there is more to Voudon than Hollywood ever knew. Voodoo is probably the best-known example of African religion although it is generally misunderstood. It is an Afro-Caribbean fusion of different religious beliefs and practices taken from the practices of the Fon, the Nago, the Ibos, Dahomeans, Congos, Senegalese, Haussars, Caplaous, Mondungues,

Mandinge, Angolese, Libyans, Ethiopians, and the Malgaches.[46] The name is traceable to an African word for "spirit". It can also be directly traced to the West African Yoruba people, while its roots may go back 6,000 years in Africa, in today's Togo, Benin and Nigeria.

What the Europeans didn't understand, they were quick to label as superstition, but studies since those colonial times have revealed that African religions were just as sophisticated if not more so than the European models to which they were compared. While there is no question that superstition was part of the African psyche of colonial times, it was also a clear element for all races during that particular time in world history and no one race had the superstition market cornered. Slaves were baptized into the Roman Catholic Church upon their arrival in Haiti and other West Indian islands, but with little Christian authority to maintain the Catholic faith, the slaves followed their original native faith, which they practiced in secret.[47] Although ancient religions such as these may seem remote, they are still being practiced by groups of Blacks, especially in large cities like New York, Chicago and Los Angeles, which are capable of supporting a variety of religious beliefs and congregations. During French colonial times, Voudon was actively suppressed in Haiti where it now flourishes. Today over 60 million people practice Voudon worldwide.

THE BIBLE AND SLAVERY

> *"The relationship of the creator to the created is analogous to that of master to slave. The religious picture of the universe is akin to a model prison, wherein inmates are beholden to the warden for their daily bread and their highest duty is to praise and supplicate him for life."*

Unfortunately, one of the most abominable chapters in American history is how the Bible was used and interpreted to justify racism and slavery. Racial relations, especially between whites and Blacks, have long been deplorable in the United States. They started out badly, got worse before they got better, and are nevertheless still poor with slim prospects of improving a great deal any time soon and religion shares a significant part of the blame.

When speaking of slavery and the Bible, the first and most obvious thing to remember is that there is no specific condemnation of slavery to be found anywhere in it. At no point does God or Jesus express even mild disapproval of enslaving human beings and robbing them of what freedom and independence they might have had. Instead, God is depicted as both approving of and regulating slavery, ensuring that the traffic and ownership of fellow human beings proceeded in an acceptable manner (1 Peter 2:18-21). In many cases, the regulations display an apparent disregard for the lives and dignity of enslaved individuals, hardly the sort of thing one would expect from a loving God. It should be observed that the King James Version of the Bible replaces the word "slave" with "servant" and in this fashion is misleading Christians as to the intentions and desires of their God. Although, slavery existed long before the "Middle Passage" occurred, the brand of slavery practiced in the United States was unique.

ISLAM AND SLAVERY

It is clear that Islam also came to the Americas with slavery and now it is one of the fastest growing religions in the world. In the United States alone, there are more than 6 million adherents. Interestingly, more than 60 percent of American Muslims are either Black or Asian with people of Arabic descent making up less than 30 percent. The majority of Arabs in the United States are Catholic Christians.[48] Although the presence of Islam is widely accepted in the Black community, compared to Christianity its adherents make up only a tiny but dedicated portion of Black religion thanks in large part to the late Malcolm X and the controversial but popular Minister Louis Farrakhan. There are other religions in the Black community, but these other religions are virtually invisible outside of the large cities that are capable of sustaining a variety of beliefs.

When speaking of religion, Americans in general and African Americans in particular tend to forget the multiplicity of faiths in the United States and instead focus on Christianity ignoring the fact that there are numerous other religions practiced in this country. Asides from the traditional denominations recognized in the United States such as Catholic, Baptist, Episcopal and Presbyterian, Blacks practice a variety of different faiths including Islam, Judaism and a variety of Caribbean and South American religions like Condomble, Voudon and Santeria.

Chapter 4

Black Belief

"The truths of religion are never so well understood as by those who have lost the power of reasoning."

—*Voltaire*

Christianity is clearly the dominant religion in the Black community, far outnumbering other faiths or religious positions and Black belief in God is unequivocally positive. Data from the National Survey of Black Americans (NSBA) indicates that approximately 84 percent of Black men and women define themselves as being very religious or fairly religious. An overwhelming number of African-Americans identify themselves as Christian and in a poll conducted by the Barna Research Group; the top-rated goal selected by 94 percent of African-Americans when asked to identify their goals in life was "to have a close, personal relationship with God", surpassing even choices of good health and comfort. In addition, a majority of Blacks surveyed believe the only reason to live is to know, love and serve God, which ranks significantly higher than either whites or Hispanics.[49]

Church is also important part of Black life with nearly 50 percent of American Blacks attending church on a given Sunday, which is about 5 percent to 10 percent higher than the national standard. In addition, 83 percent of African-Americans say their religious faith is very important in their lives compared to 68 percent of whites.[50] In 1997, 87 percent of Americans said their religious faith was important to them but in 2001 that figure dropped to 68 percent, a nineteen-point drop.[51] The International Social Survey Program received 62 percent favorable response to the question; "I know God exists and have no doubts about it," in the white community, whereas nearly 90 percent of Africans American responded favorably which is about 30 percent higher than the national average.

In fact, 82 percent of Blacks believe that God is "the all powerful, all-knowing, perfect creator who rules the world today." [52] Not only are Blacks more likely to believe in God, they are also more likely to believe their prayers are answered and in times of crisis 92 percent of African-Americans are "absolutely certain" they can count on God to answer their prayers, which is substantially more than either whites or Hispanics.[53]

In addition, Blacks tend to view their relationship with God and Jesus in a closely personal manner, in which the supernatural almost becomes a personal mentor and friend. George Barna, the President of the Barna Research Group, said, "While whites tend to be self-reliant, Blacks are more likely to rely on God. Whites persevere on their drive to achieve, Blacks do so, based on their faith. Whites turn to business leaders and government officials to represent them in the world; Blacks support their religious leaders. These two groups have very divergent strategies for interpreting and dealing with virtually every aspect of life."[54] This comment reflects tradition as nearly two-thirds of African-American adults list their pastor as a community leader, as well as a primary spokesman for the Black community, which ties in with the Black church historically being a meeting place during crises and an organizer of people.

Blacks are also much more likely than either whites or Hispanics to read the Bible, pray to God, attend Sunday school, participate in a small religious group, and have a quiet time during a typical week.[55] The religious differences also vary by region as people in the South are more likely to report being absolutely committed to Christianity, reading the Bible, attending Sunday school, and having a quiet time. They are also more likely to be born again (50 percent vs. 39 percent in the rest of the nation) and to be an evangelical (10 percent vs. 5 percent in the rest of the country).

BELIEF IN GOD

A recent CNN/USA Today/Gallup Poll indicates 96 percent of the U.S. population says they believe in God. The question that generated that 96 percent figure was "Do you believe in God or a universal spirit?" [56] During a survey conducted by the International Social Survey Program, when participants were asked to respond to the statement "I know God exists and I have no doubts about it," only

62 percent replied affirmatively, indicating that Americans aren't quite so sure of their convictions.[57]

Despite the high level of belief in God, more than 45 percent say they give priority to their own views and the views of others when deciding a course of action. Even with the high emphasis on God and religious teachings, about 50 percent of Americans say that religion has unnecessary rules and prefer the ala carte approach that allows them to "pick" and "choose" what they feel is right or what conveniently fits with their behavior patterns.[58]

THE BIBLE

The Bible is the one book most likely to be found in the home of Blacks. It is the world's best selling book and Blacks seem to read it more than the rest of the country and among households which own a Bible, Blacks are more than likely to have at least three.

Statistics for praying and reading the Bible vary widely as 94 percent of Blacks reported praying regularly compared to the national average of 77 percent and were twice as likely compared to other Americans to have read from the Bible in the past week. The national average for Bible readership is 31 percent. Research also showed that Blacks are more likely to believe the Bible is totally accurate 64-41 percent compared to whites showing a considerable gap in those who believe the Bible to be inerrant.[59]

Almost every household in America, 92 percent, has a copy of the Bible, including the homes of atheists and agnostics.[60] However, according to a Gallup poll, overall readership of the Bible has declined since the 1980's from 73 percent to 59 percent today while the same poll says that 65 percent of Americans say that the Bible "answers all or most of the basic questions of life." Curiously, 28 percent of those who agreed with this said they rarely read the Bible or never read it.[61]

In 1997, nearly 58 percent of Americans believed the Bible to be totally accurate but in 2001, that figure dropped 17 points to 41 percent, a swing of more than 30 million people. George Gallup Jr., son of the founder of the Gallup Organization said there is vast difference "between Americans stated faith and their lack of the most basic knowledge about that faith." [62] Americans ignorance of the Bible can be shown in that 12 percent of adults believe that Joan of Arc was Noah's wife and only 42 percent of Christian adults know that the Sermon on the Mount was preached by Jesus.[63]

The ubiquitous Bible is not only the best selling book in the world; it is also the most translated book in the world. It has been translated into more than 40 languages including Chinese and Braille. It decorates millions of coffee tables and bookshelves in the United States and often serves as a diary for family history. It populates courthouses and legislative digs where it is revered as talisman of truth. It is sworn on, used as a judicial prop and bumped on the heads of children during solemn events. It comes in a variety of colors including red, white and blue with gold edged pages and even tabs. It ranges in size from small enough to fit in a pocket to large enough to require both hands to lift it.

One thing about the Bible that seems sure is that not everyone agrees with it, understands it or even actually reads it. As the numbers indicate, for many the Bible serves no other purpose than as a conversation piece or political decoration. The Bible was written over the course of centuries by many different authors with different agendas, which were often prompted by political expediency rather than truth. Although the Council of Nicaea took great pains in putting it together, the Bible is filled with errors and few people understand that the Bible as it is, popularly printed, was voted into existence. The council literally picked and chose among various texts and often the Council's choices were the result of power struggles and had nothing to do with accuracy or history.

Whether anyone wants to admit it or not, the Bible is filled with glaring contradictions, bad science and numerous errors, that will not go away no matter how sincere or fervent the belief. Still, even with the number of people who claim to read the Bible, these things seem to go unnoticed, except among Biblical scholars whose research rarely reaches the regular reader of the Bible.

Interestingly, nearly all of the participants for this writing including nonbelievers and freethinkers claimed and demonstrated extensive knowledge of the Bible including its many contradictions and errors. Not only were they familiar with its contents, the majority possessed knowledge that extended well past the Bible and included the study of works by various theologians, sociologists and historians, as well as noted scientists, philosophers and humanists.

Reflecting the continued dominance of women in the church, research shows that women are twice as likely to read the Bible than men and that Blacks are more likely to read the Bible than whites.[64] Barna commented that the survey challenges some widely held assumptions. "Charismatic and Pentecostal churches are often characterized as attracting people who respond on the basis of emotions but who lack strong biblical training."

Education also has a direct influence on religious belief throughout the world, with the uneducated tending to have higher belief rates than those with advanced education. Of the nearly nine out of ten people who define themselves as Christians, seventy-two percent of Americans with a high school education or less believed the Bible to be totally accurate while only 46 percent of Americans with postgraduate degrees felt the same.[65] Nationally, less than half of all adults (41 percent) believe the Bible is totally accurate in all it teaches.

EDUCATION AND RELIGION

> *Few intelligent Christians can still hold to the idea that the Bible is an infallible Book, that it contains no linguistic errors, no historical discrepancies, no antiquated scientific assumptions, not even bad ethical standards. Historical investigation and literary criticism have taken the magic out of the Bible and have made it a composite human book, written by many hands in different ages. The existence of thousands of variations of texts makes it impossible to hold the doctrine of a book verbally infallible. Some might claim for the original copies of the Bible an infallible character, but this view only begs the question and makes such Christian apologetics more ridiculous in the eyes of the sincere man.*
>
> —*Elmer Homrighausen*

Another interesting anomaly is that most Americans do not accept evangelism as a personal responsibility even though the call for personal evangelism stems from the Bible and its call to go forth unto all nations spreading the word of God. It is controversial because it often seems to be in conflict with individual privacy. Only one-third of Christians (32 percent) claim they have an obligation to share their religious faith with those who believe differently.[66] One of the most remarkable and controversial aspects of insights into America's Christian faith is the fact that less than half of all adults (40 percent) are convinced that Jesus Christ lived a sinless life during his life on earth which is a direct contradiction of everything Christianity teaches about its namesake—Jesus.

Chapter 5

▼

Sleeping with Extraterrestrials

"...when it comes to the supernatural, ESP, psychic powers, astrology and so forth, lots of people have a different standard. They believe because they want to believe. They care less about proof because believing makes them happy."

—*John Stossel* [67]

"When you believe in things that you don't understand, then you suffer..." These words from Stevie Wonder's hit song *Superstition* seem to summarize the potential for the danger in living life unexamined. Superstition still abounds in both the Black and white communities. According to a recent Gallup poll, almost 50 percent of adults still claim to be anything from a little superstitious to very superstitious.[68] In the Black community, psychics, spiritualists, palm readers, card readers and root men and women are still making decent if not extravagant living from patrons who readily part with their money for what amounts to hocus-pocus and mumbo-jumbo.

...superstitious thinking springs from misunderstandings of probability and random processes, errors of logical reasoning, and cognitive shortcuts that sacrifice accuracy.[69]

AT HOME WITH SUPERSTITION

Haints, hexes and roots are no strangers to the Black community. Unfortunately, the belief in these unproven phenomena can lead to unreal expectations and often disappointment. In the worst cases, superstition can lead people to delay taking needed action waiting for spiritual intervention when direct action is required. In the Black community, the world of special powers such as the ability to see into the future, interpret dreams, read minds and to cast spells is real for many despite scientific evidence showing otherwise.

This superstition contributes to thousands of dollars that flow to the pockets of clever con men and women who would otherwise go broke if located in a less superstitious part of the community. Blacks are often stereotyped as being highly superstitious and although this is not the case for a majority of Blacks, there are enough who fit the stereotype to give these psychic frauds and religious shysters a good living.

Superstition has been linked to Black stereotypes in this country since the time of slavery, but just a nonformal look at the world in general shows that there are no clear signs that superstition is fading as 35-44 percent of Americans believe in some aspect of psychic phenomena including ghosts and ESP.[70, 71]

PARANORMAL IS ALMOST NORMAL

In a telephone survey regarding psychic belief of 2,392 respondents, nearly 7 percent believed in the power of psychics to predict the future, but that poll is just the tip of the iceberg when it comes to superstition in the United States.[72] A Gallup Poll conducted in June of 2001 showed the figures to be much higher. Fifty-four percent of Americans believe in the physic or spiritual healing. The survey also showed that 50 percent of Americans also believe in ESP and telepathy while another 28 percent believe that people can hear from or communicate mentally with someone who has died.[73] Poll after poll in the United States shows that Americans believe in things such as UFOs, angels, psychics, reincarnation and ghosts when there is absolutely no credible proof to support these beliefs.

Even now, almost one in four people believe in astrology. Even a former president of the United States, an avowed Christian, consulted an astrologer. In Hollywood, it is expected that a variety of strange, weird and even kinky beliefs might flow from there, but it would seem that in the age of science and technology superstition would disappear. Yet, belief in ghosts, spirits and angels is at an all time high with nearly 38 percent of Americans believing that ghosts or spirits can come back to earth in certain times and places.[74]

A Gallup Poll also showed that 72 percent believe in angels. Even hard news magazines such as Time and Newsweek have devoted special sections to discussing angels, spirits and religion in general, but have never taken a prime time look at nonbelief. Although no scientific evidence of any supernatural phenomena has ever been put forward, major news organizations have not hesitated to promote such unsupported stories. In an age that is largely ruled by science and technology, these figures are difficult to take seriously in 2003. However, numerous other polls have shown nearly identical results and new polls indicate that nearly 35-44 percent of Americans believe in at least some aspect of psychic phenomena.[75] This unfounded belief in paranormal occurrences and outright superstition has helped build thriving businesses for barely legal hucksters, spiritual con men and women, and marginal new age spiritualists.

Unfortunately, superstition is likely to lead to or cause financial difficulties making people targets for a variety of scams including unscrupulous cons by preachers and other religious fakers. Superstition's realm negates the reality of reason and reduces thinking to a useless and unnecessary burden. Regrettably, it seems that superstition is very much alive and it thrives across America and especially in the Black community where palm readers, psychics, card readers and a host of ethereal con men and women make unearned livings fleecing the gullible flock. Consulting with spiritualist and seers plays into a dual edged stereotype that projects Blacks as superstitious children who are afraid of their own shadows on one hand; or, it casts Blacks as masters of the paranormal with special connections to the world of spirits as depicted in hundreds of Hollywood Voodoo movies.

Dial A Psychic *(Contributed by Reginald Finley)*

On Sunday morning, the 15th of August, I was looking in the classifieds section of the *Atlanta Journal and Constitution*. As I was searching for a new career, I came across an ad in the counseling section which was recruiting for psychics. I couldn't believe it. "Counseling, I can do that," I thought to myself. I called the number advertised and spoke to a gentleman who informed me to meet with him at a *Shoney's* restaurant in the northwest end of town (Cobb Pkwy, Marietta, GA). When I arrived there a conference room in the back was already filled with eager people waiting to learn the particulars of psychic-hood. I apologized for being late and humorously informed them that if I were psychic I would have found the place. They all chuckled. The ringleader was a warm and friendly Caucasian female around 30ish. She began to explain the hours involved, paper work, commission structure, tricks of the trade, and so on. The concept seemed sound enough. The longer you keep the caller on the line the more you get paid. So, if you are consistently receiving calls you can make a fortune. A computer program calculates everyone's averages and distributes calls based on your averages.

I decided to give it a try. A "ring master" line was added in my home and in two days the calls came rolling in. I was taken aback at how amazingly gullible and ignorant these people were. I received calls ranging from the curious to the suicidal, from the depressed to the disheartened, from young to old. No one seemed immune. Over 75 percent of callers were female and 50 percent of those were over the age of 55. It gets worse. A startling 95 percent of my callers made insinuations, and some overtly, that they believe in a god. My first thought, "Then why are you calling me? The Bible explicitly forbids this behavior." Also, over 95 percent of my callers truly believed that I was psychic. Some even made reference to God giving me this ability as a gift, and that I should use it often. Of course the truth is that the callers had given me plenty information about themselves. Even them not speaking gave subtle clues that any observant person would pick up on. Breathing, background noise, pauses, interjections, tone of voice. All these factors play a role. I guessed rather easily whether someone had children, were married, dying, or ill. Even the sex of their children I guessed. (Hey, you've got a fifty-fifty chance of getting it right, so what did I have to lose?) No special powers here though. It was all done utilizing reason, probability, and luck. Is it by chance that I guessed that a man was dating a woman whose name begun with an "M"? Not at all. He told me. Part of his reading went as follows…

Psychic: "I don't know why, but I see someone in your life."
Gullible 1: "Really, what do you see?"

Psychic: "I see someone whose name starts with an "M" in your life."
Gullible 1: "Wow," (clue #1) "Uhhh, where did that come from?"

Psychic: (Utilizing clue #1 to suppress doubt) "I don't know, I'm certain (now I am) that someone whose name starts with an "M" will be an important factor in your life."
Gullible 1: "That's amazing! I'm dating a woman named Martha."

At this point I could have told him anything, true or false. It doesn't matter what I say at this point because hey, I'm psychic. Did I simply make a good guess? Darn right I did, but a very ambiguous one at that. He could have easily applied the letter "M" to anything. He began to assist me in trying to discover what the significance of the letter "M" was. Even if the "M" didn't pertain to his past or present, I could have easily transferred it to his future. Either way, I win. I'm psychic remember?

Another reading went as follows…

Fooled again: "Are my boyfriend and I going to stay together?" (Kind of obvious there's a problem if she's asking)

Psychic: "I sense troubling waters up ahead. I hear arguments...." (pause......)
Fooled again: "Well, yeah (surprised) we've been arguing a lot lately." (No...really???)

Psychic: "I see some children here."
Fooled again: "Yeah, we have a daughter." (I later discovered that her boyfriend has a son that visits from time to time. This added more credibility.)

Psychic: "I sense some infidelity here......"(long pause)
Fooled again: "(chuckling) "Really..." (pause again)......(quivering) "Hmmmm...."

A long pause generally denotes personal reflection. She obviously was wondering whether I knew if it was her or not. If she were guilt free she would have quickly responded with: "Who is he cheating on me with?" "Do I know her?" However, she didn't, so I saw the hole and went for it.

Psychic: (concerned) "You've cheated on him haven't you?"
Fooled again: "Oh, my god!!!! How did you know that?"

I so badly wanted to say, "I didn't, you just told me idiot!" Needless to say that at this point she was convinced. She stayed on the phone with me for a complete hour. Let's see, $4.99 a minute times 60 is, well, you do the math. Eventually, I began to feel awful perpetuating such an obvious fraud, especially since mysticism goes against everything I support. So as a result I quit. I regret that I didn't tell these people after the reading that it was all trickery and psychological games. Money, silenced me. I'm elated that I can now tell this story and be an opponent of mysticism.[76]

PSYCHICS FOR THE COMMUNITY

Television advertising for "psychics" is clearly aimed at the Black community. These ads feature a host of Black entertainers on the downside of their careers hawking psychic mediums. People pay $3.99 per minute or $239.40 per hour to talk to these hocus-pocus hucksters and it is no mistake that the Black community is targeted for such deliberate ventures. "One component of the African-American stereotype is superstition, which is manifested as excessive religious devotion and a penchant for the supernatural and psychics use this stereotype to bilk Blacks out of their money.[77]

In an essay published in the *African Americans for Humanism Newsletter*, Dr. Charles Faulkner said, "Society equates African-American religion to their viewing themselves as children (in opposition to the "father," "God"). It equates their propensity for the use of astrology to the failure to develop their ability to determine with the use of logic how to make their lives successful. It equates their acceptance of superstition as a contribution to the evolution of a fearful race of people who are prone to manipulation. And, it equates the belief in the "What goes around, comes around," concept of poetic justice to a race of people who sit idly by, waiting for some unseen force to rescue them from the evils of their society while the perpetrators of the evil go unpunished...The very oppression of African-Americans cries out for them to throw off the cloak of the supernatural, which appears in the form of astrology, ESP, palmistry, theism and ghosts—and to throw off the fear and intimidation that accompany them. Freedom requires sound, logical thinking that removes the crutches of phenomena whose existence has never been proven." [78]

The Psychic Friends Network managed to empty the pockets of thousands using its stable of 2,000 psychics to foretell the future at $3.99 a minute. The popular network fronted by former singer Dionne Warwick recently filed for bankruptcy. The company, which once raked in more than $100 million in annual revenue, should have seen it coming. Ms. Warwick's psychic friends also were unable to warn her when she was arrested at Miami International Airport after baggage screeners said they found 11 suspected marijuana cigarettes inside her lipstick container. The charges were later dropped.

Recently, popular psychic, Miss Cleo, was hit with two lawsuits from the Missouri Attorney General for allegedly violating the state's no-call law and consumer fraud statutes. The head-wrapped, Jamaican patois spouting physic regularly appears on television commercials and late night television spots promising insight in personal love life's, lottery predications and relationships.[79, 80] Unfortunately, for Miss Cleo, her physic powers did not reveal the lawsuit in the making.

Another popular psychic "pitch" is the ability to speak with the dead. Among those capitalizing on the grief industry is John Edward, (born John MaGee Jr.), host of the short-lived television show *Crossing Over* where he supposedly communicated with the dead on the behalf of their relatives. Edward has been unmasked as a fraud by James Randi as well as reports from several news organizations. Still, he and others like him make princely livings playing upon the hopes and desperation of grieving families. Several families who lost loved ones in the World Trade Center disaster allegedly contacted Edward.

Although, what he does is despicable and borderline unethical, he and others like him are only guilty of playing on people's grief for personal enrichment. However, when people die because of superstition or belief in the paranormal, it becomes an extremely serious problem. Two major problem areas are the denial or medical treatment and the selling of miracle cures and operations. Each day faith healers and psychic surgeons prey on sick people by giving them false hope that often delays pivotal medical treatment, but not before extracting a fee and leaving the patient to seek real medical care long after it is too late to help.

PSYCHIC SURGEONS AND FAITH HEALERS

The death of comedian-actor Andy Kaufman focused attention on psychic surgery when Kaufman went to a Phillipino psychic surgeon after being diagnosed with lung cancer. During the treatment received by Kaufman, the psychic surgeon removed Kaufman's diseased tissue and later pronounced him ready to return to work, which he did. Kaufman died a short time later of lung cancer and x-rays showed Kaufman's lungs to be in the same state as before the psychic surgery.[81]

James Randi, a former magician and noted debunker, has investigated psychic surgeons and found that their alleged surgery is nothing more than clever sleight-of-hand mixed with an assortment of concealed animal guts and blood. Recently, several of the most famous of the psychic surgeons have been arrested for fraud, but probably more revealing is the reliance of these so-called healers on regular medical doctors to heal them or their family members. Still, the frauds can average up to $40,000 a month income from unsuspecting patients.

THE POWER OF PRAYER?

Today there is much made about the power of prayer to help heal the sick. All three major television networks have actually televised shows talking about the power of prayer to help the sick. However, new research published in the Archives of Internal Medicine was the first to look at the negative affects of religious beliefs in healing.[82] In a study of 600 patients, of whom 95 percent were Christian, scientists at Duke University Medical Center found that religious beliefs aren't always a source of comfort when people are ill. According to the researchers, in some cases religious beliefs may actually increase the risk of death. Researchers found that the key factors that served to increase the risk of death were feelings of being abandoned or punished by God or that some patients believed that their illness was caused by the devil. Patients who reported feeling alienated from God or who blamed the devil for their sickness, had a 19 to 28 percent increased risk of dying during the following two years.[83] A Gallup poll showed that people who are terminally ill would rather have a visit from their doctor than from their pastor.

FAITH HEALERS

> *"Reduced to its basics faith-healing today-as it always has been—simply magic."* [84]

In the movie "Leap of Faith", comedian-actor Steve Martin played a sleazy evangelist who used a truckload of scams and cons to fleece the flock as a traveling revivalist. Martin's character used everything from pickpockets, con men and electronics to make his traveling show seem like reality. However, it seems that truth, is indeed, even stranger than fiction as each year millions of people are duped into parting with their money, believing in things that are patently unbelievable and exposing themselves to potentially fatal situations.

Most visible among faith healers have been Christian Scientists whose faith does not allow the use of doctors or medicines, but instead they rely on the providence of God to cure or not to cure illness with the most controversy being aroused when God does not cure an illness and death results. To followers of the faith it is God's will, but even among other religions, it is a blatant disregard for life. Each year, 10-20 preventable deaths occur among groups like the Christian Scientists and other groups with similar ideology.

Stephen Barrett, M.D., noted that there is no evidence at all that "faith" healing actually works and believes in order for "faith" healing to be even considered there must be proof. "In my opinion, three criteria must be met: (1) the ailment must be one that normally doesn't recover without treatment; (2) there must not have been any medical treatment that would be expected to influence the ailment; and (3) both diagnosis and recovery must be demonstrable by detailed medical evidence.[85] Still, a poll of 1,000 adults regarding "faith" healing indicated that nearly 80 percent believed that spiritual faith could help people recover from disease.[86]

This overwhelming faith has often led to tragedy, as people often delayed needed medical attention in hopes that a miracle would occur. An example of this tragedy is the death of an 11-year-old Oregon boy who died of easily treatable complications from diabetes after suffering painful symptoms for a week and lapsing into a coma. The boy had been dead for about three hours when detectives arrived at the family home and found about 100 people praying. Often members of these religions regularly visit dentists and optometrists, but children with life-threatening conditions are offered only prayers.

A Pennsylvania couple was convicted of involuntary manslaughter and child endangerment in the death of their daughter. The husband and wife, both members of Faith Tabernacle Congregation, were sentenced to a maximum of five years in jail for not seeking medical attention for their 16-year-old daughter, who died of complications from untreated diabetes. Another child from the same family died previously of an untreated ear infection.

An article published in *Pediatrics* in 1998 said that 172 children died as a result of the parents withholding medical care because of reliance on religious rituals and beliefs. Of that number, 140 deaths were from medical conditions for which survival rates with medical care would have exceeded 90 percent.[87] Although, there are several religions that follow this practice, the Christian Science Church is most noted for this practice. Estimates say that every month between one and five children die due to the religious beliefs of their parents.

Faith healers and the belief in divine intervention have been popular throughout religious history and there are thousands of tomes filled with episodes of miracles and magic. However, investigations into faith healing have provided no evidence of such a phenomena, even though large numbers of people believe it to be true.[88] During the 1950's, British psychiatrist Dr. Louis Rose started investigating incidents of faith healing. Over a twenty-year span, Rose investigated hundreds of cases but found no evidence of any miracle cures.

"After twenty years of work I have yet to find one 'miracle' cure…I cannot be convinced of the efficacy of what is commonly called 'faith healing'." [89] Another investigation of faith healing by Minnesota surgeon, Dr. William Nolen, also produced no results. Nolen actually attended services conducted by Katherine Kuhlman where she apparently "healed" a number of people. Nolen actually did "follow ups" with those who were healed and found no evidence of them being cured. In fact, at least one of those "healed" died a short time later of complications of the disease that had been "healed." [90] In another case, Nolen said a female patient reported that a psychic surgeon had actually removed several screws from her fractured hip, but later X-Rays showed that the screws were still there.

James Randi has done extensive investigation of claims of faith healing and has found no evidence that such claims are true. More importantly, Randi has uncovered the "tricks" of numerous faith healers and has often done so in public like he did in when he unmasked evangelist Peter Popoff on *The Johnny Carson Show* where he revealed how Popoff's miraculous medical insight was actually being delivered not by a divine communication, but through high technology by the voice of his wife who was transmitting to him through a tiny ear receiver from her position back stage.[91]

In Mathew Barry's *Adventures in Faith Healing*, he tells of how he attended a Benny Hinn Miracle Crusade that he claimed was long on hype and marketing but short on miracles. "Brooks and I wondered why Hinn didn't make an amputee's arm grow back right there on the stage. Why didn't he make a bald man grow hair? How about removing scars from a burn victims face? No. We noticed all of Hinn's healings had the common characteristics of being internal, invisible, and unverifiable."[92] Faith healing is not a new phenomenon, but it is interesting that in an age of science and technology so many people believe in it.

AFTER ALL THESE YEARS

From the beginning, religion and science have been at odds as religion has been continually pushed back by science and there is no reason why it won't continue to do so. Miracles are now the realm of ordinary science. The healing of a disease, turning one's life around, or raising enough money to build a church is all done with practiced regularity and technology and science are the major reasons.

> *"The root of the trouble is that the theory of evolution contradicts a literal reading of the first 11 chapters of Genesis."*[93]
>
> *"Christians who say they take the Bible literally are either ignorant or self-deluded."*[94]

Darwin's theory of evolution caused major unrest in the religious community when it was published in 1859 and more than 140 years after its publication, it still stirs the fires of many religionists who eventually developed "creation science" as an alternate theory. Creation science is based on a literal interpretation of the Bible, especially the creation account in the first book of the Bible—Genesis. Using the Bible as a strict guide "creation scientists" have determined that the universe is just 6,000 to 12,000 years old which flies in the face of scientific measurement that shows the earth to be at least 4-5 billion years old. Despite its religious underpinnings, "creation science" is not a theory nor is it "science" that is even marginally accepted anywhere in the world. Nevertheless, majorities of Americans believe that God and evolution are tied together, a view that is quite different from other civilizations around the world.

Less than 35 percent of Americans believe in human evolution, whereas 75 percent of Great Britain and Germany believe in the theory of evolution. Even Russia and Northern Ireland, which rank at 50 percent, surpass the United States where almost 60 percent believe in the creationist theory of evolution.[95] A recent Gallup poll showed that only 12 percent of more than 10,000 adults polled believed that "human beings have developed over millions of years from less advanced forms of life, but God had no part in this process." Most preferred the statement that "Human beings have developed over millions of years from less advanced forms of life, but God guided this process." [96] An International Social Survey Program showed that Americans ranked last or were the least knowledgeable of the 21 countries surveyed regarding the theory of evolution. At the top of the list were Japan, Germany, Canada and as well as Great Britain, Italy and Norway.[97]

The Religious Landscape

Christianity has operated with an unmitigated arrogance and cruelty—necessarily, since a religion ordinarily imposes on those who have discovered the true faith the spiritual duty of liberating the infidels. —James Baldwin, "Letter from a Region in My Mind," in New Yorker (17 Nov. 1962; The Fire Next Time, 1963).

How so many absurd rules of conduct, as well as so many absurd religious beliefs, have originated, we do not know; nor how it is that they have become, in all quarters of the world, so deeply impressed on the minds of men; but it is worthy of remark that a belief constantly inculcated during the early years of life, while the brain is impressionable, appears to acquire almost the nature of an instinct; and the very essence of an instinct is that it is followed independently of reason. —Charles Darwin, Descent of Man p. 122

CHAPTER 6

GLOBAL RELIGIOUS ESTIMATES

"The invisible and the non-existent look very much alike."

—*Delos McKown*

Global estimates for nonbelievers range from 700 million to more than 1.2 billion worldwide making nonbelievers rank third in number compared to Christianity which is first with nearly 1.8 billion adherents and Islam which is second with approximately 1.3 billion. According to the 1994 World Almanac, atheists number about 800,000 million worldwide.[98] Measures that are more current vary widely as the lists below illustrate.

Major Religions of the World Ranked by Number of Adherents[99]

Christianity: 2 billion   Islam: 1.3 billion

Hinduism: 900 million   Secular/Nonreligious/Agnostic/Atheist: 850 million

Worldwide Adherents of All Religions by Six Continental Areas, Mid-1995[100]

Christians: 1.9 Billion   Atheist/Nonreligious 1.1 Billion

Muslims 1 Billion   Hindus 781 Million

One reason for the disparity in the figures concerning nonbelief or atheism is that atheism is not an organized faction. Most religions have a hierarchical structure of which the Catholic Church is a good example. Christianity's roots can be traced directly through the Catholic Church, which is essentially the genesis of all Christianity despite the hundreds of branches that exist today. Until Martin Luther posted his 95 theses on the doors of Wittenburg castle in Hamburg, Germany, Roman Catholicism was the basis of Christianity. Martin Luther started the protest movement and the introduction of new "Protestant" religions at a geometric rate. Although Christianity has the most adherents worldwide with almost 2 billion, it is deeply divided as witnessed by the multitude of denominations dotting the Christian religious landscape and the rift in philosophical, as well as pragmatic ideology, continues as new versus old, conservative versus liberal and orthodox versus evangelical all in the name of Christianity.

RELIGIOUS SPLITS AND RIFTS

Statistics show that most religion is heavily fragmented, especially Christianity which may have more than 20,000 different sects, certainly diluting the original message with each split. The sheer number of Christian sects suggests that there is a gulf of disagreement between those who identify themselves as Christians. Christianity is split into Catholics and Protestants with the former accounting for a little over 30 percent of the Christian number while the remainder is carved up among Protestantism and its many denominations. Islam is the second largest religion with nearly 1.3 billion adherents and it is split with numerous sects ranging from mainline Islam to extremist groups that are very similar to American Christian fundamentalists. However, behind the two most numerous religious populations comes nonbelievers with nearly 1 billion. The remainders of the world's religions rank far behind these numbers with the exception Hinduism that ranks fourth with 900 million adherents.

That there are divisions and subdivisions within nearly all of the world's religions points out the lack of agreement even between like groups. As an example Christian Baptists have multiple denominations all claiming Christianity, but each is different from the other. These groups include the original Baptists, the Anabaptists and all of the following and more: Southern Baptists, Primitive Baptists, African Baptist Assembly, Free Will Baptists, Apostolic Spiritual Baptists and even Seventh Day Baptists.

Out of Africa

Religion in Africa today is made up of varying groups with nearly 315 million Christians, 310 million Muslims, 95 million who practice the indigenous religions of Africa, about 5 million who claim no religion and about a half a million atheists.[101] Islam and Christianity are powerful forces on the continent of Africa. Both have been there for centuries and both have made substantial inroads in replacing traditional religions and beliefs. The Black Catholic Congress estimates that there are more than 200 million Black Catholics worldwide with 130 million followers in Africa alone and nearly 80 million in Latin America and the Caribbean.[102] It is clear that in the north of Africa, Islam holds sway and the converse is true for equatorial and southern Africa. Combined with traditional tribal practices like Yoruba, Christianity has a strong influence in modern Black Africa as nearly 80 percent Black Africans are Christians and nearly two-thirds of African Christians are Catholic.

However, even in such an overwhelming Christian atmosphere, atheism and skepticism are not unheard of in Africa. Nobel laureate, Wole Soyinka, winner of the Nobel Prize for literature in 1986 is probably the most well-known African atheist, but he is not alone as secular humanism and rationalism are starting to gain a foothold in sub-Saharan Africa.

Chapter 7

Religion in the United States

"Our species needs, and deserves, a citizenry with minds wide awake and a basic understanding of how the world works."
—Carl Sagan (from "The Demon-Haunted World")

Christianity is clearly the dominant religion in the United States far outnumbering other faiths such as Islam and Judaism which together only account for barely 4 percent of the religious make up in the United States. Eighty-six percent of Americans identify themselves as Christians and in line with the Christian ethic of "love your neighbor," most adults in the United States show reasonable tolerance towards different religions, but surveys indicate that the same tolerance does not extend to nonbelievers. Almost 70 percent of Americans agree that freedom of religion applies "to all religious groups, regardless of how extreme their ideas are," but nearly 30 percent felt that the same tolerance didn't apply to atheists. [103, 104]

Common Ground

As divided as the Black and the white community often are they share some of the same misunderstanding and intolerance of those who do not share the same religious beliefs as themselves. Interviews with Black atheists and freethinkers revealed that they also believe that most Blacks also hold many of the same negative beliefs and that not only do some Blacks not understand either agnosticism nor atheism, but exhibit considerable ignorance and intolerance concerning both. According to the participants, most Blacks they encountered appeared to have no clear knowledge of what either term actually meant but exhibited strong hostility toward anyone who didn't believe in God or doubted its existence. Today, more than a third of Americans believe that the number of nonbelievers in the U.S. is increasing, and most who hold this view say they are bothered by it. Not surprisingly, Blacks appear to be more concerned about nonbelief than whites as nearly a third of Black poll respondents compared to 22 percent of whites said that the growing number of non-believers in the United States bothers them.

In 2001, more than 29.4 million Americans said they had no religion, which is more than double the number in 1990, according to the American Religious Identification Survey of 2001. A USA TODAY/Gallup Poll also found that only 50 percent of Americans refer to themselves as religious, which is a 4 percent drop from just one-year ago.[105, 106] The Organization of American Atheists claims that over 25 million Americans are atheists. If that is correct, when that number is combined with the number of people who are considered "unchurched" in the United States, the figure for the nonreligious can reach as high as 80 or 90 million people who if they are not atheists or agnostics are certainly "de facto" nonbelievers because of their action, or in this case—inaction.

THE SHORT END OF THE STICK

Of all the belief stances in the United States or religious orientations, atheists receive the lowest ratings, falling far behind Islam, which Americans generally tend to be suspicious of especially since the September 11, 2001 terrorist attack on the World Trade Center. Telling statistics on the unpopularity of nonbelief come from a Gallup Poll that asked people to express their willingness to vote for a candidate from various backgrounds. A decisive 95 percent said they would vote for a Black president, which was higher than the 92 percent received by Jews, Baptists and Catholics.

Women also fared well as 92 percent said they would vote for a woman. However, bringing up the rear were homosexuals and atheists. Homosexuals beat out atheists by almost 10 percent with 60 percent of people saying they would vote for a homosexual president while only 49 percent said they would vote for an atheist.[107] Still, the 49 percent figure is the highest number ever tallied since the poll was started more than 40 years ago. When a Rob Poll asked only Blacks the same question concerning voting for an atheist as a political candidate, a whopping 75 percent said no and only 13 percent said yes.[108] Most Americans, 66 percent view atheists negatively.

> *God, once imagined to be an omnipresent force throughout the whole world of nature and man, has been increasingly tending to seem omniabsent. Everywhere, intelligent and educated people rely more and more on purely secular and scientific techniques for the solution of their problems. As science advances, belief in divine miracles and the efficacy of prayer becomes fainter and fainter.*
>
> —Corliss Lamont (1902-1995)

Education and Religion

Becoming educated often jeopardizes religious belief in that education teaches people how to think and reason, as well as exposes individuals to a variety of learning experiences and information. Research shows that high education levels have a direct bearing on religious belief in that it reduces or dilutes it. Conversely, the reverse is true for less educated individuals and groups. Among the less educated nearly 75 percent of those who did not finish high school say they feel unfavorably toward people who don't believe in God, compared to just 37 percent of those with college degrees.

There is a strong negative connection between attendance and education across religious groups within the U.S. and elsewhere.[109] In Charles Kimball's book, *When Religion Becomes Evil*, he warns adherents to be cautious of any religion that tries to limit intellectual freedom and individual integrity. Education has a clear impact not only on church attendance, but also on what church one attends or which religion one joins. Researchers Bruce Sacerdote and Edward L. Glaeser found that the less educated joined strong denominations such as Baptists or Pentecostals, while the educated chose less stringent denominations like Judaism or Episcopalianism. Attendance by denomination was much lower with Jews and Episcopalians being the least likely to attend church regularly but having the highest education levels. The reasons for this disparity are complex but it is believed that high degrees of education tend to minimize the perceived benefits of religion.

On the surface, most Blacks don't fit this pattern as large numbers of educated Blacks attend church regularly and are members of a strong denomination such as the Baptists. On the other hand, 32 percent of the Black population is considered unchurched and the educational makeup of that group is largely unknown. However, across religious denominations, church attendance declines with education. Said bluntly, the educated attend church in smaller numbers than the uneducated. For instance, those belonging to the most educated Christian denomination, Episcopalianism, the median person attends church "several times per year," but in the least educated major denomination, the Baptist groups, the median person attends church once per month.[110] Presbyterians, Episcopalians and Jews are the highest education denominations and have the lowest attendance levels. The lowest education denomination is the Baptists who have the second highest attendance level. The second lowest education group is the Other Denomination Protestants, which includes fundamentalist groups and Mormons.

In his best selling book, *The Culture of Disbelief*, Yale Law Professor Stephen Carter complained that educated professionals tend to be embarrassed by belief. He notes that "More and more, our culture seems to take the position that believing deeply in the tenets of one's faith represents a kind of mystical irrationality, something that thoughtful, public-spirited American citizens would do better to avoid. If you must worship your God, the lesson runs, at least have the courtesy to disbelieve in the power of prayer; if you must observe your Sabbath, have the good sense to understand that it is just like any other day of the week." [111]

RELIGIOUS SHIFT

Information from a recent study funded by the Pew Foundation indicated that more than 58 percent of Americans say it is not necessary to believe in God to be moral and have good values, which marks a significant shift in American opinion that is more tolerant of nonbelievers. Nevertheless, nonbelief is alien to the predominantly Christian Black community. [112]

The few Black nonbelievers and freethinkers ever mentioned come largely from the "Black intelligentsia" and even Black historians speak little of nonbelief and freethought or its place in the history of African America or the Black community in general, although clear evidence of its existence is available. Aside from the negative mention of nonbelief and freethought by Black clergy, a few talk show hosts and commentators, its connection to the community remains reserved for radical activists, fringe political groups and, as far as the general community knows—there are no Black atheists.

Belief & Behavior

"The bane of hypocrisy is not its visibility to others, it is its invisibility to the practitioner." —Michael Shermer, *Why People Believe Weird Things*

"Thou hypocrite, first cast out the beam out of thine own eye; and then shalt thou see clearly to cast out the mote out of thy brother's eye." —Matthew 7:5

Chapter 8

Actions Speak Louder Than Words

"In the last analysis we must be judged by what we do and not by what we believe. We are as we behave—with a very small margin of credit for our unmanifested vision of how we might behave if we could take the trouble."
—Geoffrey L. Rudd, The British Vegetarian, September/October 1962

"The hypocrite's crime is that he bears false witness against himself. What makes it so plausible to assume that hypocrisy is the vice of vices is that integrity can indeed exist under the cover of all vices except this one."
—Lionel Trilling, On Revolution, 1963

Actions speak louder than words is a truism meaning that what one does overshadows what one says. That we often do not 'practice what we preach' is another truism that has its roots in the observance of how belief and behavior are often at odds with one another. Even the idea of Black nonbelief is met with skepticism by both Blacks and whites and part of it is based on stereotypes and part is based on fact, especially in the United States where more than 90 percent of Blacks claim belief in God. However, a closer look at belief and behavior in the Black community shows that belief has not deterred aberrant behavior. In fact, the Black community as well as the white community, seem to either forget that God is watching, not care; or, are in fact willing to gamble with immortality feeling they have time to "get right" with God before anything happens to them.

Who's Fooling Whom?

Although the number in the Black community claiming Christianity is even higher than the national standard, it is readily apparent that in both the white and Black communities there is much lip service paid to moral living as the figures do not bear out the success of religion or anything else, for that matter, as being effective in curbing bad behavior. George Gallup Jr., son of the founder of the Gallup organization saw the trend in 1995 when he said, "While religion is highly popular in this country, survey evidence suggests that it does not change people's lives to the degree one would expect from the level of professed faith."[113] A close look at professed faith and actual behavior reveals a clear disparity between the two that clearly shows that religion has little to no behavioral effect on the majority of the nation as a whole or in the Black community. This gap between believing and behaving is the indictment of those clamoring for more religion.

To put it into perspective, it is clear that behavior that goes against Biblical teaching is a sin. No one can sin accidentally for in Christianity the intent counts nearly as much as the sin. No one accidentally kills, rapes or even lies without a conscious decision to do so. Each act requires a conscious decision, which for Christians means there is an awareness of the spiritual consequences, a weighing of those consequences and finally, a decision to proceed in spite of them. An argument could be made that even considering the consequences is a sin for even to consider the consequences implies that one is not sure of the direction to take despite the stated law or rule.

Crime

The United States is a country of extremes and opposites. It has a population that is nearly 90 percent Christian and it also has the highest rates for violence, crime and drug abuse in the Western world especially in the Black community. Although crime receives a lot of attention in the United States as a moral problem, violent crime and crime in general have dropped according to a recent FBI Uniform Crime report. Yet, the fastest growing industry in America is prison construction. Already, the United States incarcerates a larger percentage of its population than any other nation in the world.[114] Nearly 3 percent of the entire population or 6.6 million Americans are in the custody of the criminal justice system, either in prison or on parole. It is by far the highest percentage in the world.[115]

Today, there are over a million Black men in prison, nearly a third of them are less than 30 years old, and that has created a permanent criminal underclass and a significant gap in marriageable Black males. Although some would try to explain this away as racism and targeting by the police, at least part of which is true, it cannot be denied that those who break the law and are caught; are put in jail.

> *"The United States is the most religious of all the industrialized nations. Forty-four percent of Americans attend church once a week, compared with 27 percent in Britain, 21 percent in France, 16 percent in Australia, and 4 percent in Sweden. Yet violent crime is not less common in the United States—it's more common.*
>
> *"The murder rate here is six times higher than the rate in Britain, seven times higher than in France, five times higher than in Australia, and five times higher than in Sweden. Japan, where Christianity has almost no adherents, has less violent crime than almost any country.... Within the 50 states, there is no evidence that a God-fearing populace equals a law-abiding populace. The Bible Belt has more than its share of both praying and killing. Louisiana has the highest churchgoing rate in the country, but its murder rate is more than twice the national average. The same pattern generally holds in the rest of the South..."* —Steve Chapman in <u>Praise the Lord, Pass the Ammo</u>.[116]

Crime rates in the United States are starting to decrease. Still, a criminal offense takes place every two seconds; a violent crime takes place every 19 seconds; a rape happens every five minutes and a murder happens every 29 minutes.[117] The FBI estimates that one in ten women will be raped during their lifetime and that more than likely the victim will know the attacker. Crime is still in the streets, but the tilt in the morality factor seems to be coming from the very people who keep bringing it to the fore. Black Americans are killing each other, going to prison, and succumbing to an assortment of addictions in record numbers and religion has not affected this sordid static in the least.

WAS IT GOOD FOR US?

As much as Americans like to blame teenagers for a variety of social ills, in reality—adults are the source of most of our problems. For instance, 80 percent of the children born out of wedlock are born to women over 20 years old, with almost half born to mothers between 20 and 29. Even the rate of sexually transmitted disease is significantly higher among adults.[118]

The same statistics hold true for abortion with less than 20 percent going to females under 20 years old. Still, relatively few Americans feel abortion should be either totally legal or totally illegal.[119] On the abortion issue 41 percent of all adults stated that abortion should be legal in all or almost all circumstances and 55 percent said it should not be legal under any circumstances or only in a few special circumstances. Just over one-third of the adult public (36 percent) contends that abortion is a morally acceptable behavior. Apparently, teenagers are targeted unfairly for the same behavior that their older siblings, parents and friends engage in at a greater rate. More startling is a Janus report showing that Christians are more inclined to have an abortion with 61 percent of those choosing to have abortions listed as Christians. The exact breakdown was 32 percent for Protestants and 29 percent for Catholics. Nonreligious women had the lowest percentage at 22 percent. Interestingly, surveys (*Janus Report*) show that only 22% of non-religious people have had abortions, compared to 32% for Protestants and 29% for Catholics.[120]

While African-American women constitute approximately 14 percent of the women of childbearing age in this nation, many abortion centers report that well over 50 percent of their clients are African-American. The nation's abortion industry reveals that abortion is increasingly becoming the option of choice for African-American women. In 1997, the most recent year for which national statistics are available, 35.9 percent of all abortions were performed on African-American women. This percentage has continued to increase virtually every year since 1973, when African-American abortions represented just 23 percent of all abortions.[121] The abortion rate (31 per 1,000 women) is approximately 2.6 times the rate for white women (12 per 1,000).[122] Studies show that black women died four times more often of illegal abortions than white women, with black teenagers dying 11 times more frequently, according to long-time pro-choice activist, Dr. Kenneth C. Edelin.[123]

Premarital Sex

Official views of premarital sex are largely hypocritical as moral conservatives are quick to condemn when teenagers are the targets, but the moral police are not so vociferous when it comes to premarital sex between "consenting" adults. More than half of Americans believe that it is not wrong for adults to engage in premarital sex, while nearly 75 percent believe it is wrong for teenagers to do so.[124] Teens seem to catch the brunt of the criticism for behavior that is not only common among adults but also is depicted as acceptable in regular television programming and movies. In other words American adults have adopted a "do as I say, not as I do" attitude regarding sexual behavior. According to the most recent data, 61 percent of all high school seniors have had sexual intercourse, about half are currently sexually active, and 21 percent have had four or more partners. Although other developed countries have similar rates of early sexual intercourse, the United States has one of the highest teenage pregnancy rates in the world. Unfortunately, about 50 percent of all unwed teenage mothers go on welfare within one year of the birth of their first child. More than 75 percent go on within five years.[125]

A 1969 Gallup poll found that premarital sex was frowned upon by two-thirds of Americans, while only 21 percent felt it was acceptable. By the early 1970s that view dropped to 47 percent, and in 1985, Gallup found a majority of Americans on the other side, with more than half saying premarital sex is morally acceptable. Today, a new Gallup poll shows that 60 percent of U.S. adults say it is okay for a man and a woman to have sexual relations before marriage.

The majority of young adults, 67 percent, think premarital sex is morally acceptable as do those 30 to 49. Both of these groups are much more liberal than those aged 50-64 where only 46 percent say it's acceptable. Only 28 percent of adults aged 65 and older say it is acceptable. Majorities of Americans also say that "living together" is a morally acceptable lifestyle with barely 40 percent holding on to the "living in sin" mentality, which says that it is morally unacceptable for an unmarried couple to live together. However, most adults are comfortable with behaviors that have traditionally been forbidden. Among the seniors who largely disagree with this stance, many couples that live together without being married for greater social security benefits in the form of additional income.

Although teenagers may not account for the amount of blame they receive, statistics show that early sexual intercourse carries the risk of contracting a sexually transmitted disease (STD), including human immunodeficiency virus (HIV).[126] Adolescents have the highest STD rates. Approximately one fourth of sexually active adolescents become infected with an STD each year, accounting for 3 million cases, and people under the age of 25 account for two thirds of all STDs in the United States.[127]

Births to Unmarried Women

Increasingly marriage rates are down and birthrates are up. The number of births to unmarried women came to an annual total of 1.3 million in 1999 of which more than half were born to women over 20 with the highest increase among Black women between 20-29. While it seems Americans may wink their eye at premarital sex between adults, nearly 39 percent of nonmarital births are due to an increased amount of "shacking up" among unmarried couples, which is a 10 percent increase over earlier years.[128]

The 2000 census indicates that, while it is not exactly becoming extinct, the American nuclear family is in definite decline. Since 1960, the percentage of households comprised of a married couple with children has fallen from 45 percent to just 24 percent. In the past decade, the number of "nonfamily" households rose at twice the rate of family households. Similarly, the percentage of single-mother families rose three times as fast as married-couple families.[129]

The Black community is disproportionately affected by nonmarital births. "Black children are only half as likely as white children to be living in a two-parent household, and are eight times more likely than white children to live with an unwed mother. For Black children under six, 'the most common arrangement—applying to 42 percent of them—was to live with a never-married mother."[130] Currently in the United States about 43 percent of Black homes are headed by women.

Today the number of children born into a Black marriage averages less than 0.9 children per marriage and today only one-third of Black children have two parents in the home." Interestingly, even with the purposeful destruction of Black families by slave masters, during the days of slavery a Black child was more likely to grow up living with both parents than he or she is today.[131, 132, 133, 134] Still, of the children born out of wedlock, only 20 percent were born to teenagers which is a significantly smaller rate compared to women over 20.

Divorce

Marital therapist and radio talk-show host Audrey Chapman worries about tomorrow. "African-Americans are the most unpartnered group in America. Census figures show that 35 percent of Americans between 24 and 34 have never married. For African-Americans, that figure is 54 percent." The chances for a Black woman to marry decrease dramatically with each year she is over thirty and if they have not married by age forty the chances they will ever marry are almost 100 percent.

Family organization and living arrangements in the U.S. have undergone remarkable change in recent times. Compared to earlier periods, Americans now marry later, are less likely to stay married and are less likely to marry after divorce. Black Americans are more likely to divorce or separate than whites. Black women also tend to separate and divorce earlier in their marriages and are less likely to remarry. Over the years, Black divorce rates, as well as that of U.S. women as a whole, nearly quadrupled. Since divorce was much higher among Blacks even in 1970, the 1990 differential is quite striking 358 divorces per 1000 women among Blacks, compared to 166 among women overall. Forty-eight percent of all Black women of marriageable age are either divorced or have never been married in comparison to 31 percent of white women.

Families tend to dissolve when married couples run into hard times today and there appears to be relatively little social pressure to force them to stay together. Nearly three in five Americans, 59 percent, tell Gallup they think divorce is morally acceptable, and another 12 percent say it depends on the situation. Only 28 percent feel divorce is morally unacceptable. Unlike the issue of sex before marriage, attitudes toward divorce are not strongly related to age, although it appears that America's seniors may be somewhat more conservative about it than those in the younger age groups.

Although divorce rates have remained stable in the United States, one out two marriages still end in divorce which has a destabilizing affect on families, birthrates and even sexual behavior. It is paradoxical that in an overwhelmingly Christian country Christians are more likely to get divorced than other religions. Nationally, 27 percent of Baptists have been divorced. The number is even higher among non-denominational Christians at 34 percent. Atheists and agnostics have the lowest rate overall at 21 percent.[135]

In the past four decades, a social and economic revolution has transformed traditional patterns of marriage and family among both whites and Blacks. In 1950, 64 percent of Black men age 14 or older were married, but by 1995, that proportion had plummeted to 43 percent. The percentage of currently married white males in the same age category also dropped, but not nearly as much, from 68 percent in 1950 to 61 percent in 1995. The divorce rate has had a negative impact on the Black community. "Only 18 percent of Black women who married in the 1940's eventually divorced a rate only slightly higher than that for white women of that era. Of Black women who married in the late sixties and early seventies, 60 percent have already divorced." [136]

The major increase in the never-married population has occurred among Blacks. Between 1975 and 1999, the percentage of Blacks that have never been married increased from 32 percent to 44 percent while the percentage of Blacks who are married declined from over 42 percent in 1975 to 32 percent in 1999, with nearly 23 percent of Black households headed by women with children.[137] Married Black women are rare. Between 1950 and 1995, the percentage of Black women 14 or older who were married fell from 62 percent to under 38 percent. Data collected by census researchers also suggest that fewer than 75 percent of Black women can expect to marry sometime in their lives, compared with 90 percent of white women.

Other data shows that between 1970 and 1990, the proportion of Black women who had married by age 24 decreased by half from 56 percent to 23 percent, while the proportion that had ever married declined from 83 percent to 63 percent.[138] Black women are also less likely than other groups of women to remarry after divorce or widowhood.

Adultery

A 1992 survey by the National Opinion Research Center at the University of Chicago showed that 90 percent of the men and 94 percent of the women surveyed felt that extramarital sex was wrong. Out of that group, 25 percent of the men and 17 percent of the women had been unfaithful.[139] A 1997 Associated Press survey showed that 22 percent of married men and 14 percent of married women have strayed at least once during their marriage. The poll also showed that there is no appreciable difference in infidelity rates between women or men. Still, 90 percent of Americans believe that adultery is morally wrong.

Conservative estimates are that 60 percent of men and 40 percent of women will have an extramarital affair. One clear element in the cheating game is that women are the victims more often than men as 80 to 85 percent of adultery victims are women between the ages of 25 and 50 years old. Seventy percent of married women and 54 percent of married men did not know of their spouses' extramarital activity.[140] Across ethnic lines, younger people are more likely candidates to cheat. In fact, younger women are as likely as younger men to be unfaithful. Interestingly, today 10 to 20 percent of spousal cheating begins as an

Internet affair in a chat room or game website.[141] These figures are even more significant when the total number of marriages involved is considered.

RAPE

In 2001, there were 249,000 victims of rape, attempted rape or sexual assault. Of these 249,000, 102,000 were victims of sexual assault, 63,000 were victims of attempted rape, and 84,000 were victims of completed rape. One out of every six American women has been the victim of an attempted or completed rape in their lifetime (14.8% completed rape; 2.8% attempted rape). A total of 17.7 million women have been victims of these crimes.[142]

It is the most often committed, least reported and least prosecuted serious crime in this country. In 2001, only 39% of rapes and sexual assaults were reported to law enforcement officials—about one in every three. Current statistics tell us that 1 in 3 women, 1 in 7 men will be the victim of a sexual assault sometime in their life.

While about 80% of all victims are white, minorities are somewhat more likely to be attacked: Blacks are about 10% more likely to be attacked than whites. In 2000, there were 1.0 victimizations per 1,000 white people, and 1.1 victimizations per 1,000 black people. Lifetime rate of rape/attempted rape of black women is almost 18.8%. About three percent of American men—a total of 2.78 million men—have experienced an attempted or completed rape in their lifetime. In 2001, one in every ten rape victims was male.

Ebony Magazine recently did a feature on sexual abuse of young black boys. About 44% of rape victims are under age 18. Three out of every twenty victims (15%) are under age 12. Of sexually abused children in grades five through twelve, 48% of the boys and 29% of the girls had told no one about the abuse—not even a friend or sibling.[143]

Less than 25% of all rapes are committed by a stranger.[144] Approximately 48% of victims are raped by a friend or acquaintance; 30% by a stranger; 16% by an intimate; 2% by another relative and in 4% of cases the relationship is unknown.[145]

PROSTITUTION

Prostitution was made illegal in almost all states between 1910 and 1915. However, it is a $14.5 billion a year business in the United States and has continued to flourish despite efforts to wipe it out.[146] It is difficult to estimate the number of persons who currently work, or have ever worked as prostitutes for many reasons including the various definitions of prostitution. However, nearly 40 percent of street prostitutes are "women of color" and 55 percent of those arrested are women of color. Even more revealing of the state of the justice system is that 85 percent of all prostitutes sentenced to jail time are women of color.[147] Nationally, total arrest figures are over 100,000. The National Task Force on Prostitution suggests that over one million American people have worked as prostitutes in the United States, or about 1 percent of American women.[148] In addition, male prostitutes also make up a significant percentage of prostitutes.

In the US alone, at least 100,000 children are believed to be involved in commercial sexual exploitation. It is believed that anywhere from 300,000 to 600,000 juveniles are involved in prostitution in the United States. Each year between 1.2 million and 2 million teenagers run away, half of them will turn to prostitution to survive.[149, 150, 151, 152]

What is not known is the number of "Johns" who seek the services of prostitutes as arrests usually focus on the prostitutes, but judging from the number of prostitutes, the number of "Johns" who make use of their service must be at least as high in number, and considering prostitutes make money by being able to service more than one customer, the number of "Johns" is at least four to five times higher.

Male prostitutes sometimes report that their clients include married men who identify as heterosexual. Judging from the arrest records that are kept and the occasional naming of the "Johns" who are busted, it is clear that Americans from all occupations make use of their services, including preachers, politicians and popular entertainers. However, customers are rarely arrested more than once for prostitution and are infrequently jailed.

Although little research has been done regarding client profiles, anecdotal reports and arrest statistic indicate that clients also vary widely in terms of race and class. In a study in London, England 50% of clients were married, or cohabiting According to another United States report, 70% of adult men have engaged a prostitute at least once.

PORNOGRAPHY

Pornography is a $12-$13 billion a year industry which is more than the combined annual revenues of the Coca-Cola and McDonnell Douglas corporations and enough to place it in the Fortune 500 along with legitimate American businesses.[153, 154] It is clear that the nation's comfort with pornography has changed as half of all adults stated that watching a movie with explicit sexual behavior is morally acceptable. Amazingly, this view was shared by three out of ten born again Christian adults and making it clear that a substantial amount of "believers" have an active role in keeping the industry alive. In like fashion, 43 percent of adults claimed that reading magazines with explicit sexual pictures and nudity is morally acceptable while more than 20 percent of born again adults felt the same way.[155]

More than 1,000 theaters show pornographic films and more than 15,000 "adult" bookstores and video stores offer pornographic material. A report from the U.S. Senate Judiciary Committee says that, adult bookstores outnumber McDonald's restaurants in the United States by a margin of at least three to one, while full-length pornographic films are raking in more than $50 million per year in box office sales.[156, 157] Ten years ago, 1,275 hard-core videos hit the market annually, compared with 11,041 for 2000, according to Adult Video News.[158] Pornographic video rental revenues jumped to $665 million in 1996, accounting for 13.3 percent of video rentals in the United States. Profits from sales and rentals of porn videos were $4.2 billion in 1996.[159]

Although pornography has long circulated in the Black community, a new element has been added as popular Black rap stars flirt with pornographic films. Recently, highly popular rapper Snoop Dogg announced that he was teaming up with Hustler Magazine and hip-hop video director Michael Martin to release a series of X-rated offerings. One of the biggest porno hits of the year was the 80-minute porno video *Naturally Naughty* from Anthony "Treach" Criss of the rap group Naughty by Nature.[160]

An estimated 325,000 U.S. children age 17 or younger are prostitutes, performers in pornographic videos according to a three-year study by University of Pennsylvania researchers. The $400,000 study includes interviews with 200 child victims and more than 800 state, federal and local officials.[161]

Pornography on the Internet

Analysts from Forrester Research say that sex sites on the web generate at least $1 billion a year in revenue.[162] In fact, pornographic entertainment on the Internet constituted the third largest sector of sales in cyberspace. American consumers spent an estimated $220 million at fee-based "adult" sites in 2001, nearly a 50 percent jump from the $148 million in 1999. Experts expect that figure to reach nearly $400 million by 2005.[163]

Alexa Research, a web intelligence and traffic measurement service, revealed that "sex" was the most popular term for which people searched. Of all the terms searched for online, roughly 1 of every 300 terms, were "sex." "Porn," along with "porno" and "pornography" was the fourth most popular search term. "Nude," "xxx," and "erotica" were also among the top 20.

A nationwide survey of 1,031 adults conducted by Zogby International and Focus on the Family, found that 20 percent of the respondents, which represents as many as 40 million adults, admitted visiting a sexually oriented web site. Thirty-seven percent of males between the ages of 18-24 admitted they had visited sex sites and almost 18 percent identified themselves as Christians. Another study found that 40 percent of pastors have visited a porn site and more than a third have done so in the last year.[164] Fifty-one percent of pastors say on-line porn is a possible temptation; 37 percent admit it is a struggle and yet, only 25 percent of pastors use filters on their or their family's computer.[165] According to a 2002 Nielsen/Net Rating Survey, there were 27.5 million U.S. visitors to adult-oriented pornographic web sites in just January of that year. About 72% of visitors were men, 28% women. According to the Nielsen Net ratings, 17.5 million surfers visited porn sites from their homes in January; a 40 percent increase compared with September of 1999.[166, 167] A Washington Times survey showed that nearly 25 million American visit pornography sites between 1 to ten hours per week with another 4.7 million visiting in excess of 11 hours per week. Pornography on the Internet has reached the psychiatrist's couch as "A recent study by researchers at Stanford and Duquesne universities claims at least 200,000 Americans are hopelessly addicted to E-porn."[168]

Children Views of Pornography

According to NetValue, children spent 64.9 percent more time on pornography sites than they did on game sites in September 2000. More than 25 percent of children age 17 and under visited an adult web site, which represents 3 million unique underage visitors. Of these minors, 21.2 percent were 14 or younger and 40.2 percent were female.[169] Nearly a third of kids age 10-17 from households with computers and a fourth of all kids 10-17 say they have seen a pornographic web site.[170]

The Internet Online Summit in 1997 in Washington, D.C., revealed that 70 percent of children accessing the Internet are doing so in public schools and libraries.[171] According to N2H2 the national average for filtering Internet access in schools and libraries is as follows: 75 percent for schools and 43 percent for libraries. A study released by the Family Research Council, Dangerous Access, 2000 Edition: Uncovering Internet Pornography in America's Libraries. With only 29 percent of libraries responding, researchers found 2,062 incidents of patrons, many of them children, accessing pornography in America's public libraries.[172]

"Some 63 percent of teachers surveyed nationwide said they used filtering software in their classrooms, an 8.4 percent increase from the previous year," said Karin Hendersin, market research director at Quality Education Data, a Denver, CO, research organization that is studying data from 400 public schools. More than a fifth of the teachers said they did not know whether filtering software was in place." [173]

At Work Pornography Viewing

One in five men and one in eight women admitted using their work computers as their primary lifeline to access sexual explicit material online [174] The Industry Standard reports that 70 percent of porn traffic occurs between 9 am and 5 pm—work hours.[175] Employees earning $75,000 to $100,000 annually are twice as likely to download pornography at work than those earning less than $35,000[176] Almost 27 percent of Fortune 500 Companies have battled sexual harassment claims stemming from employee misuse and abuse of corporate e-mail and Internet systems.[177] Additionally, the number of employees who are fired for using the company's Internet access to view pornographic sites has risen dramatically in the past four years.

STRIP CLUBS GROWING IN POPULARITY

Americans also have no problem with strip clubs as long as they are kept in the right neighborhoods, but lately, strip clubs are becoming more popular and have moved into the main stream. There are thousands of strip clubs located throughout the United States and not just in the Sodom and Gomorrah of big cities but in small municipalities in states like Minnesota, Iowa and Nebraska which are all heavily Christian populations.

Annual revenues at some clubs are as high as $8 million, and some employ as many as 200 dancers."[178] In California alone, there are an estimated 7500 full-time dancers and another 5000 part-time.[179] Politicians are slow to move against strip clubs because each of these clubs provides thousands of jobs and produce billions of dollars in revenue. Interestingly, the strip industry brings in millions of dollars in tax revenue and a large portion of it goes to law enforcement.

SPOUSAL ABUSE AND CHILD ABUSE

Black women face a higher risk for being killed by an intimate than women of other races. Black women are also more likely to murder an intimate. Nearly one out of three American families experience some degree of domestic violence and their children are more likely to witness it. Battery within American homes inflicts more damage on American women ages 15-44 than rapes, muggings and automobile accidents combined. [180] Figures show that domestic violence is the single major cause of injury to women. The FBI estimates that husbands or boyfriends batter a woman in the United States every 15 seconds and nearly 30 percent of female homicides are caused by spousal abuse.[181]

Nearly 60 percent of battered women are beaten while they are pregnant, often in the stomach. Even more frightening is that 70 percent of the men who batter their wives physically or sexually abuse their children. Each year more than 2 million children are beaten by a family member.[182] The Bureau of Justice projects that nationwide almost 4-6 million women are victims of domestic violence. Since only 10 percent of these episodes are ever reported, the actual figure is probably much higher.

Nearly one-third of American women (31 percent) report being physically or sexually abused by a husband or boyfriend at some point in their lives and studies show that child abuse occurs in 30-60% of family violence cases that involve families with children. [183] Violence by an intimate partner accounts for about 21% of violent crime experienced by women and about 2 % of the violence experienced by men.[184] In 92% of all domestic violence incidents, crimes are committed by men against women. In 1996, among all female murder victims in the U.S., 30% were slain by their husbands or boyfriends.[185]

DRUG ABUSE

Teenagers ranked high in drug abuse, but not as high as adults, especially adults between the ages of 20-29. There is also significant use of illegal drugs in the above 30 crowd.[186] Drug use among American adolescents in 1999 "continued at much higher levels" than in the early 90's according to Monitoring the Future a teen drug use study conducted at the University of Michigan's Institute for Social Research. The report indicated that 73.8 percent of 12th grade students say they have used alcohol during the past year and 43.1 percent say they have used some illegal drug during that same year.[187] According to the 2000 Partnership Attitude Tracking Study, an estimated 23.6 million teens are in grades seven through 12 in America today and 11.3 million of them (48 percent of the teen population) have tried illegal drugs.[188] In addition, between 1992 and 1999 teenage pot smoking doubled, as did the strength of marijuana, making it even more intoxicating.[189]

Approximately 11 million people use marijuana on a regular basis and almost 2 million use cocaine regularly with Blacks constituting 15 percent of current U.S. drug users and 15 percent of cocaine users.[190] Now, Americans have found a new high as millions of drug tests shows that amphetamine use jumped 17% in 2002 and is up 70% in the past five years. According to ASAP Family: Drug and Alcohol Statistics, 10 percent of all American workers have an alcohol problem and 6 percent of all American workers have a drug problem. Currently, the illegal drug industry ranks in size with Mobil Oil as the second largest business in the United States—only Exxon is larger making cocaine the leading cash product at $26-32 billion per year.[191]

The United States is the number one consumer of illegal drugs in the world with U.S. citizens spending more on illegal drugs than the gross economy of many countries.

ALCOHOL ABUSE

However, alcohol is still the drug of choice with more than 100 million Americans using alcohol every year and 11 million minors who drink illegally. Drugs and alcohol play a significant role in crime statistics. In 1980, only 6 percent of prisoners were jailed for drug offenses. Now, that figure has reached 23 percent in state prisons, while the numbers for federal prisons jumped from 25 percent to 60 percent as nearly 6 of 10 are accounted for by drug or alcohol related offenses.

Predictably, statistics show that alcohol is involved in 30 percent of suicides, 48 percent of robberies, 50 percent of homicides and 52 percent of sexual assaults and with over one-third of Americans reporting that drinking has caused family problems. [192, 193]

Getting drunk is considered morally acceptable among one-third of the population. Almost half of all non-born again adults said drunkenness is morally acceptable, but only one out of five born again individuals concurred. Still, Americans have relaxed their opinions on many things once thought reprehensible and now even the use of profanity is deemed morally acceptable by almost 40 percent of those surveyed.

Commercial liquor distributors have a strange relationship within the Black community. They are one of the largest financial supporters of Black events such as concerts, art shows and sporting events while at the same time Blacks are disproportionately consumers of the products that these companies manufacture. Cigarette and alcohol commercials far outnumber other types of advertising in the Black community. Annually, alcohol is responsible for more than 100,000 deaths.[194] Alcohol use also affects driving statistics as just under half of all Black drivers, passengers, pedestrians and cyclists killed in motor vehicle crashes had been drinking.[195] Findings from the National Roadside Surveys for 1973, 1986 and 1996 show that in each year Blacks were more likely than Whites to have blood alcohol levels above .05 and 1.0.[196]

Degrading Music

Blues and rock traditionally walked a fine edge when it comes sexual content and raw language, but much of today's music crosses the line where traditional forms just skirted the edges. Although music is hardly a crime, it is clear that much of the music in today's Black community is at odds with the highly religious view held by others. One of the biggest negative features is how Black woman are treated in rap songs as women are frequently referred to as bitches, hoes and worse. Yet, it is not unusual to see the makers of these records be rewarded on national television to give thanks to God for their musical success. "…the miseducation of millions of Black males and the creation of a climate of violence and intimidation that threatens millions of Sisterz in the 'Hood."[197] It is another instance of stated belief and blatant disregard in actual behavior.

SMOKING

During the early 90's smoking dropped off among all groups in the country but in 1999 the figures started to rise again and now smoking among high school students is up more than 30 percent over the last six years.[198] However, the largest increase in smoking is among Blacks and the Department of Health and Human Services Centers for Disease and Prevention says if the current trend continues, an estimated 1.6 million Blacks who are now under the age of 18 years will become regular smokers and about 500,000 of those smokers eventually will die of a smoking-related disease.[199] Each year approximately 45,000 Blacks die from preventable smoking-related disease, while tobacco related disease kills about 430,000 annually. [200, 201]

Smoking is responsible for 87 percent of lung cancers and Black men are at least 50 percent more likely to develop lung cancer than white men. In addition, Black men also have a higher mortality rate from cancer of the lung and bronchus.[202] Although smoking prevalence rates were similar among Black adults (26.7 percent) and white adults (25.3 percent) in the United States, Black men (32.1 percent) smoked at a higher rate than white men (27.4 percent).[203] Experts say smoking increases the risk of stroke, which is associated with hypertension and is a major cause of death in the United States. It is well known that hypertension or high blood pressure is twice as high among Black men (53.1 per 100,000) as among white men (26.3 per 100,000) and twice as high among Black women (40.6 per 100,000) as among white women (22.6 per 100,000).[204, 205]

In addition, smoking contributes to heart disease that is the number one killer of Black women, according to the American Cancer Society.[206]

GAMBLING

Gambling was in the national spotlight recently after it was revealed that former Secretary of Education, William Bennett is a high stakes gambler. Normally, the issue wouldn't be of that much interest, but Bennett's books and speeches espousing traditional virtues have made him rich and famous. He is the writer of the best-selling *The Book of Virtues*. Bennett has been a national leader in espousing moral behavior and he has been quick to rain his scorn on everything from drug use to wife swapping, but he comes up noticeably short when it comes to gambling and apparently with good reason.

Like Bennett, religion has been quick to bemoan the vices of drinking and gambling but it seems it has had little affect on either. The amount of money bet legally has jumped 3000 percent in the last three decades from about $17 billion in 1973 to more than $800 billion today. Gambling rates have actually increased over the years. Until 1977, gambling was a crime in 49 states and now it is on the verge of becoming a national pastime.

A recent Gallup Poll showed that 63 percent of American adults approve of gambling. In 1984, only Nevada and New Jersey had legalized gambling, but now there are more than ten states that allow gambling including Louisiana, Mississippi, Arkansas, Indiana, Iowa, South Dakota and Colorado.[207] LaFluer World Lottery Almanac reported that in 1984, 17 states plus the District of Columbia had lotteries; now 36 states including DC have lotteries, which are now the most popular forms of gambling in the United States.[208]

A study by the university of Chicago's National Organization for Research (NORC) found that pathological, problem and at-risk gambling was proportionately higher among Blacks than other ethnic groups.[209] According to a 1996 Gemini Research, 10 percent of the nation's gamblers have a compulsive gambling habit with the majority residing in Nevada the first state to have legalized gambling.[210] Gamblers Anonymous, founded in 1957, now has 2,000+chapters worldwide, and the American Psychiatric Association has now added, "compulsive gambling" to its official Diagnostic and Statistical Manual of Mental Disorders.[211] According the International Gaming & Wagering Business Magazine, legal wagering topped $482 billion in 1996 and lottery ticket sales sold almost $29 billion.

Cheating

If this isn't disturbing enough, it also appears that Americans have a problem with cheating. In 1998, the Internal Revenue Service reported that it lost nearly $195 billion to fraud, tax evasion and cheating. IRS officials said the problem is growing among some of the most respected portions of the community including self-employed doctors, lawyers and other high-income Americans who do not have W-2 forms filed with the IRS.[212] Estimates of the number of people who cheat on their taxes range from 20 percent to as high as 75 percent. To many, beating the government out of money is an approved practice but in reality, it is stealing. Interestingly, 55 percent of people under 25, compared to 75 percent of people over 64, think it is absolutely wrong, not to declare all one's income to the IRS.[213]

Recently, several students at a West Coast school were dismissed after it was discovered they cheated on a pivotal test. A new book, *Student Cheating and Plagiarism in the Internet Era: A Wake Up Call* says that 80 percent of high school students admit to cheating. Authors Ann Lanthrop and Kathleen Foss also say that 34 percent of teens said their parents never talked to them about cheating.[214] An Associated Press poll was more generous indicating that 56 percent of American parents teach honesty to their children.

Lying

The bar for lying is difficult to gauge because it is so widespread. Surveys indicate that 91 percent of Americans admit to lying and nearly 45 percent say they lie on a regular basis. There are many reasons for this epidemic of prevarication and many of the reasons are good, such as lying to avoid hurting someone's feelings or lying to protect a family member, but most are lies for no specific reason. A Report Card on Ethic of American Youth in 2000, found that 92 percent of the 8,600 students surveyed lied to their parents in the past year.

Lying takes many forms. One instance of lying is making false claims on employment applications. Younger adults are much more likely than older adults to believe there is nothing wrong in making false claims in a job application.[215] Fifty-one percent of adults under 25, compared 72 percent of those over 64, believe it is absolutely wrong to exaggerate one's education or experience in a resumé or job application.

Music Theft

At any given time there are more than 20 million people downloading music from the Internet illegally. Law suits shutdown illegal sites like Napster but new sites are flourishing. According to a recent PEW Report many people believe that downloading music online is not theft, but the courts have held that it is and as such each day millions of American are stealing music. How much? Even the industry analysts aren't sure, but downloading copyrighted material without paying for it is illegal and estimates say that the recording industry is losing billions of dollars each year to music pirates which includes illegal downloads of Christian music by Christian music lovers.

Shoplifting

Recently, film star Winona Ryder was convicted of grand theft and felony vandalism for shoplifting in Beverly Hills.[216] The statistics on shoplifting are sobering. One in eleven Americans shoplift, but a shoplifter is only caught once every 49 shoplifting episodes. When they are caught, they are turned over to the police only 50% of the time.[217]

WHITE COLLAR CRIME

> *Those who have more power are liable to sin more; no theorem in geometry is more certain than this.* —Lord Acton, quoting Baron Gottfried Wilhelm von Leibnitz (G. E. Fasnacht, *Acton's Political Philosophy*, p. 134),

White-collar crime seems distant to most Americans; yet, it costs the United States more than all other crimes combined. With the recent scandals at Enron, Tyco and Worldcom among others, Americans have suddenly become aware of crime in corporate America. Greedy corporate executives and their cronies have stolen billions of dollars and wrecked the lives of thousands of employees as these companies line up to declare bankruptcy. These corporate crimes also may force the United States to answer some tough questions about itself, such as: Have we become a nation of thieves and lairs?

The Enron bankruptcy and ensuing scandal involving Arthur Andersen's accounting practices is a typical example of corporate fraud. Enron rode to the top using questionable bookkeeping practices which the Arthur Andersen firm approved. Enron is just one case. Each year corporations go out their way to disguise profit to either hide earnings or overstate them in order to influence stock prices. Because of teams of legal experts, corporate citizens are some of the worst abusers of the public trust. In 1999, a nationwide study of more than 15,500 corporations indicated that 41 percent had federal or state lawsuits pending or on the record.

In March of 2000, *Mother Jones* magazine reported that corporate profits were up 8.9 percent that year, but corporations paid 2.1 percent less in income tax. Further clouding the issue, are the often shady bookkeeping practices that many corporations use for reporting financials. In 1996, large corporations reported $119 billion less income to the IRS than they did to their shareholders. It is common for multinational corporations to avoid taxes by buying and selling with their own foreign subsidiaries at substantially reduced prices. In fact, by doing so, multinational corporations were able to skip almost $45 billion in income taxes in 2000.[218]

According to the National Association of Attorneys General, business fraud costs the nation nearly $100 billion a year. The most obvious of these white-collar crimes is embezzlement and insider trading, such as the saving and loans scandals of the 1980's which will eventually cost the taxpayers around $1.4 trillion dollars when it is over. Neil Bush, former president George H. Bush's son, never served time in jail for his part in running an S&L into the ground, but with increased scrutiny it is unlikely today's corporate culprits will be so lucky.[219] People seem to engage in "white-collar" pilfering because they can do it with little chance of being caught as there are no corporate police and even then, unless the crime is unusually shocking, the worst penalty is dismissal from the job without charges being pressed. Rarely does the punishment fit the crime, as sentences tend to be more lenient than one would receive from a $200 heist at a local convenience store. That is not always the case, but it happens enough to make taking the chance worth the effort for some people.

Crimes that are not quite as obvious such as the knowing manufacture of faulty goods, monopolistic practices, corruption in public offices and corporate violation of federal regulations add another $250 billion to the thievery festival. Few people stop to consider crime outside of police blotter staples of mayhem and theft, but as statistics show there are crimes committed by corporate conglomerations that hurt individuals and the entire United States economy.

If insurance fraud were a legitimate business run by a legitimate company, that firm would rank in the Fortune top 10 every year, said Jim Quiggle, senior official with the Coalition Against Insurance Fraud in Washington, D.C.[220]

Crimes such as health care fraud, insurance fraud and corporate tax evasion cost the United States more than $200 billion annually. The cost of health care in the United States topped a trillion dollars in 1997 and fraud has helped pushed the cost of healthcare to those levels. The National Health Care Anti-Fraud Association estimates that 3 to 5 percent of health care dollars are lost to fraud each year, which represents almost $50 billion.

According to FBI statistics, nearly 35 percent of all FBI fraud cases are in health care. Health care fraud occurs in a variety of fraudulent reimbursement and billing practices practiced by American hospitals, doctors and other health care providers. The Inspector General of the U.S. Department of Health and Human Services reported to Congress approximately 14 percent of Medicare claims dollars ($23 billion) were paid inappropriately due to fraud and/or abuse and/or lack of medical documentation to support claims, according to the Irving Levin Association Inc. In 1998 and 1999, health care was the second highest FBI investigation category. Some experts say that fraud affects nearly 10 percent of all healthcare billings. Since 1992, the FBI has increased the number of health care fraud investigations conducted by nearly 500 percent. Even those using medical coverage cheat and abuse the system. The NICB estimates that workers compensation fraud costs the insurance industry $5 billion annually and FBI statistics indicate that as many as 10 percent of all disability claims involve some type of abuse or fraud.[221]

The notorious "Willie Horton" political ads used by former President Bush's election campaign helped put a Black face on crime in the United States. That, along with the steady stream of Black offenders paraded across the evening news helped many Americans buy into long held stereotypes helped maintain that picture, but that has changed as corporate scandal has put new face on crime in the United States. For so long a Black face has represented crime in America, but with each breaking corporate scandal it should be apparent that criminal activity knows no colors or class. Most recently, homemaker maven Martha Stewart is under indictment for alleged insider trading and soft drink giant Coca-Cola recently admitted financial improprieties.

The Enemy is Us!

Not only are corporate executives and their cronies suspect, the entire workforce, Black and white, is under suspicion and with good cause as each year American businesses loose billions of dollars to internal theft. Most Americans consider themselves honest, law abiding citizens and certainly do not imagine themselves to be thieves, but the statistics show that more than 50 percent of Americans engage in some form of "white collar" crime causing a staggering $200 billion annual drain on the economy. The $200 billion thievery figure surpasses the amount for all other types of theft combined, including robbery and burglary.

When thinking of "white collar" crimes, images of conniving embezzlers, stock swindlers and boardroom bandits come to mind, but the truth is that major larceny is perpetrated by gangs of moms, dads and "regular working stiffs" who use the workplace as their "personal" shopping mall. These corporate crooks are indiscriminant in their pilfering taking everything from school supplies for their children to furniture for their homes.

Some of the most popular items boosted include long distance telephone calls, express mail, regular postage, office supplies, light bulbs and toilet paper. Items as large as televisions, copiers, computers and even chairs find their way to employee's homes and those of their friends. Amazingly, most don't see it as theft. Instead, it is seen as a company "perk", but put simply—it is stealing. The range of items taken can be as small as pencils, pens and paper clips, but when multiplied by half of the working population the cost of these seemingly innocuous items quickly runs into pilferage costing billions of dollars.

None of this takes into account the number of "faithful" employees who regularly gouge their employer on their expense reports or take sick time to perform personal errands. A man or woman caught shoplifting some of these same items from a convenience store would be guilty of theft and would be subject to prosecution under the law. Although this would be a minor incident, the consequences would be different. One would go home and the other would go to jail—hardly an equal punishment for the same crime of theft.

When asked why this change has occurred, Barna stated that religious institutions have failed to present a compelling case for a Biblical basis for moral truth. "Most people do not believe that there is any source of absolute moral truth. Even born again individuals are abandoning the notion of law based on scriptural principles," which is another way of stating what should be obvious by now and that is that religion has little to no effect on human behavior. [222]

It is clear that crime in the United States is not dominated by any one group. Who winds up in our criminal justice system is largely due to proximity and opportunity. There are no police in the corporate boardroom and the chances of being caught for regular street crimes bearing the fancy names like embezzlement and fraud are almost nil. If there is an arrest, the chances of the perpetrators serving hard time is also nil.

None of the facts and statistics are difficult to find and the only reason they appear in this writing is because of the idea of the United States being a Christian nation, which if not saying the opposite, at least says that the Christian ethic, although highly touted, is not practiced as rigorously as one might expect from a nation that claims an 86 percent rate of Christianity. In fact, it shows that Americans are largely hypocrites when it comes to stated beliefs and practiced behavior.

CHAPTER 9

NO ONE IS IMMUNE

"For lack of intelligent guidance, then, the Negro church often fulfills a mission to the contrary of that for which it was established. Because the Negro church is such a free field...it seems to that practically all the incompetents and undesirables who have been barred from other walks of life by race prejudice and economic difficulties have rushed into the ministry for the exploitation of the people...Almost anybody of the lowest type may get into the Negro Ministry."

—Carter G. Woodson [223]

It would seem like those most directly involved in religion would be least susceptible to the ever present tug of the secular world as opposed to those who are a part of the flocks, congregations and followers who make up the body of the church. Unfortunately, church leaders are just as susceptible, if not more so, to the same temptations of the secular world and the spotlight that is brought to bear on religious leaders is even more intense. Many church leaders become targets because of who they are, including female spiritual leaders as well. The American public expects a higher degree of rectitude from its spiritual leaders and for the most part, they have delivered, but scandal has never been too far from religion.

Theft, fraud and blatant stealing are a documented part of early Christian church history. The church finally put a stop to the run away behavior of its "holiest' members and once the Reformation took place such behavior decreased, but it didn't disappear. The most recent large scandal involved high profile preacher the Rev. Henry Lyons, former leader of the National Baptist Convention. Lyons was caught in an illicit affair by his wife. However, being caught in the affair was the least of Rev. Lyons problems. Not only did Rev. Lyons carry out an illicit affair with Convention publicist Bernice Edwards that became public, Lyons embezzled more than $4 million from the National Baptist Convention of which he was the elected leader for millions of Black Baptists. Lyons showered his mistress with expensive jewelry and furs bought with the embezzled funds and even purchased a house in his mistress's name using the embezzled money, but the whole scheme came down when his wife burned down the house of his mistress.

Apparently, no one was looking when Lyons was elected National Baptist president in 1994. Previously, Lyons was accused of bank fraud in 1981, paid $85,000 restitution, and served a year of probation. Rev. Lyons lover, Bernice Edwards pleaded guilty to embezzling $60,000 in 1994 from an alternative high school she had directed.[224] Rev. Lyons is in the penitentiary for the next six years for crimes, but the list doesn't stop there. There are hundreds of such cases across the Unites States each year; the only difference is because of Lyon's high profile bringing more attention. However, when it comes to stealing in the name of the Lord, Lyons is not the only preacher fleecing the flock in the Black community. The charlatans and pulpit pimps come in all colors.

Unfortunately, for the unscrupulous and dishonest, religion offers larcenous con men and women the ultimate dodge in that there is no way to ascertain the truth of the promises these charlatans pass out like free tickets to heaven. Because the greatest rewards of religion are in the afterlife, there is no way of proving these hucksters wrong as the dead cannot file complaints with the Better Business Bureau and that is what these criminals rely upon—gullibility, blind faith and an unwillingness to question.

Despite the good works performed by the majority of the clergy, a few money hungry crooks cast all clericals in a bad light bringing distrust and negativity to the very religions in which they purport to so fervently believe as they become wealthy and increasingly removed from those who support them. The saddest part of this felonious profiteering is that the people who make these demagogues rich are the very people who can least afford it. It is no mistake that many of these preachers target the Black community of which pollster George Gallup says, "American Blacks are, by some measure, the most religious people in the world." Unfortunately, this also makes them easy prey for the unscrupulous among the clergy. It is clear that the ministry provides little protection against human nature and weakness as the litany of light-fingered felons below attests.

Oklahoma evangelist James Roy Whitby was convicted of swindling an 83-year-old religious widow out of $25,000. Later, he was charged with selling $4 million in worthless Gospel Outreach bonds. Also charged in the same scheme was convicted swindler the Rev. Tillman Sherron Jackson of Los Angeles, who had previously bilked the born-again in the Baptist Foundation of America—a $26 million fraud that resulted in congressional investigation.

Faith healer LeRoy Jenkins of South Carolina grossed $3 million a year by selling miracle water, prayer cloths and healing T-shirts to believers who watched him on 67 television stations. Jenkins ended up being sentenced to a 12-year prison term for conspiring to burn the home of a state trooper who had given his daughter a speeding ticket, burn the home of a creditor and mug a newspaperman who had exposed his money abuses and drug arrests.

The Rev. Hakeem Abdul Rasheed was convicted of mail fraud in California where he once operated a $20-million a year church in an Oakland movie theater. The Rev. Robert Carr of Durham, N.C., was sentenced to 10 years in prison for taking paychecks, food stamps, and welfare checks from members of his Church of God and True Holiness. In Chicago, The Rev. Roland Gray was convicted of theft, fraud and conspiracy and served two years in prison after falsely collecting $43,000 in welfare checks and food stamps. Welfare fraud slipped into Washington, DC where Bishop Lucius Cartwright and Pastor Albert Hamrick were sent to jail for embezzling $250,000 while administering food stamp distribution.

FLEECING THE FLOCK

Every year millions of people are bilked out of their hard earned money by purloining preachers, felonious faith healers and a variety larcenous psychics, mystics and paranormal charlatans whose only real ability is their remarkable proclivity for relieving trusting dupes of their funds. Sometimes the amounts are small ranging from a few dollars up to a few hundred dollars. On the other hand, people have had their life savings cleaned out by these unscrupulous fakers. Unfortunately, those who are bilked are usually those who can least afford it coming from the ranks of those living on fixed incomes or the poor. They are also the least likely to believe they have been bilked even if the culprit is caught in the act. Still, in most cases the money is given willingly regardless that often they are persuaded into giving by promises that cannot be kept.

Still, it is only money. Charismatic religions, or those religions that depend upon the leadership of one man or woman, are big business today and the number of megachurches has steadily increased even though they are clearly one-man or one-woman operations that are usually characterized by sumptuous surroundings, extravagant dress and lavish life styles. However, these enterprises are also the most likely to abuse the trust of their followers. Abuse ranges from simple deception and false promises to punishable offenses such as mail fraud, racketeering and embezzlement.

PROSPERITY PREACHING

"The line between foolishness and fraud is thin." [225]

Prosperity preaching's basic premise is that God wants us to be successful, which includes material wealth and all that is associated with it. Prosperity preachers are not new phenomena in the Black community. In the early 1900's, colorful preachers like Daddy Grace and Father Divine drew large congregations and became wealthy because of their charisma and their preaching a doctrine of personal prosperity. Money and religion have been intimately tied together from the beginning and it was no different when Christianity rose to power during the decline of the Roman Empire. Over the centuries, Rome-based Christianity collected vast fortunes in gold, art and property and individuals leaders of the church and their families became extraordinarily wealthy. The material corruption of the early Christian church eventually led to the Reformation and a bloody time in Europe, but money and religion remained inextricably intertwined as the church still wielded considerable influence because of its money and possessions. Today money and religion remain unyieldingly interconnected and not always to the benefit of the followers. It is no different with the Black church.

The Rev. Frederick Eikerenkoetter, who is better known as Rev. Ike, is considered the modern day model for prosperity gospel preaching which spawned a whole school of prosperity preachers including Creflo Dollar and Benny Hinn who have become fabulously wealthy preaching the Gospel. Recently, Rev. Ike's career received a needed boost when his show began airing on the Black Entertainment Television network. Black Entertainment Television (BET) is one of the most watched television networks in the Black community and it regularly features a host of television evangelists. The once Black owned network was bought out by entertainment giant Viacom for $3 billion, but the nation's largest

Black television network came under criticism for allowing evangelists who have been discredited for financial improprieties, ethical lapses and even fraud have access to its airways.

Among those televangelists are known fraud Peter Popoff, the much investigated Robert Tilton and prosperity preachers like Reverend Ike and Benny Hinn. In an article published in Salon Online Magazine, University of Virginia professor Virginia, Jeffrey Haddon, said that "a network that pats itself on the back by saying it serves the Black community ought to stop selling time to people who take advantage of them." [226] Texas Attorney General Dan Morales said that Tilton is "raping the most vulnerable segments of our society—the poor, the infirm, the ignorant...who believe his garbage." [227] According to a recent piece in Liberty Magazine, at the height of his evangelical stardom the Robert Tilton Ministries was taking in an estimated $80 million per year, giving Tilton a salary of $400,000.[228]

Rev. "Ike," the founding father of the modern "prosperity gospel" movement on the airwaves, has been promising believers that in exchange for their cash, God will shower them with material reward. "The LACK of money is the root all evil," is Rev. Ike's signature phrase. The flamboyant New York preacher regularly wears $2,000 suits, his fingers drip with diamonds and gold, he owns 16 Rolls-Royces, and he has luxury homes all over the country.

Creflo A. Dollar is a more recent "prosperity gospel" salesman. He and his wife, Taffi, head the 35,000-member World Changer Church "megachurch" congregation in Atlanta, Georgia. Like Rev. Ike, Dollar promises the faithful that they will be blessed with wealth and prosperity courtesy of Jesus Christ. So far, it has worked for him. According to the Atlanta Journal Constitution, Dollar drives a Rolls-Royce, flies around the globe in his private jet, and has a $1 million house in an upscale Atlanta neighborhood." [229]

Fund raising for these "televangelists" range from religious self-help books, videos and tapes to prayer cloths that have been personally anointed and sell for as much $20 to prayer tunnels and even corn meal that has been blessed and sent to the donator with a special blessing. Religious charms, holy hankies, "prayer tunnels" and other ruses for extracting money from followers are often perfectly legal under the First Amendment. Promises of wealth and prosperity, though, can be dangerous vehicles in taking money—and hope—from those who can least afford it.[230] Despite how many people may be hurt by this holy hucksterism, usually it is only financial taxing and extremely embarrassing. Obviously, this is not the case when savings accounts are wiped out or people are put under financial stress because of money hungry dream hustlers.

SHOW ME THE MONEY?

Churches need money to operate and to do the work they do best, but how much money is enough money for the church leader? Judging from the prosperity evangelists, apparently there is never enough money, as money always seems to be a key topic or advertisement for their religious "pitch."

As a rule, being the pastor of a church is not a lucrative profession. Many preachers have outside jobs just to make ends meet and even then many often funnel their personal funds back into the church to help further church outreach programs. Most pastors are not rich. For the most part pastors do not receive extravagant salaries with compensation averaging around $39,000 annually across the United States. For many, being a pastor often requires a second job to make ends meet. Generally, it is not a lucrative business, but there are many who are prosperous. The Bible even makes reference that you cannot dedicate your life both to God and to getting rich, but it seems that is not the case with some of the most popular pastors in the Black community.

But as mega-churches continue to siphon off members from smaller congregations to attended churches that literally seat thousands every Sunday, it becomes curious as to whether these megachurches are houses of the Lord or temples to Mammon. These megachurches rake in thousands of dollars each Sunday and are housed in huge complexes that cover acres of land. In the Black community, often the pastor and their spouse, of these megachurches are paid princely salaries and have such perks as helicopters, planes and even chauffeured limousines to help them get about.

> "Do not store up for yourselves treasures on earth, where moth and rust destroy, and where thieves break in and steal. But store up for yourselves treasures in heaven, where moth and rust do not destroy, and where thieves do not break in and steal. For where your treasure is, there your heart will be also. (NIV, Matthew 6:19-21)

Many see no incongruity in preacher's living the life styles of the rich and famous, but it is hard to skirt the issue of money, possessions, and what the Bible has to say about them. It is even more difficult to see the people who help make the megachurches prosper, give money that they can't afford to give and even worse, it seems that no one has any qualms about taking it.

But it is not just the megachurches that focus on money. Some churches in the Black community actually ask for financial statements from its members so they can "help" them figure what its members need to tithe. Not to be bypassed by the digital age, some churches accept credit card donations and debit cards as well, making it easy for member to give money they don't have to give.

Churches also often identify money givers in the church by actually asking those who have contributed $1,000 to stand, and then asking all who contributed $500 to stand and it goes on and on until it finally reaches the $5 dollar limit. Part of this is done to give recognition to those who have donated, but it is also done to shame others into giving more, or play upon people's egos so they can be identified among the big givers.

Basically, this surface research shows nothing more than human beings being human beings. This in no way absolves either the religionist or the nonbeliever of their transgressions, it simply points out that religion hasn't had much affect in curbing the excessive behavior of humanity and that there is no logical reason to assume the more religion will make a difference especially considering its track record, in both the Black and white communities.

SEXUAL IMPROPRIETY

> *Since the primary motive of the evil is disguise, one of the places evil people are most likely to be found is within the church. What better way to conceal one's evil from oneself, as well as from others, than to be a deacon or some other highly visible form of Christian within our culture?...I do not mean to imply that the evil are anything other than a small minority among the religious or that the religious motives of most people are in any way spurious. I mean only that evil people tend to gravitate toward piety for the disguise and concealment it can offer them. Martin Buber*

The Catholic Church Trips

With the recent sex scandals involving the Catholic Church, sexual impropriety among the clergy is under heavy examination. Each day it seems that another case of sexual molestation by a priest or other clergy comes to the fore. As much as the world is surprised, it is a surprise of forgetfulness. Several years ago sex scandals rocked the Catholic Church, but that scandal died out and was replaced with O. J. Simpson. Sixty Minutes did a report on priests who sexually abused members of their congregation and received nothing more than a transfer to another location. The report included an overview of a New Mexico retreat where errant priests were sent for rehabilitation. Nothing has changed.

Sexual impropriety is as old as religion itself. History recorded sexual abuse and misuse in the Catholic Church from its beginning. It is unfortunate what is happening to the Catholic Church, but it is not the only denomination burdened by sexual misbehavior in its ranks, it is just the most visible because of its size. In the Roman Catholic Church, over 800 priests have been removed from ministry because of allegations against them. More than 1,400 insurance claims on the books and the Church has paid out over $1 billion in liability with nearly an estimated $500 million pending. One noted expert claims that there are over 5,000 priests with some type of allegation against them. If this is true, then there are at least 1,000,000 direct victims of clergy sexual abuse and between 4-6 million indirect victims in the U.S.[231]

Sexual Misbehavior

The subject of illicit sex barely crosses the lips of today's clergy who now seem to look the other way when it comes to adult behavior of this type and maybe with good reason. A survey of Southern Baptist pastors by the *Journal of Pastoral Care* said that 14 percent of the pastors surveyed admitted to engaging in inappropriate sexual behavior. The same pastors reported that they had counseled at least one woman who reported having intercourse with another minister.[232] If the recent "love child" scandal involving the Rev. Jesse Jackson is any indicator, it is clear that not even the clergy is immune to the whims of human behavior. However, Rev. Jackson was not the first prominent preacher caught with his pants down. The Rev. Jimmy Swaggart was caught with a prostitute after he was exposed by former a church member.[233]

In fact, a 1997 Newsweek article pointed out that various surveys show that as many as 30 percent of male Protestant ministers have had sexual intercourse with women other than their wives.[234] A survey of Protestant clergy by *Leadership Magazine* found that 12 percent admitted to sexual intercourse outside of marriage and that 23 percent reported doing something sexually inappropriate with some one not their spouse. The same researchers also interviewed a thousand Leadership subscribers and 45 percent admitted to sexually inappropriate behavior and 23 percent to extramarital intercourse.[235]

The Presbyterian Church stated that 10-23 percent of clergy have "inappropriate sexual behavior or contact" with clergy and employees. The United Methodist research showed 38.6 percent of Ministers had sexual contact with church members and that 77 percent of church workers experienced some type of sexual harassment. The United Church of Christ found that 48 percent of the women in the work place have been sexually harassed by male clergy. The Southern Baptists claim 14.1 percent of their clergy has sexually abused members.[236]

As far back as 1983 in a doctoral thesis by Richard Blackmon, 12 percent of the 300 Protestant clergy surveyed admitted to sexual intercourse with a parishioner and 38 percent admitted to other sexual contact with a parishioner. Although the actual extent of the problem is unknown, the significance of clergy sexual abuse is acknowledged by the denominational leaders of all Christian churches.[237] Since the founding of the Christian church in Rome, scandal has surrounded Christianity. In early Rome, the Holy Fathers of the church engaged in every conceivable misconduct imaginable including unsanctioned sexual relations and adultery to rape and sex with children. The early popes not only engaged in illicit sex but also often sired entire families of illegitimate children, while others kept mistresses and used church funds to pay for the services of male and female prostitutes.

What is happening today seems to be no more than an example of people succumbing to human weaknesses and depravity. Religion has not changed this behavior and more headlines are forthcoming as more people come forward to report sexual misbehavior among the clergy. The big difference is the level of hypocrisy demonstrated by those who claim spiritual and moral leadership which makes it that much more reprehensible.

Going Against the Grain

There is something feeble and a little contemptible about a man who cannot face the perils of life without the help of comfortable myths. Almost inevitably some part of him is aware that they are myths and that he believes them only because they are comforting. But he dares not face this thought! Moreover, since he is aware, however dimly, that his opinions are not rational, he becomes furious when they are disputed. —Bertrand Russell, Human Society in Ethics and Politics (1954),

CHAPTER 10

▼

BLACK NONBELIEVERS

"It is an interesting and demonstrable fact, that all children are atheists and were religion not inculcated into their minds, they would remain so."

—*Ernestine Rose*

Going against the grain like rowing against the current always make for a more difficult task. Why anyone would willingly submit themselves to such unnecessary difficulty is hard to understand. However, when dealing with human behavior based upon ethics, principles and reason, it becomes clear that the answer has nothing to do with ease, but with honesty. Over the past three years, I have collected some general information regarding the opinions of Black atheists, skeptics and freethinkers that may foster some understanding of how and why anyone would live a life free of religion. After gathering and compiling information from the respondents to my surveys, as well as obtaining their individual stories, it became clear that living a life according to their belief was more important to them than going along with the status quo.

WHY DO BLACKS BECOME ATHEISTS OR AGNOSTICS

There is a popular misconception among "believers" that some terrible experience drove the nonbeliever away from God and this is a position that those surveyed found not only troubling but also "insulting." Another misconception is that people choose to be atheists or agnostics when those surveyed said it was not a choice but a reality. Many tie atheism to rebellion against religion and authority, but that is not the case according to those surveyed. It seems that people lose faith when religion has nothing substantial to offer.

Those who describe themselves as atheists or agnostics responded negatively to questions asking them why they became agnostics or atheists, indicating that such questions implied that something is wrong with them, or that some terrible thing must have happened in their lives to make them take such a stance, and highly resented the implication of such thinking. The basic reason cited for their nonbelief was simply "a lack of evidence." Oddly, one of the biggest influencers or proof sources for nonbelief are "the people who call themselves Christians." All felt that "Christians themselves" are the worst advertisement for Christianity, saying that each knew too many Christians whose behavior didn't match with their announced beliefs. Also, each felt that their varying degrees of disbelief accorded them a certain amount of freedom by allowing them to escape from "second guessing" and "guilty feelings."

For those who once belonged to organized religion loosing one's faith is not taken lightly, especially if it has been a major part of ones life. It is a traumatic experience marked by constant questioning, second thoughts and finally resignation. However, it was pointed out that everyone is born an atheist and that it is an accident of proximity that determines religious make up. If one is born in the United States, more than likely that child will accept Christianity. If one is born in Egypt, there is a high likelihood that one will follow Islam.

WHO, WHY AND WHERE

Who are these Black nonbelievers? They are your neighbors, your friends and even your relatives. Most nonbelievers don't advertise their nonbelief as a matter of respect and as a matter of expediency. Asides from their lack of belief in any God they are no different from anyone else. They are patriots. They are concerned with the welfare of others. It would seem that the ideas and beliefs held by atheists and agnostics would make them almost exact opposites of most Americans, but that isn't the case. Most nonbelievers I interviewed were what anyone would say are "average Americans." Nothing distinguished them from other Americans except their nonbelief. Otherwise, they are mothers and fathers, teachers and coaches and just about everything under the sun considered normal.

Where do these people come from? Everywhere! Responses came from all across the United States, from New York and Los Angeles to Amarillo and Alaska. Replies came from those as young as 13 to 72. The survey group included professionals such as doctors and lawyers, librarians, a radio talk show host, registered nurses, an army sergeant and two former preachers. Education ranged from graduate degrees to high school degrees, as well as a large measure of self-education. Respondents included men, women and a variety of sexual orientations.

There was no "typical" nonbeliever or freethinker. The majority said they came from Christian families and once attended church regularly with their families. Nevertheless, the majority said they stopped attending church as soon as they were able to make the decision to stay or go themselves. Not surprisingly, the Black agnostic and atheistic experience does not seem to differ much from that of whites except that Black nonbelievers are a minority within a minority. Strangely enough, some say they still attend religious services for weddings or funerals, but some say they also attend to make business contacts, see old friends, and listen to good music or to enjoy a good show.

My natural doubts grew stronger and I began to suspect that there was no one at the helm. My change produced much anguish and some conflict. I've found liberation in my conversion to atheism/humanism/freethought.
—*John Arnold*

FAMILY LIFE

Three respondents claimed never believing in God or a Supreme Being. Although nearly three-fourths reported attending church with their families, the remainder said they were never directed toward organized religion although all claimed they received strong moral and ethical direction from their parents and felt no pressure from their family to do otherwise.

While at least half said that their stances had caused some "ruffled feathers" in their families and among their friends, they also said that once the initial shock wore off, everything returned to normal, although several said it is still an issue for some of their friends and family. All said their friends and family initially expressed disbelief and were asked, "what happened?" which is one of the things most did not want to hear. As indicated earlier, all believed that nothing had happened other than "a logical thought process" that made them think different.

I think the fair thing to say is that my family is less concerned about my religion and my religious practice and more concerned about my behavior, accomplishments, and responsibility. —Naima Washington

TRADITIONAL GOD

Belief in the traditional God of Christianity was dismissed as unreasonable and requiring a measure of blind-faith, that as one respondent said was "unacceptable." In fact, they felt there was something wrong with those who believed in the "magic and superstition" of an invisible God. Most respondents said they came to their beliefs early in life; many before they reached 20 years old and that there was no trauma or "earth shattering experience" that suddenly changed them. Most said they literally outgrew the God "concept" or never had it to begin with.

Despite the overwhelming tonnage of misery in this world God always gets credit for being merciful because humans are trained to expect nothing more from life than to take the next breath. —Sid Davis

I just think that there's no proof that God or any place such as heaven or hell exist. So, I choose not to believe, in what I don't know. —Wanda LeVine

I don't believe in God anymore than I believe in ghosts, demons, angels, fairies, goblins, trolls, tooth fairies, Santa Clauses, rabbits that lay eggs, great pumpkins, flying purple people eaters, vampires, werewolves, gargoyles, leprechauns that live in my cereal, or any other mythological character that was invented for one reason or another. —Sid Washington

…I wish I could have had a kinder more gentler god in my childhood!! It's the type of church I was in, rather than religion in general I think, my mom was a Pentecostal faith healer, so I was constantly exposed to fundamentalist ideas, and hearing all the time about bad things that happen to people when they turn back on the faith (like diseases coming back, etc)…I still feel bits of anxiety at times when I talk about god not existing, like he's going to get me for that comment! "—Carlo Harris

The Bible

Of the thirty respondents selected for this writing, only two feel the Bible is a book that is divinely inspired or a revelation from God. However, none of the respondents think the Bible can in any way be taken literally, with one respondent describing parts of it as "moronic" in reference to Balaam's talking ass and "not as believable as Aesop's Fables." Nearly three fourths of the respondents feel that the Bible is purely the work of men, "men ignorant of the laws of science and filled with superstition." In addition, most felt the Bible is too open to interpretation to ever be useful as a guide, saying that "people interpret the Bible anyway they want" depending upon their personal agendas. They see the Bible as largely a collection of myths and fables "put together by a bunch of superstitious men hundreds of years ago."

Opinion on the Bible ranged from outright disbelief of the entire book as the work of God and denial of Jesus Christ as Lord and Savior to belief in Jesus as a historical figure, but not as a supernatural being or the Son of God. Many cited the Bible as being filled with "errors and contradictions" which they said definitely proves that it could not be the work of an all-knowing and all-powerful God. Those who professed belief in a "supreme being" specifically denied that it could be the God of the Bible saying that the God of the Bible is "too much like man" citing repeated incidences of violence, pettiness and jealousy, which are more human than Godly. However, the biggest indictment of the Bible was regarding its lack of concern for human life. Readers said they literally lost count of the people killed after the first book of the Bible—Genesis.

> *"God" didn't write the Bible, man did and man makes mistakes and embellishes. Even if it was the "word of God" at one time, the translation's, writes and rewrites over the centuries have lost the original meaning—especially the King James Version (note, that's "version" and not "translation").*
> *—Eddie Daniel Glover*

> *Any all-knowing entity should have been able to not only write a book in such a way as to leave no doubt regarding its message but to also make that book tamper-proof. —Naima Washington*

> *I consider Mark Twain's The Adventures of Huckleberry Finn more sacred and at least it's a good read. —Omari Christian*

> *...one need not look at history for the sins of Christianity. The pages of the Bible itself clearly shows the horror. Imagine the events of the New Testament taking place instead, in the Jim Crow-era Deep South. Imagine, if you will, a young, 30-something Black man who speaks out against the injustices being suffered by his people. He is arrested by the authorities, questioned, beaten, and nailed to a piece of wood and left to hang until dead. I wonder if this could in fact be the real cause of why some within the community have resisted portraying Jesus as a Black man in their churches. Would portraying the bloodied, beaten body of a Black man suffering on the cross finally reveal to Christians how truly vicious Christianity really is? The cognitive dissonance alone would probably force many to make unwelcome parallels between the plight of Jesus and the long, painful history of segregation. —Frances Parker*

Knowledge of the Bible

Also, most felt that a majority of those who call themselves Christians know less about the Bible than the average atheist because "they have not searched" and are largely "followers" and have no real understanding of the Bible or what it says. Most felt that few Christians have actually read the Bible and suspect that most others have only brushed over it and have no deep comprehension of it. It appears there may be some merit in their argument because as the amount of Americans who read the Bible on a regular basis has steadily declined and that among those who agree with biblical teachings most have never read the Bible.

SUFFERING AND PAIN

Respondents were also unanimous in feeling that an all-powerful and all-loving God is incongruous with the amount of pain and suffering in the world, citing ethnic wars, terrorist bombings, AIDS and starvation in Africa, as well as, religious wars in Sri Lanka, the Middle East and India. Others said they could not reconcile a God who "allows such suffering among his children" to be a God worth praising or even acknowledging. A majority felt that if an omnipotent and omnibenevolent God existed, then "that God would not allow the amount of suffering and pain that is apparent in the world." Others said if God exists then he is not all-powerful and loving or that he doesn't care, which most indicated that to even consider such a spirit would be ridiculous.

I reject the possibility that any God worth his or her salt would allow this to go on. —Sid Davis

There is a lot of needless suffering on the planet. If religious people truly believe that suffering is God's will then they are con artists when they collect money claiming that the money will help to relieve the suffering of others. After all, if it is God's will that people suffer then why would the religious community attempt to alter the will of God?—Naima Washington

MORALS AND ETHICS

Most feel there is a "clear" line between morality and religion with many feeling that religion actually retards moral growth by absolving individuals of responsibility in the present world and providing loopholes for doing almost anything and being forgiven, diminishing any motivation to strive for the betterment of this world. Several cited the Ku Klux Klan as a clear example of the divide between religion and morality, saying that although the KKK is a Christian organization, it hardly represents the tenets of Christian philosophy.

Questioned as to how they maintained moral and ethical standards without a religious code for guidance most said they did not need religion to be moral, although many said there is some good advice in some religious teachings, "but not any that can't be found elsewhere." In fact, most said that except for a few they feel that religion has no impact at all on the way people behave saying it was all a matter of "personal choice." "Nothing has changed man's inhumanity to man" is the consensus of the group surveyed. For themselves, a majority said they set their own moral guides using some variation of "The Golden Rule" to cause no harm to anyone and to avoid usurping another's individual rights. In addition, most respondents believe "reason and logic" are keys to understanding and leading a moral and ethical life. Some indicated that morality develops out of a concern for others, which is also another version of the Golden Rule and an offshoot of humanism.

Basically, I hold the objectivists view: Cause no physical harm or usurpation to another person or that person's property. —Chris Felton

The fact that there's no heaven or hell does not give me permission to hurt others, even those who spout what I consider to be absolute nonsense.
—Naima Washington

INTELLECT

Interestingly, the respondents were unanimous in targeting religion as anti-intellectual, anti-progressive and a "blind" follower of the status quo, citing how Christianity sided with slavery, fascism and often stands against science. On this issue, most felt the church has no moral standing even to "suppose" that anyone should trust it. A clear majority felt that "organized religion" was against "using our minds or asking questions" and uses that stance to avoid doubt from its followers or to avoid any discomfort in the church. However, most also felt that the "insistence" on not thinking and the pure "reliance" on faith actually did more to encourage disbelief and promote doubt by evading questions or making it seem wrong to ask them. Most indicated that it was not rebellion that led them away from religion, but more of an interest in "what wasn't being said and why".

> *Now, they were trying to tell me basically not to think too hard, or question, the Bible. Unacceptable!* —J.R. Ector

> *Things that concern me, like in the Pentecostal church, there is such a lack of understanding and appreciation for science, that they take the Genesis account literally!...I truly believe that Christianity has enslaved our intellects and shackled us in fear. Christianity has not pulled us together as many Christian theists would assert. I maintain that it has done exactly the opposite.* —Frances Parker

WOMEN AND THE BLACK CHURCH

Again, on this question there was unanimous belief that the Church and the Black church in particular has been less than observant of women's rights. Many cited the male domination of Black religion on both a local and national level, while others referred to Biblical passages supporting the mistreatment and denigration of women. In addition, there is significant research to support this and most of the respondents were familiar with it, including Biblical references that denigrate women and in effect make women less than second-class citizens, (Ephesians 5:22-24). Most are also aware that Christian religion's leadership is dominated by men at more than 9:1 ratio, even though women now account the majority of church membership, as well as, making for the majority membership in church programs.

It is also clear that the men have no desire to change the situation as the Bible speaks directly of women being subservient to men. The women in this survey made it clear that they understood that the Bible was written by men and that those men were following the traditions of that time in history, but they also said that some men want to keep women subservient today and that was not an option.

> *When I consider the poor treatment of women at the hands of most organized religions, I certainly see cause for women all over the world not to show up at their house of worship next Friday, Saturday, or Sunday!*
> —Naima Washington

GOD AND CHILDREN

This topic aroused significant comment outside the intended scope. A majority felt that although parents may feel that they are doing the right thing by getting their children involved in religion at an early age, those interviewed see it as risky and potentially harmful. Of most concern is religion's potential to stymie intellectual growth by its call for the subjugation of the intellect and its insistence on blind obedience to authority. All agreed that religion loads children with unnecessary guilt and shame for imagined sins and had serious concerns about introducing children to the concept of God, in particular the Christian concept.

> *My children realize that the concept of "God" is like a more potent version of the concept of Santa Claus. There are a few books they have which are very good for teaching them the importance of scientific thinking and reasoning, but the one I favor is entitled, "Just Pretend—A Freethought Book for Children", by Dan Barker.* —Chris Felton

> *Attempting to keep children in the dark is never an intelligent way to raise a child into a responsible adult, and failing to give children age-appropriate information about life is totally irresponsible!* —Naima Washington

The young mind cannot distinguish between fantasy and reality. So to introduce it to religion and present its stories as fact is wrong. Also, the children should be given the choice if they wish to be involved in religion. It should not be forced upon them. When they are old enough they will ask questions and the parents should be there with the proper answers.
—Eugene Globe

AFTERLIFE

Descriptions of a heavenly afterlife are often the subject of Sunday sermons where a perfect life is depicted as a reward for service and faith here upon earth. However, the survey consensus was firmly against the possibility of an after life. Even the two deists who replied thought the possibility of an afterlife sounded like "silly children's fantasies." Once again, respondents referred to the man made descriptions of heaven as unimaginative and even dull and called the desire to enter heaven as wishful thinking and an inability to accept that we are not special.

> *There is no afterlife. Mark Twain was asked if he feared death. He responded something like "I was dead thousands of years before I was born and I didn't suffer the slightest inconvenience from it."* —Omari Christian

FUNDAMENTALISM

The recent upsurge in fundamentalist Christianity also stirred most of the respondents negatively and contrary to what most might think, they believed that fundamentalism would eventually so cripple Christianity as to make it ineffective, or that it may eventually lead to its death. Most felt that religious fundamentalists lacked depth, understanding and are extremely intolerant and bigoted. Failure to acknowledge reason and logic were recurrent themes in the answers concerning the negativity of fundamentalism. A majority felt that the horrendous suicide bombing of the World Trade Center is a prime example of fundamentalism stretched to the limits.

> *Fundamentalism presents an opportunity to see religion functioning without its kid gloves. Its naked unapologetic authoritarianism doesn't sneak up*

on you. It loudly condemns, it emotionally and physically attacks, and in many instances, it kills. —Naima Washington

Fundamentalism harms the course of religion because it consistently defends tenets that are indefensible. In addition, fundamentalism is very controlling and binding. People do not want to be slaves to a belief knowingly. Fundamentalism will fail. —Reginald V. Finley

It exposes the level of extremism to which some religionists are willing to go. —J.R. Ector

BLACK REACTION

Responses were mixed on this topic, but all said most Blacks were surprised and "didn't know what to say" about their nonbelief. Many of the respondents found it humorous. Several said some people thought they were "devil worshippers" or "Communists", expressing disbelief that anyone harbored these kinds of thoughts. Most attributed these reactions to "ignorance and bigotry." However, all said that there was a clear indication that some how "your worth as a human being" had suddenly dropped.

Their tolerance for people who believe something different from what they do—is zero. —Eddie Daniel Davis

They truly believe that atheism is synonymous with evil and Satanism, that atheism is a "white man's belief." Many I've talked to have never even heard of a Black atheist. Many don't believe a Black atheist exists. —Reginald V. Finley

Nonbelievers clearly swim against the tide and most people are raised to believe that your life is guided by two forces, one good and the other one evil. For them, a non-believer is someone who is guided by evil forces. —Naima Washington

To be honest, I am quite surprised how many of my friends and colleagues both Black and white are supportive even though they disagree. I do have people who say they will pray for me. But they do not say this in a malicious, judgmental way, but in a respectful manner. —Wayne Evans

INTOLERANCE

Although none have been physically attacked, several mentioned verbal altercations with "over zealous Christians" who mostly called them names and voiced hostile threats. Most said the attacks were harmless although some found a certain humor in them because the attacks always came from what they called "love thy neighbor" Christians and that they were not surprised by the intolerance. Because of potential danger almost half of the respondents asked that their names not be used and requested a pseudonym saying they feared alienation and repercussions on the their jobs, in their communities or from their friends and acquaintances. Of those identified, approximately half of that number are social activists regularly promoting the division of church and state, opposing prayer in schools or the posting of the ten commandments among other social issues. Only two were aggressively anti-religion saying that organized religion is not only "irrational and dangerous" but that it should be banned from the world.

> *The profession of a belief in God is very important in the Black community while it shows little tolerance for nonbelief.* —Naima Washington

RELIGION

Despite coming from a variety of Christian denominations, including Catholics, Baptists and even Pentecostals, most cast a skeptical eye at the organized religion of their parents, either dismissing it outright or ignoring it all together. On average, most feel that organized religion promotes "ignorance and complacency" and is anti-intellectual while actively "denying the progress of science." Even with that outlook, most believe the Black church is useful in providing social services and bringing important issues to the public spotlight.

Although most disregard organized religion, they also indicated they did not want it to go away, but were mainly concerned that religion "continues to promote superstition, arrogance and intolerance." They felt that if the supernatural elements and the "denial of realism" could be removed from organized religion it would be more effective in finding and keeping followers while also acknowledging that if these items were removed that more than likely religion would fail.

Still, I must say that because of the heinous and atrocious conditions Blacks encountered through slavery, religion played a major role within their lives.
—Chris Felton

As for myself again, I am highly critical of organized religion—highly critical! —Charles Cooke

Religion doesn't make you a responsible person. It makes the devil responsible and makes the believer the devil's co-defendant! —Naima Washington

THE BLACK CHURCH

In general, most feel the Black church is an important historical institution and highly useful entity citing how the Black church once served as a meeting place during slavery where plans were made and ideas came about. Many said that the Black church still serves as a buffer against racism and as voice for those who can't speak for themselves, but they also said they felt that today's church in the Black community promotes "helplessness and superstition" that leads to "passivity" and acceptance of intolerable conditions. "Many believe that it is our plight to suffer" because they will be rewarded when they die. Others called religion a form of mental slavery, but most still see the Black church as a source of unity in the Black community, but they also said they believe that "unity" is dying out.

Proselytizing

Views on proselytizing were unanimous and blunt. Proselytizing is looked on as an "obnoxious" and "rude" behavior that "speaks poorly" of the religions that espouse such action. There was no equivocation on this point. A Public Agenda report supports their view, as most Americans believe that proselytizing is not acceptable behavior. Respondents listed "door-to-door" proselytizing as especially "obnoxious."

> *I don't want them to become atheists and have no interest in trying to get them to live life on my terms but should they want to look beyond their current beliefs for answers, I would actively support their efforts if they wanted my help.* —Naima Washington

Church and State

As far as mixing religion and politics, all said they think it is a bad idea, citing instances such as the Inquisition and the Crusades to the mixture of religion and politics in such disparate places as Ireland, Iraq and Israel where "Holy wars" are still in progress. And, with the World Trade Center terrorist attack all agreed that fundamentalism gone awry is to blame for the terrorist attack. Several cited American fundamentalism as dangerous to the separation of church and state predicting a return to the "Dark Ages" if fundamentalism manages to impose its will upon the country.

> *This trend interferes with the rights of others to follow their own faith and belief. The politicians that are doing this have only one religion on their mind, "Christianity." No doubt about it. That's just plain wrong. The first settlers left Europe because of this same type of mentally. —Reginald V. Finely*

School Prayer and the 10 Commandments

Prayer in school also prompted much the same responses as most felt that any prayer in school was bound to offend someone, especially non-Christians or even Christians who believe differently from others. The Ten Commandments fared no better and most viewed them as "historically" ineffective and not adequate as "they have had little affect in the Christian community."

> *Just another ploy by the religious to thwart the separation of Church and State and get prayer back in school. They should be separate. —J.R. Ector*

> *The problem with it is because the Ten Commandments are a Christian document. Muslims, Bahai's and others would be forced to review this document. Not only that, it's a lie. The Ten Commandments presently presented were destroyed by Moses in an angry fit. The second set that God commanded Moses to make are an embarrassment to Christianity. That's why they are not used today, although God commanded that this second set was to override the first. In addition, the Ten Commandments are not practical in today's complex society. They need to post the US constitution in school not the Ten Commandments. —Reginald V. Finley*

The All Everything God

Most also had tremendous problems with the concept of an all-powerful, all-knowing and all-loving God. One key area of argument the interviewees brought forward was the conflict between the concept of an all-powerful God and the clear inability to do anything in real terms with clearly viewable results. They also pointed out the seeming contradiction between God's omniscience and the idea of free will, saying that if God knew the future of man, he would have known that the creature he was making was going to sin. Meaning, if God knows what we're going to do, how can we do anything other than that which he has foreseen? A particular issue for most was the idea of evil and an all-knowing and all-loving God.

> *If God created everything, then why did he create evil? If he didn't create evil, then he must not be omnipotent. If he is the ultimate origin of evil, then he either isn't as good as we think, or is powerless to stop it. —Reginald V. Finely*

Organization and Authority

All tended to shy away from groups such as atheist, agnostic or humanist organizations because they felt that organized groups always degenerate into quasi-religious modes after doctrine begins to take over. However, not all felt that way. Some felt that it is important to become involved in social actions, particularly involving the church and state, but also just to help enlighten and educate others to "another reality".

BREAKING AWAY

When reality and religion are in conflict some cannot reconcile what is taken on faith and their perceptions of reality. It is at this point where many atheists and agnostics suffer the pains of breaking free of religion. Although many atheists and agnostics stopped believing in the God of the Bible at an early age most reported that shaking the indoctrination of religion hasn't been so easy. Some religionist might say that this is God's way of working through the individual but nonbelievers would be quick to deny this saying that it is merely a matter of breaking a childhood habit that developed when they had the least defenses and knowledge.

One respondent said that "religion is like an unwanted guest, it never leaves unless you put it out and even then it keeps trying to sneak back." Others echoed that sentiment indicating that introduction to religion as children leaves an indelible mark that is always there despite the efforts to be rid of it. Some reported fighting battles with what they termed unnecessary guilt because of what they perceived as the result of early religious training.

> "...the most nerve racking part was leaving behind the idea that I was divinely protected, and realizing that anything could happen to me at anytime, just like any other person...so basically it was a loss of security.... I've always had the divine punishing God concept, and so when I committed a 'big' sin like premarital sex, I felt that God would punish me severely for the deed, so I worry myself to death about retribution, and now that I don't believe in a God, that sense of retribution is still with me...and still tend look at certain events as 'omens' of impending disaster! —Carlo Harris

Many spoke of wishing that their parents hadn't introduced them to religion saying that in some ways they felt some animosity even though they were sure their parents did not mean any harm and were only doing what they thought was right. It is a fascinating "Catch-22" conundrum. How could a Christian parent not introduce their children to their religion? It would seem that a Christian parent would be remiss if they did not introduce their children to Christianity and would have no way of knowing that in the future that early religious indoctrination "might" cause problems for their children.

> "I grew up in a church that would talk about god's wrath and people would 'prophecy' about upcoming funerals, and as kids we were so scared that we would be the next one in the casket.... My pastor used to say, If you want to fool around (sex), then god will 'AID' you...it's hard to get those things out of your psyche, if ever...People who didn't grow up in a strong religious environment can't understand that, but it's interesting that it didn't effect most of my cousins like that because they never gave the sermons much thought, because I've always been the type to reflect and take things of 'ultimate' significance seriously..." —Carlo Harris

For the child of a religious upbringing breaking away into nonbelief and skepticism can be traumatic and is not easily accomplished despite overpowering doubts and scientific fact. It is even more difficult in the Black community because of the high degree of religiosity demonstrated at all levels of the Black community where invocation of the name of God or Jesus accompanies even the most mundane before dinner blessing to X-rated entertainment and comedy. It may seem a small issue but for those breaking away from religion it is no laughing matter as the shedding of years or training and indoctrination that was implemented during the most formative years, when we all are most vulnerable, requires a change of self and rejection of many things that were once believed to be true.

Most felt that no parent willingly subjects their child to harm and are just not aware that sometimes there are negative affects of early religious indoctrination although they have been documented for years. Alternately, the group also felt that early religious training was also harmful to those who continue on in their faith saying that they believed that many become unable to deal with reality and reject or avoid any real thinking to avoid putting their religious beliefs against nature and reality.

Religious addiction is a term with which I am familiar. It usually refers to someone who is overly religious to the point that it is unhealthy. Usually that person lives a life that is very much out of contact with reality, concentrating almost exclusively on religion often neglecting family, friends and careers for religion. From an atheistic viewpoint it takes on an entirely different meaning. To some, religion is a harmless drug that gives its users comfort and usually causes no ill effects. Problems only arise when intellect and logic in conflict with religious dogma. When the mind can't resolve an issue without magical thinking the quest to do so becomes unacceptable.

Breaking the habit of religion is just as difficult as giving up smoking according to many I spoke with who characterized religion as a "mind altering drug." With the exception of a few most of the participants said they were introduced to religion as children and had no choice in the matter. In many ways, the parallel between drugs and religion is appropriate in that both are used to fill a void in the lives of the users. Similarly, neither the drug user nor the religionist is aware they are hooked until they try to stop and it is at this point the clear difference between the two becomes apparent. Drug dealers knowingly sell addiction to those with the price of a fix, whereas those who introduce others to religion have only the best interests at heart, as they are our mothers, fathers, families and friends.

In many ways it is highly similar to drug or alcohol addiction in that all the addict ever cares about to the exclusion of all else is getting their next result fix. There are many people who could be considered very religious or even overly religious to some, but they are not religious addicts. They are not controlled by religion and live normal lives managing to keep things in perspective.

> *"I often times find myself crossing myself before I eat, as if I should still be giving thanks to something or someone for my food! I always catch myself, and say 'Who am I praying to?' It is an annoying habit that I have, even though I've been an atheist for a little over 4 years." —Frances Parker*

Religious addicts become strict religious legalists and interpret religious dogma literally, making no exception for anything between Black and white. They try to live their lives according to unbendable religious rules and regulations and more importantly, they seek to make others adhere to the same unyielding philosophy. In advantage, they also tend to believe they have a special or exclusive connection with God that no one else has including same faith believers.

> *"The most difficult part for me is people in my life that insist on having me participate in the old rituals and celebrations, i.e. Xmas." —J. R. Ector*

The personality of the religious addict and the drug addict are very similar in that they are both marked by tremendous need and emptiness common to the addictive personality. Like any addiction one of the most difficult things to do is break the habit, the addiction referred to by those I spoke with is possibly the most difficult portion of addiction, and that is breaking the habit.

> *"The most difficult part was the lingering doubt. "What if I'm wrong" type thoughts plagued me. The drug addict analogy is a good comparison to describe how it feels to leave religion or anything for that matter that you have been doing for a long time. I also felt left out and kind of like a weirdo because everyone is all talking about God and going to church and all, but I had no one to talk to about my atheism." —Kareem Lane*

During my research, I surfed across a web site for recovering religious addicts. Like other recovery programs, the Religious Recovery program is a twelve-step platform that includes many of the same steps included in drug and alcohol addiction programs. Interestingly, several respondents said that if allowed to choose for themselves that they might have chosen religion. However, most indicated that having the choice would not have made a difference, in that they believed that atheists are always atheists.

THE IMPORTANCE OF COMING OUT

Being an atheist and being identified as an atheist, are two distinct propositions. No accurate count can be made of the nonbelievers who keep it to themselves to avoid unpopular positions of the known atheist. The key benefit to staying invisible is to avoid negative public scrutiny and possible repercussions. This "stealth" existence is often easy to maintain and does not put the pretender in danger of repercussions unless they are found out. In a community, especially one as religious as the Black community, claiming atheism is surely not a way to generate positive support, while staying hidden may actually result in acceptance.

Nevertheless, most that I interviewed felt that is that most feel that it is better for the individual to come out in their atheism, feeling that the down side of remaining anonymous is a destructive psychological tug of war. Those who stay hidden always fear being found out. They fear the very real repercussions such a revelation will have on family and friends. At the same time, there is a desire to reveal the secret just to be rid of the pressure of keeping the secret hidden. Few actually lose friendships and family relations over such revelations, but that doesn't mean there won't be negative reactions. Families often wonder "where they went wrong" as if there is something they could have done to prevent it, without realizing that it is a personal choice but once the initial shock wears off most relationships are healed and the world keeps turning.

This is only a summary of the opinions of a select group of people I talked and corresponded with on a variety of subjects relating to their atheist or agnostic positions. All have been cooperative and open in replying to such a sensitive topic.

CHAPTER 11

THE INFIDELS

"They were allowed to stay there on one condition, and that is that they didn't eat of the tree of knowledge. That has been the condition of the Christian church from then until now. They haven't eaten as yet, as a rule they do not."

—*Clarence Darrow*

REGINALD FINLEY

I guess deep down inside I have always felt that something was wrong with the world but I could never put a finger on it. When I read *Atheism-The Case Against God* by George H. Smith, it all became clear. I have always been an atheist. I personally believe that we are all inherently human (not evil or good like many religions teach), and are animals of nature, capable of wondrous and unfortunately, even horrendous things.

My siblings think I am crazy and lost but they leave me alone about it because they know I am not going to change. I am probably a better person for my atheism because I do what's right just because it's the right thing to do, not for fear of eternal retribution. If anything, I probably pull from a variety of belief systems that improve the human condition, secular and non-secular. Our constitution is one of them. I truly do not believe that if everyone stopped being religious that people everywhere would start going out killing each other. I have more faith in humanity than that.

Using the Bible as a moral guide has some very serious issues because of the many contradictions of its own doctrines. The entire Bible has some serious moral dilemmas that clergy do not tell their congregations. Not only that, religions is slow to evolve. Many religions are fundamentalist, literally taking the Bible as inerrant and they do not leave room for the possibility of change. Many of the Bible's antiquated religious laws have no place in today's highly evolved scientific and technical society.

Fundamentalism is dangerous. If it weren't for secular laws, Christians would still be running around burning people at the stake and beating women in the streets. All in the name of their God. I truly believe that Christianity has enslaved our intellects and shackled us in fear rather than pulling us together as many Christian theists would assert. Christianity makes their followers self-righteous, bigoted, and cruel all in the name of their Jesus. Many Christians are taught that they can do wrong as long as they pray about it. However, a nontheist will burn for all eternity just because one does not believe. Where's the morality there? I don't see it.

Christianity harms us by not giving us a true moral basis to follow and suppresses our ability to learn and critically analyze data. The Bible is solely anti-science and reason and that's why our children are empty. That's why our children turn to gangs and violence because they are not taught how to deal in an ever-changing world. Just praying about your problems won't take them away. However, that's what most of our children are taught.

I used to be Christian. In fact, I used to teach Bible study, I sang with a gospel group, and I began to see just how cruel many Christians were. I no longer wanted to be part of such a self-righteous, hypocritical group. That's when I found atheism. Organized religion shackles and debilitates the mind. Most organized religions teach, "My God is better than your God" which is a quick and easy step to separating us as humans. Finally, I started to see the church as a place for people to fellowship, network, see who's wearing the best clothes, release guilt for all the sinning they did during the week, and see who can catch the "Holy Ghost" (sacred air) the most.

However, I do truthfully acknowledge the work that religious organizations have done for the homeless, sick, and poor. Let's not forget that there are also secular organizations like the Red Cross that assist people. Unfortunately, everyone is giving his or her money to religious organizations instead and now President Bush is trying to get us to pay for faith-based services, which is a clear violation of the separation of church and state. His religious proposals and bills have a good chance of going through as most people don't see the wolf hiding in the Armani suit just waiting to bring the church and government a little closer together. Didn't work for Rome and Afghanistan, won't work for us.

This trend of mixing religion and politics interferes with the rights of others to follow their own faith and belief. The politicians that are doing this have only one religion on their mind—Christianity. There is no doubt about it and it is just plain wrong. Shall we not forget that the first settlers left Europe because of this same type of mentality?

Still, it will not go away as long as the ultra right and fundamentalists try to put the 10 Commandments in our schools along with implementing school prayer. The problem with this is that the Ten Commandments are a Christian document. Muslims, Bahai's, Hindu's and others would be forced to review this document that isn't true. Not only is it a lie, the Ten Commandments presently presented were destroyed by Moses in an angry fit. The second set that God commanded Moses to make are an embarrassment to Christianity. That's why it is not used today, even though God commanded that this second set was to override the first. In addition, the Ten Commandments are not practical in today's complex society. They need to post the US constitution in school not the Ten Commandments.

Believe it or not, this fundamentalism binge actually harms the course of religion because fundamentalist consistently defend tenets that are indefensible. Among the fundamentalists, there is a general unwillingness to accept criticism although they are quite ready to dish it out and they believe that we should respect their opinions over empirical evidence. That's ridiculous. It's the old "because I said so", argument from false authority. In addition, fundamentalism is very controlling and binding. I truly do not believe that people want to be slaves, and in this fight for freedom, the failure of Fundamentalism and possibly Christianity is inevitable.

To set the record straight, I am not a bigot, racist, evil, immoral, nor amoral. I am an atheist, without theistic belief. My thoughts are free. Everyone should think freely but act responsibly. History has shown us that dogmatic religions are dangerous because it preaches falsities; falsities, which influence the way "followers" perceive others right to life, liberty, happiness, and justice. It also alters ones ability to reason and weigh evidence. Abiding by fallacious doctrine always seems to harm people. We should always seek the truth, not assume it.

One of the reasons I started doing the radio show is to bring voices of reason and logic to as many as I could. The Infidelguy radio show is just part of the package. The Infidel Guy Audio Show is for everyone. I hope we all continue to learn and realize that there is still much left to learn in this Universe. It is my intent to inform theists and non-theists alike that it's okay not to believe. What father wouldn't want you to use your mind critically? Only an evil dictator would demand such submission. Considering the history of all the violence, torture, death, sexism, and racism in this world, I'm surprised that anyone can truly believe in a loving anthropomorphic deity.

Unfortunately, most blind closed-minded fundamentalists don't know the differences in faith, reason, truth, reality, and belief. It's all the same to them. However, there are great differences in what we believe, what we want to believe, what we know, and what we want to know. This is one of the reasons I started the Infidelguy Radio Show so I could inform and educate as well as give others a chance to be heard.

Bio: Reginald Vaughn Finley has rocked the freethought community with his dedication to educating the world through his webcast at www.infidelguy.com. Better known as "The Infidel Guy," Mr. Finley is a 27-year-old native of Atlanta and was born into a home of agnostic theists. Now an explicit atheist himself, Finley is active in the freethought community and is known for his debating abilities. An atheist in the proverbial foxhole, Finley has been in a variety of overseas missions as a US Army infantryman and later became a federal law enforcement officer. He is an avid reader and writer and has published articles about his experiences as a psychic for The Psychic Network at the Secular Web and in various freethought magazines and newsletters around the country. The Infidel Guy is known internationally with his website receiving over 200,000 hits a year. He is the creator and Webmaster of "Black Atheists" (www.Blackatheists.com) a site dedicated to dispelling the myth that there are no Black atheists and establishing a method for Black atheists to contact each other.

Finley attended Georgia State University, City Colleges of Chicago, St. Leo College and has an in-home library, which consists of hundreds of books on philosophy, science, and theoretical astrophysics. He is on the Board of Directors for the Atlanta Freethought Society, a member of Georgia Humanists, American Atheists, The Planetary Society and The Council for Secular Humanism.

FRANCES PARKER

I was born in Baltimore, Maryland in 1968, and adopted two years later. My adoptive family was typical of many African-American families—extremely devout. I was raised in what was a very typical Pentecostal household, where Jesus came first. Now I am an atheist and my atheism tends to show up in my writing a great deal. My mother was a Pentecostal Fundamentalist and my father was a non-practicing Catholic.

Our home, in Prince George's County (Northern Maryland), was brimming over with religious plaques, pictures and tons of bibles. We (absent my father) went to church every Sunday, sometimes twice on Sunday and there was bible study and choir practice during the week. When I was a teenager, I was confronted head-on by the misogyny and patriarchy of the church. The preacher, a Black man born and raised in Jim Crow-era Georgia, was convinced that women would go to hell if they wore slacks, make-up, earrings, or cut their hair! Needless to say, this was a very chaotic time in my life. I eventually left that church (much to my mother's dismay).

I slowly began thinking about religion and God, and one thing that helped me a lot was watching a Bill Moyers special on PBS. The program highlighted an American anthropologist by the name of Joseph Campbell, and the series was called *The Power of Myth*. Watching that program got me on the road to examining religion in a historical, sociological and anthropological context. However, one sister, a devout Pentecostal, said she would pray for me.

Recently, a friend and I were discussing how there is a chasm between the intellectual progress that was made in Europe (the Enlightenment, Renaissance, etc.), and the knowledge of the average person in this country. We also noted that this chasm is wider still for African-Americans, who usually aren't exposed to Bertrand Russell, Kant, Nietzsche or Hume.

For me, it all started with a dissatisfaction with the whole organization, or should I say mismanagement, of the Black Pentecostal churches, the high levels of ignorance and miseducation of the Black clergy and the incredibly narrow-minded, patriarchal mind-sets. I consider myself a humanist, treating others with decency and trying to stop suffering if I see it. That's how I live.

Religion can be extremely disturbing. In the Pentecostal church, there is such a lack of understanding and appreciation for science, that they take the Genesis account literally! The idea that god made his 'son' suffer for the supposed sins of others and all the brutality in the Old Testament, makes it hard to believe anybody could take it seriously. The Bible is not sacred or divinely inspired. There are stories in it (Balaam's talking ass) that make Aesop's Fables look like poetry!

I will say that the Black Church and Christianity, to a certain extent have been helpful to African Americans. It was the only institution that Blacks could participate in and control for so long. In fact, the AME church was formed because of the racism in the White Methodists churches during slavery. However, there is also something in Christianity, particularly in Black churches, that tells its adherents to ignore the world around them, and rely on something supernatural to solve their problems.

Christianity, from its very inception, has been opposed to humanity's progress in science, education and the elevation of women. The Fundamentalist Pentecostals, in particular, are killing Christianity. Of course, I have no problem with that because it is long over due, but sometimes I can't believe that other Christians sit idly by and let these people rant and rave and generally make a fool of their religion.

Religion, in my opinion, plays only a minor role in high moral standards. I've known enough ministers to know that, but it still serves an important, sociological function. Many Blacks still feel that American society is hostile towards them, and the church lends them psychological support, but unfortunately, Black churches are not very progressive.

Bio: Frances is 33 years old and lives in Northern Prince George's County, Maryland. She was born in Baltimore and grew up in middle-class suburbia in Prince George's County. She is unmarried and an aspiring novelist. Her first novel, *Bad Faith* was published by iUniverse.com in April 2001. She works as an Information Technician with the Environmental Protection Agency in Washington, D.C. and in her spare time she reads philosophy and literature, and writes constantly.

NAIMA WASHINGTON

I was born into a Catholic family and from the beginning my mother had no reservations about beating me with a rope, an ironing cord, or a mop or broom handle. The mistakes I made as a child were no different from anyone else's my age, but I paid a heavy price for making them. My mother was a product of the church. She learned its lessons well and ended up a twisted, close-minded individual.

My stepfather was an alcoholic and a child molester, and like my real dad, he only had a fourth grade education. When I got tired of ducking and dodging his hands as well as his habit of exposing himself to me. I told my mother but she didn't believe me. By the time I was 14-years old, I had endured whippings, a loveless home, sexual molestation by two grown men, and an attempted rape (not by my step-father).

Keeping children in the dark is not an intelligent way to raise a child into a responsible adult, and failing to give children age-appropriate information about life is totally irresponsible! As a young adult, I attempted to retreat into religion, but the more I retreated, the lonelier I became. From time to time, I donated what little money I had to this and that evangelist, went to this and that meeting and still felt disconnected. I wasn't able to attend many meetings because of work and just not having the time. So, outside of the radio broadcasts and the printed materials I received in the mail, my indoctrination was not great, but I attempted to remain religious.

Ultimately, I sought refuge in marriage. Getting married was a very bad idea. The bad marriage, however, led to my beginning to fully understand one of life's many important lessons. No matter how bad things were, I was going to have to take responsibility for myself, stop making excuses, and think about what I needed to do to have the kind of life that I claimed I wanted. The day that I decided to stop begging, pleading, and praying for changes to take place in my life was also the day that I decided think and act like an adult.

After nearly two years of marriage, I finally packed my things and left the last violent household that I ever had to live in. I also became an active participant in my own life. I left the make-believe world and began to examine the real world of those who hold power and privilege. I also became a community activist and a tenant organizer in my apartment building. I soon realized that the suffering around me called for more positive and decisive actions—not prayers.

Growing up, the one thing I could never figure out was the question of poverty. Religions are known for begging in the name of some god on behalf of this or that group of poor people, but I couldn't understand why some countries are poor and others are rich and why some people are poor and others are rich. I struggled with this question for many years as I grew up around decent honest people who were intelligent and hardworking but had little to show for it. Why couldn't people like that have more money?

I started to search independently. I decided to get some books, read, think, explore, and get better ideas. If I came up with some wrong answers, so what? The world wasn't going to topple over because I got something wrong. But, I wasn't going to feel any better about my ability to think for myself if I continued to accept things because that's what I had been told.

It took a few years for me to get to the point where I was challenged to re-think the purpose of religion and belief in a god. I realize now that I had probably met atheists before but I was not open to their way of thinking. Plus, it was not until I had a one-on-one discussion about belief in god that I was able to understand that believing in a god was a choice. I was taught all of this stuff since I was a small child, and I was also taught to be fearful of the unknown.

The very idea of not being able or allowed to question something is a cruelty. Anything that cannot stand up to examination will fall and it ought to. Punishing, ostracizing, torturing, jailing, and killing those who question the existence of a god, religious authority, political parties, kings, presidents, governments, etc., will never legitimize any of these so-called authorities.

Once I resisted the crippling messages of the church that claimed that the church, god, men, and my parents or husband represented the ultimate authority figures in my life I was able to act in own best interests. I have no doubts that trying to live a life that is ethical, compassionate, loyal, positive, generous, and civilized is worth more than having membership in every single religion on the planet. The one thing that I've learned from atheism was that I must take full responsibility for my own actions.

Most people in my life who believe in a god are doing the things that they feel are necessary to live the kind of life that they want to have. I don't want them to become atheists and have no interest in trying to get them to live life on my terms but should they want to look beyond their current beliefs for answers, I would actively support their efforts if they wanted my help. On the other hand, I have no interest in living life on their terms either.

Generally, I don't enjoy talking about religion. For one thing, I find it deeply offensive for people to tell me that I need to join their religion, read their texts, and get right with their god, as though I wouldn't have ever thought about these things without their unsolicited advice. Just like religious people can't conceive of either changing their faith, or dropping it altogether, I can't conceive of turning to those practices which I view as degrading as well as unintelligent.

The fact that there's no heaven or hell does not give me permission to hurt others including those who spout what I consider to be absolute nonsense. But, many religions have no problem calling for the punishment of those who do not see things as they do. In their opinion, worshiping the "right" god may even give them the authority to take the life of so-called nonbelievers.

I've also come to realize that many people do not understand the term atheist, and over the past few years when asked what religion I practice, I say I'm a nonbeliever. This is unequivocal and for anyone who is in doubt it very plainly gives them my status: I am just the opposite of who they are.

Some people are offended when I say I am a non-believer. I never ask about their religious beliefs and when I say that I am a nonbeliever, I'm answering their question. Believers believe in many things: devils, omens, ghosts, palmistry, witches, aliens, talking snakes, angels, faith healing, astrology, evil spells, saints, fairies, hexes, transubstantiation, reincarnation and even satanic-possessions. I guess it never occurs to people that I could ever be offended when they claim to be a believer!

While I feel that it is necessary to try to be as honest as I can about my status, I admit to not pressing the point. I also very much dislike people assuming that because I don't challenge everything they say that I'm in agreement with them! Religious belief is deeply personal and I don't want to get into debates about my religious status any more than about my sex life or my finances. Nor do I want anyone to think that I feel that I have to defend my nonbelief status any more than they feel that they must defend their religious choice.

Sadly, when someone lives their life according to what is right, decent, and just, and has no interest in religion or a god, this is somehow seen as unacceptable. Of course, if they are criminals, they can always be prayed for! But what is most troubling for those in the religious community is someone who lives a decent life and who is also a nonbeliever because theists are so accustomed to people lying, claiming to be believers, and making excuses for not engaging in religious rituals. The truth of the matter is that the non-church-mosque-synagogue goers stopped going for the same reason I did. There was simply nothing going on in those buildings that interested them.

I have no idea as to how many people have changed religions, were brought up to believe one thing, and made a different choice later on in life. So did I. I chose not to believe. But, what do I believe? I believe that the human race has the potential for achieving happiness. We can achieve happiness by making positive and constructive use of our talents, skills, and resources.

One of the most intelligent institutions ever created is the secular government, and it is supposed to protect us from those who seek to do harm even if they claim to have religious reasons for doing so. But, I am very clear about one thing: as long as people are afraid to speak their minds, ask questions, disagree, express doubt or disbelief about anything under the sun, there is no freedom; and where there is no freedom, there are no "true believers!"

Bio: Naima is a community activist in Washington, DC, and work as an administrator. She is knowledgeable of various theological stances and remains current on the struggles of women.

Chapter 12

Other Black Atheists

"Good people will do good things, and bad people will do bad things. But for good people to do bad things—that that takes religion.

—*Steven Weinberg*

Since I wrote the first draft of this book, I have contacted and remain in contact with numerous Black atheists, agnostics and humanists. What follows are the original comments I received from the initial group I surveyed.

Glenn Ellison Jr.

I was born in Georgia in 1942 and was raised in a good Methodist Family. I also had a strong Baptist influence from my grandfather. When I left home in 1960 on my way to college, I was grounded in what we called "The Word." Even though I had a lot of religious training, I always had my doubts. I remember reading a book when I was young about the earth and it's evolution. That book put the real doubt in my head and I could never agree with 6,000-year-old earth "theory" again.

When I was in Viet Nam doing the late 60s, I had lots of time on my hands with nothing to do. To pass the time I decided to read the Bible in it's entirety to give me more insight into God. During my stay there I read it from Genesis to Revelation. The more I read the less I believed it. That was the first step toward nonbelief. I found the Bible to be full of stories and fairy tales designed to make people understand the beginnings of their world. It did not coincide with logical facts and when it is read as a book, it was not realistic nor convincing.

That is when my world began to fall apart. All the things I had held dear over the years didn't fit into the new world I had discovered. It is very hard to just disregard what you learned while drinking mother's milk. I went to church, I prayed, I joined youth groups at church, and I volunteered to teach Sunday school but nothing helped. I had lost my faith in God and the Bible and I could not make myself believe again.

After I figured out that I couldn't make myself believe something my mind could not accept, I had to convince myself that I was the force behind my life and I had to be the one that is responsible for me and my family, not an invisible God. When I accepted that fact, I felt better than I had in many years. I was truly a free man. Life finally made sense to me and my world finally began to fit together. That was more than 30 years ago and I have never looked back.

For those who still believe more power to them. If it makes their world fit together, so be it. For me, I don't need that any more. There is no God, I'm in control of my life and I feel great.

CHRIS FELTON

People speak of Black atheists as if the two terms are supposed to be inherently oxymoronic. Though I am not the proverbial lamb who advertises his beliefs amongst the wolves, I am extremely proud of my decision to choose reason, rationale, and freethought over mysticism and superstition. To me, religion has only a minor role in the morality of society. It plays a role only to the extent that it reflects the moral and ethical standards as already established by benevolent and rational human beings without the inclusion of religion. In other words, the only genuine "standards" that religion offers to society are the ridiculous reasons behind its morals and ethics: fear of hell and greed of Heaven and "God's" favor. Basically, I hold the objectivists view: cause no physical harm or usurpation to another person or that person's property.

I "officially" realized my atheism, and denounced mysticism, on November 1, 1998 and at this point, I think my family and friends are pretty much ignoring my nonreligious stance. I grew up in a religious home, and have studied several religions since then, but the great turning point for me came when I was a student preacher in the Memphis School of Preaching during the summer of 1998. Because of the fundamentalist teachings of the school and the subtle racism, I quickly began to see the Bible, religion, and "God" as mere tools, crutches and feeble expressions of man.

Two of my greatest concerns with religion is that those involved with organized religion will unify for what I consider to be the two most destructive acts against society: merging church and state and pronouncing killings as justified or excused in the name of their religious beliefs. If religion and politics continue to slide toward each other, we are heading for serious trouble. Ruth Hermence Green said, "There was a time when religion ruled the world. It is known as the Dark Ages," which is where we'll be if it happens again. Personally, I believe that organized religion has caused more death and social destruction to human beings than any other malady!

Still, I must say that because of the heinous and atrocious conditions Blacks encountered during slavery, religion played a major role within their lives. This facet of a slave's life was taught and handed down to the descendants of the slaves as an integral and necessary part of life. So, in that way Christianity has "helped" the African-American community because it served as a sedative to soothe the despair, anguish and cruel physical and mental torment of the slaves, but it also acted as a stimulant giving many slaves just enough hope to continue their daily tasks and chores without breaking down or committing suicide (which occurred among many slaves).

Even though the church's involvement with community affairs still helps, today, that same sedative/stimulant has many African-Americans hallucinating because the drug is no longer needed. It is now weakening the mind of the believer because it causes them to evade reality and rational thinking and to continue to limp along with the crutch of mysticism. Yet, because the church continues to evolve as the most powerful and "entertaining" social organization within the lives of many Blacks it manages to exist.

It is my opinion, that the "Black Community" ridicules and shuns agnosticism and, especially, atheism. I am concerned that many Blacks will continue to be blind and crippled to reason, thus form irrational decisions pertaining to social and intimate relationships; the stronger or more fundamental the belief, the more irrationality within a person's life. The crux of this problem? A lack of concern or care for this "earthly" life and a strong yearning for and movement towards a life in "heaven."

It is almost impossible to avoid God in some shape or form in this country. With so much religion in the air, it is difficult to keep children focused. They are young and don't understand what it all means, but they pick up things easily, without realizing what affect it could have on their lives later. My children realize that the concept of "God" is like a more potent version of the concept of Santa Claus. There are a few books they have which are very good for teaching them the importance of scientific thinking and reasoning, but the one I favor is entitled, *Just Pretend—A Freethought Book for Children*, by Dan Barker.

As for me, I tend to govern myself by taking advantage of anything that contributes to my happiness. However, I understand that, in general, the "long-term" approach is the most beneficial and rational way to achieve that happiness. I understand that happiness is not necessarily an 'unbroken chain', nor is it permanent (nothing is), but it is more attainable and enduring when the proper actions have been taken to best benefit the physical and mental condition of the human being. Growth and development always stand upon the prerequisites of consistency, patience, perseverance, and varying levels of discomfort.

EDDIE DANIEL GLOVER

I am an atheist and believe that religion is a form of class control. Religion is a device used by the ruling classes to keep the masses under control. I have had a problem with organized religion for over 40 years and haven't attended church during this time.

I don't know for sure what I am, although I must certainly say that I am not a theist in any form, which would make me an atheist, but I'm still open to possibilities as always. I just don't think there are many possibilities that I haven't already explored and I don't think I'll see any in my life time. I call myself a humanist, but that's just semantics. Basically, I know I have no belief that the God of Christianity exists and that's the one I know the most about. Of course, the others haven't seemed to come about very often either. So, I guess they are figments of somebody's imagination.

Religion as a changer of human actions is a lame excuse. Look at the amount of Black on Black crime being committed today by people who call themselves Christians. We all know what's right and wrong and don't need religion to tell us this. Still, even with the purported good that is does, it's the blind faith and lack of free thought in all religion that I find disturbing. I know "God" didn't write the Bible, man did and man makes mistakes and embellishes. Even if it was the "word of God" at one time, the numerous translations, writes and rewrites over the centuries have lost the original meaning—especially the King James Version (note, that's "version" and not "translation").

Overall, I think religion limits initiative and self-determination. Too many Black people fail and instead of trying again or trying harder, they have the excuse that "it's God's will" and divest themselves of all responsibility in their lives.

This movement by Right Wing groups to get more religion into society disturbs me. Church and State are supposed to be separate. The Constitution promises freedom of religion and freedom from religion and that freedom is gone when Jews, atheists, Hindus or Rastafarians, etc. are forced to engage in Christian rituals. America was founded on religious freedom and to take that freedom away takes away a major part of America.

I know that most Blacks have a very low view of atheists. Whenever I mention my beliefs, I'm called a Satanist (which is silly, because if I don't belief in God, I obviously don't believe in Satan either) or I'm "crazy" or "confused" and don't know the "Truth." In the Black community tolerance for people who believe something different—is zero.

Bio: He is 57, divorced with three children, work as a management consultant, live in the Philadelphia Pa. Area, undergraduate in accounting, MBA Finance. He grew up in Memphis, Tennessee and has lived in the Philadelphia suburbs for the last 25 years.

SID DAVIS

Why Don't I Believe in God? I could reiterate any of the points Bertrand Russell made in his book *Why I Am Not A Christian*, but by the time I read that very entertaining collection I was already an atheist. I could discuss the hypocrisy of my church, describe my ten years there as a Sunday-school student, and later as a young man who had returned from a year of college only to be asked by the elders to weave tales of big city wickedness, but you've probably heard versions of that story from others.

Instead, I'd like to explain my beliefs by drawing a parallel. There is an interesting statistical principal called "Gambler's Ruin." Here's how it works: in gaming there's a house and a gambler. Let's say you're the gambler and you're betting on coin flips. Any time you flip a coin the odds are fifty-fifty on which side it will land. Thus, you should do no worse than break even if you always bet on one side. However, the same coin, bound by the same odds, might land twenty times in a row on heads. The house, with unlimited funds, has enough money to cover this quirk of odds, but you, the gambler, do not. So whether it takes five losses in a row, or ten, or fifty, the gambler will always bust out, and the house will always win.

God has the odds stacked in his favor as well. If you wake up in the morning and stub your toe, you'll probably look at it and say, "Thank God it isn't broken." If you break the toe you'll say, "Thank God I didn't fall and break my leg." If you get in the car and crash into a tree you'll say, "Thank God I wasn't going faster." If you're going fast enough to break a collarbone you'll say, "Thank God, at least I didn't break my neck." Lose an arm and you'll say, "Thank God, at least I'm still alive." And if you are killed, someone in your family will say, "At least he didn't suffer." Thus God gets credit for being merciful no matter what tragedy befalls us—no matter whether children starve, or nuns are raped, or great leaders are assassinated. I reject this reasoning as nonsensical. If God exists, he deserves the blame for these things.

Despite the overwhelming tonnage of misery in this world God always gets credit for being merciful because humans are trained to expect nothing more from life than to take the next breath. Where did this belief come from? Who trained us this way? These are rhetorical questions, of course, because organized religion's hand in this belief couldn't be more obvious. The next question isn't rhetorical. What could it possibly profit our world's religions to teach us we can expect nothing from life?

The answer to that question might explain why ministers are always wealthy, why the Vatican is the largest corporate landowner in the world, why business and religion are bedfellows worldwide. I reject the idea that I must expect nothing from life while those whose job it is to provide spiritual guidance accumulate wealth.

Religion is used as an opiate to quell the displeasure of those who possess nothing. This opiate is sold to poor folk so that the wealthy can pillage the world without anyone raising a fuss. It's the corporations of the world (both legitimate and illegitimate) riding piggyback on the Gambler's Ruin concept who propagate this notion. If we expect no more from life than to be allowed to take the next breath, what do we care if our neighborhoods are razed or gentrified, filled with crooked police or inundated with drugs, as long as we can take refuge in the arms of our god?

In order to debate Biblical content one must pretend that what is written in there isn't a total fairytale. So I'll do that to make a few points, but please understand that I don't for one second believe any of it is true. As I said before, religion is merely an ingenious scheme to make money. And religious people are not bothered by this, even though the teachings of Christ are at odds with those of what I like to think of as the Cult of Profit. The only recorded instance of Jesus losing his temper occurred when he attacked the moneychangers for doing business in the temple. This couldn't be a more direct example of his belief that to make profit upon the powerless is the most heinous of sins. Think of it—Jesus forgave harlots, thieves, lowlifes of every stripe, but he could not stomach the moneychangers. He knew his greatest enemy was greed.

Jesus' teachings have been historically ignored by Christianity, as was abundantly proven when King James retranslated the Bible in 1611 and changed words such as "debt" to "trespass" in the Lord's Prayer. There are those who believe he did this to appease business interests of the day, who were looking for a mandate from Religion to exploit the emerging non-serf classes. Obviously, forgiveness of debt, as in the original Lord's Prayer, is a tenet which precludes profiting from other people's hard work. This is something, by the way, which Christ specifically forbade in his oft-quoted "Seven Woes" speech in which he told the Pharisees that they were sinners who would "bind others to lift heavy burdens but would not themselves lift one finger to move them." (I'm paraphrasing here)

In our day, the Cult of Profit has grown so huge that they have their own commandments. One of the most familiar of these is: "It's business, not personal." This simple phrase, which is part of the popular lexicon now, excuses any act short of murder to achieve one's ends. Thus, we have supposed Christians in the business cult committing every Biblical sin even while excusing themselves for these acts because they have no personal animus toward those they ruin and rape. I just love this twisted, funhouse-mirror reasoning. Perhaps it explains why we executed Nazis for their war crimes yet allowed the owners of Mercedes, BMW, and Volkswagen to go unpunished, though they profited more from genocide than any concentration camp commandant.

I reject the possibility that any God worth his/her salt would allow this to go on. This is more than just one instance historical suffering we're talking about; our world tolerates genocide even today (think of the six million that will die in Africa this year while AIDS drugs are withheld because poor tribespeople have no money to offer greedy pharmaceutical companies). Is there a way to change this amoral landscape? In the most general sense, knowledge and education can help us at least be less exploitable. But there's a problem—our churches are anti-education. Jesus, Muhammad and Buddha loved simple folk, so we can guess that God must also. Why would God create a world of simple folk and then allow this quality which he loves so much to be the catalyst for his children's enslavement?

Here in America we laugh at simple folk, blame them for their lot in life, ignore their misfortune, and arrest them so we don't have to look at them. When the Pope came to Denver for World Youth Day about eight years ago the first thing the city did was roust the homeless along the pontiff's route so he would not have to see them. Would God allow this to occur under the nose of his presumed servant? I reject this possibility. While we're on the subject, would God allow any servant—even the pope—to claim anything remotely resembling equal standing with him? In the Old Testament, men were blasted out of existence for such effrontery. Nimrod brought disaster to all of humanity for shooting an arrow at the sun. Where is this hands-on God now that we have video cameras to document his acts?

Some Bible scholars say that Jesus taught us to rely less on miracles than on ourselves. This is a desperate argument that holds no water. Jesus never taught humanity not to expect divine intervention. His presumed resurrection is a complete refutation of that belief, because if life is a test of faith he wished us to pass without leaning on the crutch of miracles, not coming back from the dead would have been a good way to start.

The religious like to fall back on a particular argument which has gained enough primacy that it has even been floated in a certain mainstream movie I won't bother to publicize by naming. They say they know God exists even though there is no proof. They then ask you if your father or mother loves you. When you say yes they ask you to prove it. That might baffle a few high-schoolers, but not anyone with a brain. The proof that human love exists lies in the simple fact that a human tells another human how they feel. Listen for God to declare his love and you'll hear a silence so ancient and so encompassing that it is, for most, too horrible to contemplate.

And therein lies the reason for belief in God, in religion, in the whole absurd costume party. The permanent end of what we are, of our memories and our mortal spirit, is too horrible for most people to deal with. But the only way to avoid death is never to have lived at all. And for me that makes the choice simple. I would rather have lived than not. Even if it means dying a Godless death that lasts forever, I would rather have walked this earth than not. I have lived an uncommon life so far, even by the standards of those who seek the uncommon. Despite that fact, all of my uniqueness will wink out of existence one day. Yet, nothing can change the simple fact that I've seen more and accomplished more than I ever would have thought possible when this whole thing began.

When the time comes for me to go I'll look back on a life that is its own monument. I know this through a faith of my own—atheism.

Bio: Sid is a coordinator at an international cable television station based in the Los Angeles area. A former magazine editor, he has written two novels, both with subtly religious themes, and is at work on a third. He is an amateur photographer and artist who has had his work published in various small magazines. He is a musician whose band toured for years and released two CDs. He is single, and when he isn't at the television station or in front of his novel, he reads, plays music, takes photographs and travels.

CHARLES COOKE

Why do some Blacks embrace religion? Why don't some Blacks embrace religion? I would suspect that there are common and distinct answers to both of these questions, which affirm each other, but I suspect that it has something to do with early training.

I "label" or define myself as "agnostic" because I neither believe nor disbelieve. I grew up Episcopalian until about the age of six. Afterwards, going to church subsided, as it was no longer "mandatory," meaning my parents did not drag me there. I enjoyed church as a kid, not for the religious ceremonies but for the children's activities—doughnuts, cookies and go-carts. It was probably an innocent indoctrination of the mind that starts the same way as the little white kids whose parents are KKK and drag them along to those types of religious activities.

As an adult, growing up in a rough and impoverished neighborhood during the 60's and 70's, religion served no purpose in my life. Religion like all things must serve some purpose or meet some human need of which other than as entertainment I am doubtful. I had an older sister who became a Jehovah's Witness. She died of cancer. I have another older sister who is a Jehovah's Witness. My Mom age 73 still goes to church as does another older sister.

As for me, I am highly critical of organized religion—highly critical! I associate religion (whether one calls themselves Christian, Baptist, Catholic, or other) as being the "opium of the masses", not in the Marxist sense, but in the brain-dead sense. Speaking to religious folks is like speaking to a rhetorical politician about serious issues in need of solutions for which only rhetorical responses are given—stupidity!

Perhaps with the exception of how religion was used in the Civil Rights/Black Power Movements (pro/con), I cannot think of anything "good" about religion whatsoever. I associate religion with most things "stupid"! To me religion is an organized body of mythical/superstitious knowledge that is used by priests, ministers, organizations and individuals to "control" how folks think, what they think, and therefore their behavior.

All bodies of knowledge do the same, whether religion, science, or other. But I find religion to be the most pernicious of all. I see it as a circular, rhetorical, body of psuedoknowledge without any empirical base except those that tend to be invented. And because religions associate themselves with a supernatural being, it is difficult to examine it, deconstruct it, expose it for what it tends to be most times in practice—human beings "interpreting" scriptures and their own beliefs to others in order to advance their own secular self-interests.

I see religion preying upon the poor, women, minorities, children, and homosexuals either to control them or to banish them. This is why I never have embraced religion, don't attend church, and probably will never embrace any particular religion. To me religion is one of the most regressive mind-control (and historical mind-fuck) acts in town and remains such.

Does this mean that no such thing as a God or Gods exists? Of course not! It means that when you have a race of beings interpreting and trying speak for something they claim to be so magnificent, omnipotent, then you will have those interpretations that express themselves in some pretty savage, hateful, oppressive, and stupid ways.

I think without the sciences, rational thought, and faith in our human capacity to learn, grow and love, religion would have all ready plunged us into—extinction. Because we are primitive, savage, ignorant, materialistic, and egoistical, we will continue to need all bodies of knowledge (including religions) as checks and balances and hopefully as catalysts of learning, growth and love!

So, as an African American, I believe there could be a "divine intelligence" (call it God if you want—singular or plural). I've been "socialized and indoctrinated" to believe such! Also as an adult, I would like to think there are higher levels of existence. However, I also temper those religious beliefs with secular logic, reasoning and knowledge—checks and balances.

I don't feel the need to pray to some supernatural being. I don't feel the need to engage in Sunday or daily rituals to show such a being I value or am subordinate to him or her. Notice I said "need" —back to that functionality/social-programming thing I mentioned.

I feel like if such a Being or beings exist then he or she will know "what time it is and why we do what we do or don't do, and telling me I'm going to burn in hell or not get a first class ticket to Heaven—hardly proves persuasive. To the contrary, it makes me that much more a non-believer. A supernatural being would not have to coerce or frighten anyone into enlightenment! This is my heretic story in a nutshell as to why I'm an agnostic—meaning a tad bit hopeful and a huge bit secular!

J. R. Ector

I never did buy into the whole God, religion thing as a child. I attended St. Joseph's Catholic School from 1st to 6th grade and I started to question what I was being taught around the age of 10. I couldn't understand why there was no mention of the dinosaurs we studied about in the Bible. I never did get a good answer for that and I've been a skeptic ever since. I am curious by nature and strive to know how things work and why things are as they are today.

I tolerated Catholic school for the rest of that year and told my parents I wanted to go to public school. Since we were about to move down South I was told to wait for that and half way through 6th grade, we moved and I gained my freedom from Catholicism. Unfortunately, my Mother wanted to fit in the South and decided that we would "all" attend Southern Baptist services.

Needless to say, I hated going to church but I had no choice in the matter. My mother stopped the arm-twisting at age 16 and that is the last time I have attended a church service outside of weddings and funerals. I didn't put a whole lot of thought into religion again until I went to college and had to choose some elective courses. This lead me to a philosophy course titled "Philosophy of World Religions". This course covered all world religions from a philosophical standpoint. It showed me that basically religions and Gods were invented by man out of ignorance of the natural world. Animist thought there was a wind God because the wind blows etc.

From that point forward, I looked at everything I was taught in those daily religion classes in my early Catholic school days with a skeptical eye. I never much liked the rituals and other trappings of religion anyhow. Now, they were trying to tell me basically not to think too hard, or question the Bible. Unacceptable!

Yes, it is a lonely feeling at times being a minority among minorities but—that is the price of superstition-free existence. People are either shocked or appalled when they find out I'm an atheist; even the most wicked of the "faithful". Their hypocrisy is the most galling of all their foibles. Some of them actually believe what they're saying they just don't believe it applies to them! Others are just opportunists fleecing their flock. The ultimate irony is that they call themselves sheep. The division amongst the same sect is another glaring contradiction. Why are there different kinds of Baptists? Southern Baptists, Cornerstone Baptists, 2nd Street Baptists, Pentecostal Baptists, Four Square Baptists, etc.

Why are there Black churches and white churches of the same denomination? If we are all "Gods children", why can't they pray in the same building with people who don't look like them? Still, the scariest ones are the fundamentalists who believe that God is on their side hence whatever they do is all right. This includes murder, rape, torture and genocide. The term "Holy war" turns my stomach. Thou shalt not kill, except if you're a (insert religion). A very scary concept of a Manifest Destiny. My research showed me that ancient people out of ignorance dreamed up Gods because they didn't understand the natural world they lived in.

They have certainly refined their stories over the centuries but still the fact is that you don't need faith. You know it or you don't. Just because you don't know the answer or can't explain something, does not mean that there are Gods, goblins, devils or fairies. The fact that religions say it is blasphemy to question God's word is very telling. Don't question what we're telling you, just believe. They obviously know that if you think too much all of the holes and contradictions in their dogma will be exposed.

It is extremely hard as a single, Black, male atheist to find Black women who don't think that superstition is a virtue. So, dating is to say the least challenging.

I'm not going to pretend that I believe all the nonsense my family believes, it's just not worth it to me and the ones who are "Fundies" know better than to foist their God upon me, lest I give them a Bible lesson. The fact that so many atheists are more familiar with the Christian Bible is also very telling. The Bible has numerous inconsistencies and also, I've done research on how the Bible was canonized. It was not an exactly holy procedure.

The guilt and shame of religious dogma is designed to keep you dependent on the church to save your soul. This can go to extremes when religious leaders convince followers that God wants them to kill infidels and that they will be rewarded in heaven for their heinous acts. All of these aspects of religion are the things that caused me to at first doubt the messengers and to finally find evidence that they are just as likely (or more likely) to commit crimes and take advantage of the weak minded as anyone else. These curiosities lead me to read about all aspects of life including history, philosophy, and virtually all of the sciences.

Bio: J.R. lives in Springfield, VA and is unmarried. He is a software engineer and a member of American Atheist. J.R. is an avid skier and belongs to Black Ski Inc. based in DC. Of course, most of them don't know he's an atheist. He says, "I only talk about it when they ask."

Kareem Lane

I don't believe in God anymore than I believe in ghosts, demons, angels, fairies, goblins, trolls, tooth fairies, Santa Claus, rabbits that lay eggs, Great Pumpkins, flying purple people eaters, vampires, werewolves, gargoyles or a leprechaun that lives in my cereal, but I understand how we have become indoctrinated to follow others lead.

In most circles of the Black community, people are raised to have some kind of "respect" or awareness of a God. I believe part of the reason so many Blacks are religious, or claim to be, is a fading since of unity. It wasn't that long ago that the only people standing up for African-American rights were highly publicized religious leaders. Martin Luther King Jr., the Rev. David Ralph Abernathy, Malcolm X, Rev. Al Sharpton, Rev. Jesse Jackson etc., all of who came from the church.

And where did these leaders congregate? Where did/do they speak? If you want to find large groups of Blacks, where do you go (other than prison, where the opinions don't count anyway or the clubs where they usually don't care)? You go to church! Overall, general community unity is dying out and with it, this strong hold that religion has on our community.

As we progress into the future, more and more Blacks will start their own businesses, more will go to college, more will go to the military, more will have access to the internet and more will be better off. There will be more exposure to other religions, other races and other cultures and as we gain more and more exposure to the world, we become less and less alike.

We become more of a blended, general populous than of a simple, minority one. This is why I believe religion as a force is, in some ways, making its way out of the Black community. However, despite our progress, we are, just as any other race, still intimidated by the burdens, stresses and ills of life and society and it still makes it just a little difficult to admit to a reporter or even to themselves that THERE IS NO GOD.

Bio: Kareem manages a convenience store in Atlanta. He spent four years in the marines. He is 26 years old and unmarried. He enjoys kickboxing, viewing movies and eating out.

OMARI CHRISTIAN

I used to believe there was a God and, like my parents, it was sexless. I can basically say that life made me a nonbeliever. I must first be thankful that I was not raised religious, or I would have taken much longer to arrive at the conclusion I have arrived at now.

My brothers are both just nonreligious, but my mom is Science of the Mind and my dad goes to Agape and basically they believe that there is a God, but it has no gender and that it resides within each of us. We're supposedly all connected spiritually. Although I only humor my mom on special days, like Mother's Day or maybe Easter, my dad tries to get me to go to his church every Sunday I spend at his house but I usually stay at home.

Overall, my philosophy is to be nice to people. Ever since 1st or 2nd grade, I remember that "niceness" was one of my more important virtues. I have also always used the proverb, "Do unto others as you want them to do unto you." Yes, Jesus did say this, but so did Confucius and a few other people before Jesus.

What about the Bible causes me concern? The whole book! Not many people realize that the entire book was written, edited and put together by people. I consider Mark Twain's "The Adventures of Huckleberry Finn" more sacred because at least it's a good read.

The very first thing that troubled me about the Bible—I remember my mom telling me it troubled her, too, when she was explaining why she wasn't Christian is the Adam and Eve thing. The first people were African, as fossils indicate. They wouldn't have names like Adam and Eve or even their Hebrew equivalent. And where are the dinosaurs? What about the extinct animals and missing links? Australopithecines are nowhere to be found in the Bible.

Why was God so prevalent thousands of years ago? The people that talk to God today are just considered crazy, even by the religious. Religion breeds superstition and ignorance. It's used to justify tragedies. It holds back science. It breeds shame, guilt and intolerance.

Religion helps some people to think that there's someone watching over them. It also helps to enjoy life when you're conceited enough to think this was all for us. I don't need those assurances. You're born. You live. You die. There is no afterlife. Mark Twain was asked if he feared death. He responded with something like "I was dead thousands of years before I was born and I didn't suffer the slightest inconvenience from it."

Bio: Omari is a native of Los Angeles and is currently attending UC Berkeley where he majors in computer science. He also enjoys acting and is active on campus with various theatre groups.

EUGENE GLOBE

It is not that I began to disbelieve, it is that I never believed and wanted to know what makes someone want to believe. Reason and logic are primary. Feelings do not dictate my actions, because as I see it religion does not play a role in morality or ethics. I will judge people based on their actions, not their words because you do not need religion to live a high moral or ethical life.

I cannot see how Christianity has helped in all of this. It has done massive harm in the way of Black people waiting for death thinking that there is a better life waiting for them somewhere "out there." Death is the end of life, so for someone to tell me that there is an after life means that they themselves have died and came back to tell me about their experience first hand. Since I don't know of any one who has done this wondrous feat, I cannot spend my time thinking about it.

Socially being an atheist makes it very hard to date, because when someone discovers you are an atheist their attitude changes toward you and you suddenly find yourself in the "friend zone" if they continue talking to you at all. However, It depends on the geographical location, if you are in the south people have less tolerance for nonbelievers. If you live in the north, there is more, because there are more nonbelievers in the north.

I know that for many of us whether or not to attend church is not an option. Children go to church with their parents because they don't have a choice and I'm sure all parents mean well. My parents did the same, but I believe introducing a child to the supernatural at such an early age may not be a good strategy. The young mind cannot distinguish between fantasy and reality. So to introduce it to religion and present its stories as facts is wrong. Also, the children should be given the choice if they wish to be involved in religion. It should not be forced upon them. When they are old enough they will ask questions and the parents should be there with the proper answers.

Bio: Eugene runs his own business in Houston, TX.

WAYNE EVANS

My story of atheism is not eloquent or dramatic but it is practical. My thoughts on atheism are similar to the reasons cited by Clarence Darrow in *Why I Am An Agnostic*. It was written almost three generations ago, but for those of us who view the world more scientifically than literally, some of his ideas still hold true.

How long have I known I was an atheist? Probably all my life, but come to really have the cognition at age 12, and verbalize it by age 14 or 15. It is amazing, growing up in a Southern Baptist home, my mother was quite tolerant. Actually, surprising. To be honest, I am quite surprised how many of my friends and colleagues both Black and white are supportive even though they disagree. I do have people who say they will pray for me. But they do not say this in a malicious, judgmental way, but in a respective manner.

Bio: He is a divorced father of two, who is currently engaged to a woman—a Black woman who is also atheist.

JOHN ROGERS

Why do Christians think that some event could make a person an atheist? The only thing that happened to me was that I opened my eyes and looked around. The creatures on this planet are far too similar. If anyone believes man and ape have nothing in common—they are blind. With recent DNA discoveries scientific proof now exists that shows we are 98 percent the same creature. The only difference between man and other animals is the size of the brain and our ability to use it better.

Other animals have different parts superior to man, such as a dog's hearing, an elephant's trunk, a gorilla's ability to live with his own kind, etc. We are not special. There's nothing waiting for us when we die. If there is it's also waiting for every other creature on earth. We have the ability to use our brain better, but we are also the most heartless killers on earth, with a Bible which forgives us for our actions. Man had better pray there's no God, for if there is a Heaven it will be a very desolate place.

Bio: John is an accountant and lives in the Midwest, Chicago area.

Chapter 13

▼

Atheist Essays, Letters and Conversations

"They were allowed to stay there on one condition, and that is that they didn't eat of the tree of knowledge. That has been the condition of the Christian church from then until now. They haven't eaten as yet, as a rule they do not."

—*Clarence Darrow*

Are Black People Too Religious? by Patrick Inniss

African Americans are too religious. For that matter, of course, any religious person is too religious. But even for the tastes of mainstream, religious America, Black people are too religious. The religiosity of the Black population has often been praised and admired by religious leaders, and religious institutions have formed the anchors for many Black communities, and incubated generations of Black leaders. At the same time, however, this tendency toward the spiritual has constituted a major element in the negative image of Blacks, and now stands to hamper the development of African America in almost every area.

One reason for this is that Black religious traditions and institutions are held in less high regard than their white counterparts. That is hardly any surprise. Members of any religious group generally tend to discount the validity of other religions—it's usually part of the doctrine. In the case of Black people in America, however, the religious experience is seemingly judged by whites to be so "over the top" that it violates the solemnity and inscrutability that in the European tradition separates true religion from false beliefs. In the European tradition, people in true communion with God are transcendentally peaceful, whereas people who are possessed of the devil are energetic and lively. Mainstream African American religious tradition, in its often raucous celebration of religious zeal, violates European sensibilities.

Black religious devotion has not been held as being sacred in the same sense that European belief is. Such is obvious in the media where earlier this century the humorous portrayal of African American religious ceremonies was almost a comedy cliché. How often in that era was fun poked at white services? Black religion has been often viewed as less than its white counterpart and the African American as not devout so much as ignorant and superstitious. But what does it matter what whites think of Black religion?

All aspects of African American culture (if one can, for sake of argument, define such a thing) have, at one time or another, been vilified. While white criticism of Black religious belief is certainly motivated largely by racism, and ignores the fact that Black religious practice is more like European practice than unlike it, nevertheless there could be some validity to these indictments of Black faith. Could there be a large element of superstition?

Who is to define religion as opposed to superstition? There is no clear line. This obvious truth is reflected in the fact that, although rarely stated in such a manner, most believers regard superstition as other people's religion. Black people have often been viewed as practicing some "primitive" form of Christianity heavily tinged with "superstition." At Black churches, religious services are commonly conducted with an extra helping of moaning, chants, and, in certain sects, writhing about on the floor. Not that white churchgoers themselves do not occasionally display such spirit-filled antics, but in the collective mind of the American public Black people seem to be the champions of being overcome by their religion.

In the battle of reason versus ignorance the perception is that among Blacks, reason often comes out the loser. Such a conclusion, of course, ignores the abundant mumbo-jumbo factor of European religious practice, but trying to determine whose religion is more reasonable would be like arguing over the relative merits of Batman and Spiderman. It seems clear that much of society has formed an opinion of Black religions as being in some way inferior, while at the same time perceiving Blacks as being more devoted to their religion and spirituality.

This enhanced sense of spirituality, however, extends well beyond the domain of mainstream white religious belief in both directions. On the one hand Blacks are viewed in the classic Stepin Fetchit mold, being so dim-witted that they are befuddled to the point of terror at the mere suggestion of the supernatural, and even the mention of a ghost is enough to send the largest Black man diving under the nearest bed. At the other extreme Blacks are depicted as masters of the occult, with unearthly abilities to bring supernatural forces under their control. Black people are imagined to have a special ability to commune with the spirits and invoke occult forces. Voodoo is viewed as not much more than a Black version of the popular conception of witchcraft, that conception itself being a gross distortion of reality. The Salem witch-hunt began with the suspicion that a Black woman was calling upon malevolent spirits, and the media still present the image of the extra-sensory Black person, as in the movie Ghost.

The perceptions of Black people as stupid and uneducated is inextricably linked to their image as excessively religious. It is certainly true that less educated people are frequently more religious, and to the extent that educational opportunities for the African American community have been less than the population in general, it is hardly surprising the Blacks should be, on average, more religious. But other factors are at work, as well.

The story of how the church came to assume such a prominent position in the Black community is well known. Religious leadership came to the fore primarily by default. Certain arguments may be made about the role of religious leaders in traditional African societies, but virtually all other means of organization and community action were foreclosed for many years. Black political action was effectively stifled, especially in the South, until just a few decades ago. Black economic development and the formation of a viable presence within the business community faced similar restrictions. Black professionals were often few in number and shut out from the networks that provided their white counterparts with political clout.

The Black church was present in the community often as the sole focus for meeting and organization. The image of Black people gathered together in churches remains, to this day, a relatively benign tableau in the American psyche, combining elements of safe, traditional values and non-threatening social impotence. High rates of church attendance in Black communities is the legacy of this dominance of religious institutions. The ascendancy of the church is a pathological aberration, the result of the same forces that have brought about epidemic unemployment and drug usage. As an adaptation to the blatant racism of previous years, it has obviously outlived its socio-economic function. Any defense of the value of the Black churches is directly impugned by the crime and suffering outside their doors every day.

As a manifestation of the oppression of Black people in America, reliance on religion and similar patterns of irrational thinking can be addressed in much the same manner as the problems of employment and drug abuse. Emphasis has to be placed upon the provision of education and economic opportunities. But this should be a priority for all persons regardless of ethnicity. The burden of religious hucksterism can only be removed from poor people's backs through the removal of the impediments that lead them to seek these miracle cures. Lenin pretty much had it right with that remark about religion being "the opium of the people." You can't stay on that kind of medicine forever.

Patrick Inniss is a member of the African American Humanist Board of Directors and former President of the Northwest Humanist Association in Seattle.

WE ARE CONDEMNED BY FRANCES PARKER

During a recent conversation with a friend, I learned of the abrupt cancellation of her wedding plans. You see, the Lord had informed her that her intended was the wrong mate for her. With heartfelt gravity she had exclaimed, "I asked the Lord to fix that situation for me, and he did!" While my first reaction was annoyance, I had to concede that my friend's attitude was a combination of both religious and cultural factors. We as African-Americans have been socialized to equate moral behavior with supernatural beliefs. While this erroneous idea is believed by many theists, within the African-American community it is an idea that is embraced with unquestioning enthusiasm.

Christianity is the foundation which our forbears built their new-found freedom upon. With slavery abolished, also gone was their dependence on their slave-masters. No longer did they have anyone deciding every aspect of their lives. But in a hostile world torn apart by war and economic collapse, they needed something constant and unchanging, and they were told that the God of Christianity 'changeth not'. But the 'word of God' seemed to echo the very things that their slave-masters had told them. They were further assured by the clergy that if they remained meek, humble, and docile in the face of racial hostility, that they would gain entry to a better world where there was no suffering or heartache. The promise of heaven was too tempting to pass up, particularly after hundreds of years of slavery. So, instead of the whip to keep them obedient, they had the Bible. The shackles of slavery was replaced with the shackles of religion.

Now, over a hundred years after the abolition of slavery, African-Americans still continue to relinquish their will and their lives to something or someone else. Countless numbers of us now leave our entire life in the hands of an intangible, mysterious, invisible deity. From pulpits, we are still admonished to 'wait patiently on the Lord', 'let Jesus work it out' and 'turn it over to the Lord'. While these seemingly virtuous sentiments are echoed in the Bible, it is interesting to note that these very sentiments are contrary to the concept of free will! Yet, many within the African-American community continue to remain psychologically paralyzed by the Christian scriptures. But not to worry, since we are assured that 'We can do nothing without God'.

This entire mind-set which is so part and parcel of the African-American experience, seems nothing more than cowardice dressed up in noble words. It is a mind-set that, like slavery and Jim Crow, has denied many of their self-reliance, courage, and even their free will. There is something disturbing about one who is unwilling to take charge of their own life and make choices for themselves. But since the Bible is replete with Scriptures that command the complete surrender of one's life, a cowardly existence is made noble by religion.

The famous French philosopher, Jean Paul Sartre wrote: 'Man is condemned to be free; because once thrown into the world, he is responsible for everything he does'. Freedom, true freedom, comes from the very sobering realization that we are responsible for the choices we make. Our choice of a mate, a career, a home—these choices and countless others, are up to us; and we are condemned to live with the consequences of every choice we make. That is a life of courage, a life of integrity and a life of dignity.

Until the African-American Christian purges him or herself of a mind darkened with servitude and fear, then they will never fully understand what our forbears struggled so hard to obtain—freedom.

African-American Atheism and the Appeal to Culture by Frances Parker

I recently heard a popular African-American news commentator disparage atheism as something 'out of Europe.' He went on to lament the absence of spirituality and 'God-talk' within public discourse. As an African-American atheist, I have a few comments to make regarding such remarks.

First, let me state that African American atheists are no different from atheists of any other racial or ethnic background. Most African-American atheists have read, studied, pondered and debated every angle concerning the existence of God. We have consciously decided to live without the counsel of bishops, reverends, evangelists, and deacons. To live in a culture that has a fondness for mysticism and considers critical thinking tools of Satan, can be a trial. Second, anyone who lives without religion will undoubtedly, from time to time, come up against hostility and religious bigotry, which is almost always fueled by ignorance and misinformation.

African-Americans are some of the most religious people in this country. The struggle for freedom was built on the seemingly Christian ideal of the inherent humanity of all God's children. Biblical stories such as the Exodus from Egypt, the Resurrection and the Second Coming of Christ have had an incredible impact in the cultural formation of African-Americans. Our music, our literature, and our folklore all praise the nobility of the slave, who in the mire pit of oppression, looked towards Heaven. Therefore, one need not be surprised by the vehement opposition taken by many within the community.

One should not be surprised by high levels of religiosity among oppressed peoples. In regards to the African-American community, I often think of the oft-quoted words of Marx 'religion is the opiate of the masses and the sigh of the oppressed'.

One may wonder how or why a people would continually look toward a supernatural being for their deliverance, instead of looking for more realistic means to attain their goals. The dependence on the Black church is to be expected. During the long history of segregation, when Blacks were barred from full participation in America, the Black church provided not only the foundation of the Black community, but also helped Blacks gain experiences that they could not gain elsewhere. The Black minister, who within the White world was bound to have his rights violated, was an important, spiritual leader within the religious subculture. Blacks, within their neighborhood churches, engaged in administrative duties and were able to interpret the scriptures from the Black experience.

Within the Christian framework, suffering is synonymous with virtue; needless to say, it is believed that the more a people suffer, the more righteous they will be in the eyes of the Heavenly Father. In Norm Allen's *African-American Humanism: An Anthology*, the syndicated columnist and psychiatrist, Charles Faulkner says, 'The Black churchgoer can find a loving and understanding "Father" in the church, which provides an escape from fear and trouble. It is a way to get back at the evil world or at least to insure that the evildoer, White or Black, will be punished—if not in this world at least in the hereafter. Retribution will surely take place and the "weak shall inherit the earth." The Bible promises it.'

The Jim Crow-era Black had more than simply the unknowable future to worry about. In a world that considered him less than human, where lynchings were simply a part of the Black experience, the Black Christian reasoned that there had to be some divine justice, some divine purpose for his suffering. Judgment had to come from 'on high'. In the eyes of the Lord, everyone was equal, and everyone would be judged.

While it is true that atheism (within the West) has its roots firmly planted in the intellectual traditions of Europe, to simply dismiss it, or any idea, based solely on its cultural antecedents, is incredibly erroneous. This fallacious argument is what I term the 'Appeal to Culture.' This argument is generally masked in more traditional fallacies, such as Argumentum Ad Hominem or the 'No True Scotsman.' Usually, the 'Appeal to Culture' rears its ugly head in political debates (pro or anti-affirmative action), or socio-cultural debates (abortion, homosexual rights, feminism). The argument simply assumes that any position that is favored by the majority (white media), or has its roots in white grass-roots movements, is automatically incorrect, and is ultimately hostile or antithetical to the concerns of the African-American community. Accusations such as 'You're not Black enough' or 'No real Black person would oppose affirmative action' are examples of this. Therefore, any African-American who expresses views that deviate from what is considered traditional African-American thought, are often faced with this fallacy.

If this argument is taken to its logical conclusion, however, one would have to dismiss practically every aspect of what is considered Western civilization, everything from architecture and literature, to economics and political systems. In fact, African-Americans would pretty much have to toss out much of the humanities and the sciences. Interestingly enough, the 'Appeal to Culture' could also be used to attack Christianity as an European construct, since it was forged in the political and cultural turmoil of the Greco-Roman world. After all, this is the argument leveled by many Black Muslims. One could also point out the fact that much of the brutality and bloodshed endured in Europe (the Crusades, the Inquisition) was instigated by the Church.

But one need not look at history for the sins of Christianity. The pages of the Bible itself clearly shows the horror. Imagine the events of the New Testament taking place instead, in the Jim Crow-era Deep South. Imagine, if you will, a young, 30-something Black man who speaks out against the injustices being suffered by his people. He is arrested by the authorities, questioned, beaten, and nailed to a piece of wood and left to hang until dead. I wonder if this could in fact the real cause of why some within the community have resisted portraying Jesus as a Black man in their churches. Would portraying the bloodied, beaten body of a Black man suffering on the cross finally reveal to Christians how truly vicious Christianity really is? The cognitive dissonance alone would probably force many to make unwelcome parallels between the plight of Jesus and the long, painful history of segregation.

This portrayal will hopefully get the African-American Christian to think. At least, he'll know not to dismiss an idea because it 'comes out of Europe'.

DIVINE PATERNAL ABSENCE? BY ADRIAN ARCHER

We often hear about the affects of paternal absence—particularly in the context of the Black family. Paternal absence is often associated with delinquency (i.e., violent behavior), feelings of hopelessness and despair, and social and psychological confusion. While these characteristics may indeed accurately represent the situation of many single fatherless households, they also seem to characterize the human race in general. This raises the question of whether the earth is suffering from divine paternal absence. When we see the violence, hopelessness and social, political and religious confusion it would seem like the answer is yes. When we look around at the state of humanity today our condition does not seem to reflect that we are the children of a benevolent and concerned heavenly father. An honest look at the starvation, natural disasters, religious and political violence, confusion and war would I believe lead us to the conclusion that we are all bastards!

If God could be taken to court, He would certainly lose custody of the world. If any human father treated his children the way God treats us, he would be considered negligent at best, and at worst down right abusive. Ninety percent of the world lives in varying levels of poverty and want, while only ten percent enjoy luxury and ease. If we say that we in West are blessed, the question arises: what about the rest of the world? What kind of father only takes care of ten percent of his children? Can you imagine a father with ten children who only shows concern for the needs of one of them, and leaves the other nine to suffer? What do we call such a father—partial perhaps, but certainly not omni-benevolent.

Someone may respond by saying it is because of our sin why we suffer. But, what sin are all the starving children in Africa atoning for exactly? And why does it seem as if some of the most "evil" people prosper while the weak continue to be subjugated. What kind of father would allow one of his daughters to abuse her defenseless younger sister—then says that he doesn't want to intervene because he doesn't want to limit the older sister's free will. Doesn't the Bible say something to the effect that a man should be able to keep his house in order? How about God taking his own advice for a change! So the question remains, is our planet suffering from paternal absence? Well if there is a God, and he is not absent, then he certainly makes a horrible father. But judging from the symptoms that characterize planet earth, and those commonly associated with paternal absence, then it does not seem far-fetched to suggest that God (if he exists) is an absent father. I think the divine paternal absence thesis would help explain a lot of what we see around us day after day, how about you?

THE LAST UNFAVORABLE MINORITY BY CHAKA FERGUSON

America may not be the most tolerant country in the world, but the majority of the country at least realizes that being intolerable is taboo in a climate of political correctness. For example, while many Americans may disagree with homosexuality on religious or other grounds, polls find that the favorable ratings of gays and lesbians are much higher than in the past. Some people may not personally like homosexuals, but when asked their opinion of gays and lesbians, they know to respond favorably.

The same is true among Black Americans and Jews. Both groups in the past had highly unfavorable ratings among the public at large (white Americans generally) and were easily dismissed as inferior or discriminated against (in the case of Blacks) or maligned (both Blacks and Jews) by the majority.

Nary will one find a poll today with high unfavorable ratings of either Blacks or Jews. In fact, both groups enjoy high favorable ratings among the American public (whether these favorable ratings are superficial or not is not essential to this essay. The point is that regardless of a person's real views, they most likely will answer in the favorable when asked their feelings about most groups, regardless of their true feelings, as not to be perceived as biased.

It may be said that for reasons of political correctness or cultural sensitivity, even the most hardcore bigot or anti-Semite will, when asked by a pollster, say they are not a racist. Few will admit to their bigotry. But there is one group that even political correctness can't save from public discrimination—and that group is atheists. The climate of tolerance disappears when it comes to the godless and those who choose to live life free of religious mandates.

According to a recent Pew Research Center on Religion and Politics (http://www.people-press.org/reli00rpt.htm) poll, more than half of Americans have an unfavorable view of atheists. Muslim Americans, who practice a religion that seems not to be regarded very highly in this country, had a favorable rating of 50 percent and unfavorable of about 30 percent.

By contrast, atheists had a favorable rating of about 32 percent. Atheists are a small (between 8-10 percent of Americans are atheists according to various polls*) and relatively silent part of the population, especially when contrasted with the much smaller and much more vocal homosexual community.

Atheists make a slightly smaller group than Black Americans and Hispanics, and are roughly equal to or more than the Asian American population and much larger than the American Indian population.*There are laws (which I definitely support) that protect these groups from discrimination based on ethnicity, religion, race and national origin. While there are too few, many jurisdictions in America have laws on the books that protect sexual orientation also.

Most Americans support civil rights laws that protect people from discrimination. And this country looks askance of those who show intolerance towards other groups. The question, then, is why is public perception of atheists so unfavorable when bigotry is scorned in this country?

What have atheists done to draw public animosity? My answer to the question is that, while the poll may be accurate, it is inherently flawed. Most people don't know any atheists (since most atheists seem to stay in the closet and keep their non-beliefs to themselves), and therefore form their opinions based upon what they are told by their preachers (imams or rabbis). Most theists probably work with, go to school with, are married to, have children, parents or a best friend who is an atheist and they don't even know it.

Secondly, the media basically ignores atheists. Even when it comes to church-state separation issues, rarely does the media seek opinions or insights from atheists. Our voices are seldom heard. Thirdly, most atheists, out of fear of retribution, keep quiet about their non-belief. Therefore, while theists may know a person who is an atheist and have high regard for that person, they don't know that person IS an atheist. The majority of atheists are upstanding people, but no one knows since most of us hide in the closet.

This poll should be a wake up call for atheists. We no longer should let our image be created by self-aggrandizing preachers who distort our character and slander us at every turn. If we don't speak up and explain our beliefs and non-beliefs to the public, the clergy will surely step in and make us out to be villains, anti-American and immoral.

How many times have atheists been asked if they worship the devil? How many times have atheists been blamed for school shootings and other social problems from teen pregnancy to drug abuse?

We must counter this stereotype. Atheists have started no Holy Wars, have not shot up abortion clinics, strapped bombs to ourselves and blown up buildings and innocent people in the name of god, withheld medical care from a family member or friend in the name of faith healing, bilked millions of people of billions of dollars through religious scams, etc, etc, etc. We are not the culprits, but all of society's ills are lumped onto our shoulders.

As long as we hide in closets and refuse to explain out position to the public, we will be maligned by those who find us a convenient scapegoat. Personally, I don't believe that half of the country views atheists unfavorably. They just don't know that we are among them _ including their closest friends and family.

But politicians respond to polls. And if the polls say the American public doesn't regard us very high, they will follow in tow. We should not allow ourselves to be at the mercy of religious hucksters whose influence, though waning, still has clout among certain segments of society. Civil rights for atheists and other non-believers hangs in the balance.

ATHEISTS AND AGNOSTICS—ANY DIFFERENCE? 2001, A DISCUSSION FROM THE BLACK FREETHINKERS WEBSITE

We've been discussing the finer points of atheism and agnosticism outside of the forum and we wanted to bring a new question to the group. Are there really agnostics, or are agnostics just atheists with another name, or are agnostics those with faltering faith/belief [or something similar]. One side of the argument says that if you don't know if there is a god or not, then you don't believe there is a god. So, if agnostics do not believe there is a god, then they need to call themselves atheists.

I agree that an atheist is someone who denies or doesn't believe in the existence of god. (I have honestly never truly understood the logic behind atheism because by definition, atheists have the burden of proving that there is no god. How can they do that?) For me there is a big difference between believing and knowing. Believing means having confidence in the truth or existence of something not immediately susceptible to rigors of proof. Knowing, for me means to be aware of something or to recognize something.

An agnostic, for example is someone that believes it is impossible to know whether there is or is not a god without sufficient evidence. We don't have the burden of having to prove anything; we just kind of sit on the fence and wait for the atheists and theists to battle it out and present us with facts rather than faith or non-faith to make us choose unequivocally which path is the "right" path. In other words, agnostics don't really believe in anything except what can be proven. I don't think that means agnostics are just "thinking theists/deists" with shaken faith who hope that someone on either side will give us that one elusive fact that will make us get off the fence.

For me there is a big difference between believing and knowing. Believing means having confidence in the truth or existence of something not immediately susceptible to rigors of proof. Knowing, for me means to be aware of something or to recognize something. I do not know that god exists; however, I believe that it is possible for god to exist. I think that atheists do not believe in this possibility.

xxxxx

I am atheist, according to the white man's dictionary. I don't believe in his "god" or, anyone else's. I 'm not sure you know this, but, speaking just for me, I made the mistake of thinking Freethinkers, were a group of atheist. If, I had known this wasn't the case, I would not have involved myself in conversations involving people who define themselves as agnostic. Only, because, I'm not there, an, I have no desire what so ever to convert anyone. I found out about Acharya S's *The Christ Conspiracy*, after I was told about the Infidelguy's site. Apparently, Ms. Acharya has broken ranks with the "Roman Empire Order of Mary, and, Christ." My point is I would have joined in that level of consciousness. I jumped the gun joining Freethinkers, thinking everyone was atheist. It was a joyous moment, no matter how brief.

Not only did I think these people were atheist, but, people of color, out of the closet. I was wrong. If I may, you mentioned supernatural. The so-called supernatural, has been made super, due to lack of understanding, regarding all senses of the physical body. We all were told about the five senses, seeing, hearing, feeling, smelling, taste. We have, to my knowledge, two more senses. These senses are latent in some of us, an, active in others. What these last two senses enable us to do is see, the unseen, and, travel there about. Some people call it magic, whatever. Amber, do you think, it's a coincidence that the moon takes twenty-eight days to go through her phases, an, a Woman's menstrual cycle is also twenty-eight days? This may appear unrelated to what you addressed, however, I like connecting the dots. I hope this E-mail doesn't offend anyone, and, the content of the matter discussed takes precedence over any errors. To the serious student of knowledge, I hope not.

xxxxx

If I may interject, I would like to first point out the fact that atheism and agnosticism are not mutually exclusive (as Amber pointed out). The agnostic first would need to ask themselves, "Okay, if there may be a God, what God would I be willing to accept." Inevitably, every aggie I've spoken with cannot seem to conjure up one, without vast amounts of fantasy and paradoxes. In which case even the agnostic is defaulted to the atheistic position.

As an atheist, I also make no positive claims about the God concept. Therefore, I am defaulted to the "a" theistic stance. The negative stigma attached to atheism are from those who do not understand it, i.e. the religious or pseudo-scientific people.

An asantaist is one that doesn't believe in Santa Claus. This statement doesn't say that there is no Santa, just that the person doesn't believe in Santa. Agreed, some atheists do indeed take more of an explicit stance in their atheism and state that there is no God, atheos. The definition of "God" however would have to be universally consistent and not self-contradictory. Not one person has defined God devoid of paradox; hence, God (every definition given) does not exist. Simple isn't it.

xxxxx

Just ranting. BTW, I call myself an agnostic atheist as well. Agnostic means, no knowledge. Even if there was a God, it would be beyond my knowledge due to its eternal super nature. If I made the positive statement that there could be a God, but it's nature is unknown, I would then be an agnostic theist. (Unlike deism which positively states there is a God.

Anyway, all in all, the proof is in the pudding. The person who has the concept, has to prove it. Just as if a person makes a claim that Pink Unicorns live somewhere in the Universe. I have no proof of Pink Unicorns, nor do I need to make a positive assertion toward the existence of them. I am defaulted to aunicornistism, (without belief in Unicorns), however, if one were to ask me if it's possible that organisms somewhere in the Universe could fit our general description of Unicorns, I would have to concede that it is possible, but unknown.

Which is an agnostic position as well, and I am still without unicorn belief (aunicornist). See? One can be both.

THE CRISIS OF THE RELIGIOUS BLACK INTELLECTUAL BY NORM R. ALLEN, JR.

Today the theologically oriented Black intellectual is enjoying tremendous popularity. Such thinkers as Cornel West and Stephen L. Carter have been featured in major media throughout the U.S.

What Black religious intellectuals have in common is the belief that faith in God is imperative if society is to survive and improve. These intellectuals have made important and profound observations on modern culture, society and history. But, paradoxically, while their deeply held religious convictions help them to examine many of the important questions in modern life, these very convictions severely hamper their intellectual depth.

Perhaps the major problem stifling the Black religious intellectual is the idea that his or her religious text is absolutely perfect and not to be held to the same standards of scholarly analysis as other texts. Though the believer might be willing to acknowledge that his or her sacred text is open to various interpretations, the text itself is never questioned.

Cornel West has written and spoken against xenophobia, sexism, homophobia and various other crimes against humanity. But one has to question the seriousness and courage of any thinker who professes to fight against such problems without acknowledging that the problems have been condoned and encouraged in the Bible. (Contrarily, Black religious intellectuals do not hesitate to point out the positive ways in which culture and society have been influenced by the teachings of various religious texts.)

The dilemma faced by Black religious intellectuals is that they advocate solutions to problems which were largely created or exacerbated by religion. These thinkers cannot be sufficiently critical of religion because they are very dependent upon it. They are therefore condemned to be limited in their perception and understanding of the problems they seek to solve. Furthermore, they are convinced that they will alienate the masses of Black people by becoming too critical of religion.

Cornel West and Bell Hooks are strong advocates of "Black critical thinking." In their book Breaking Bread, Hooks says she was upset because she did not believe that West had attacked sexism with enough force. But neither West nor

Hooks acknowledge the fact that sexism is consistently supported in the bible that, ironically, inspires their feminist views. While both thinkers acknowledge the sexism that exists within the Black church, they do not accept the fact that the Black church is acting consistently with biblical teachings regarding the treatment of women. And while both thinkers are critical of the misogynistic lyrics and images in the popular media, they do not acknowledge that centuries of biblical teachings helped to mold such hatred and disrespect for women. (Books such as Annie Laurie Gaylor's *Woe to the Women—The Bible Tells Me So* adequately prove the sexist mentality of biblical writers.)

Most Black intellectuals have denounced slavery as a moral evil. They have also acknowledged the church's role in supporting the institution. But the leading Black religious intellectuals will not admit that slavery is condoned in the bible. (Forrest G. Wood's *The Arrogance of Faith* brilliantly demonstrates how the bible was used, misused and abused to perpetuate slavery and segregation.) How can serious scholars be critical of Christians for having practiced slavery without being critical of the book that gave the institution moral respectability?

Stephen L. Carter, author of *The Culture of Disbelief* and an Episcopalian, discusses the many differences of opinion among members of his religion. It does not seem to strike him as strange that though the bible teaches that "God is not the author of confusion," the members of his religion seem to be thoroughly confused on many subjects. Furthermore, Carter believes that one can have a dogmatic belief in the bible and still engage in public discourse without reason being the arbiter in disputes. He even argues that creation scientists are as logical as scientists.

Carter is a self-proclaimed liberal who opposes sexism, xenophobia, slavery, etc. And like West, he prefers to ignore the fact that such "sins" are condoned in the bible. But while the anti-slavery opponent might argue that the bible never condones slavery, the advocate of slavery knows better. The same holds true for sexism, xenophobia, homophobia, genocide and many other undesirable forms of behavior condoned in the bible.

Those who are well read in the areas of history, philosophy, freethought, science and comparative religion wonder whether such Black religious intellectuals sincerely believe what they profess to believe regarding religion. Some probably do. But others believe that the masses will not accept leadership that is not religious. West believes that the church is the only "organic institution" in the Black community, and the only institution with historical roots strong enough to liberate Black people.

Black religious intellectuals who embrace this view will always be unable and/or unwilling to understand the profoundly negative impact that religious texts have had upon Black people, culture, history and society unless they are willing to examine those texts in an uncompromising manner. And this is most easily done if such theists embrace a religion like that practiced by the Unitarian-Universalists, i.e., a humanistic religion.

A humanistic religion enables many to remain spiritual while still being sufficiently critical of religious texts which have been largely responsible for encouraging negative behavior. At the same time, these religionists might embrace the positive teachings of religious texts. The point is that many religious humanists realize that all religious texts are at least partially the product of human beings and must be examined in the same manner as all other books. Any intellectual who does not realize this will necessarily be severely limited in his or her ability to understand culture, history and society. Moreover, reluctance to critically examine religious texts unwittingly contributes to the oppression of the groups that Black religious intellectuals seek to liberate. The Black religious intellectual must be committed, not to defending the faith, but to finding solutions to the problems confronting his or her people. If such solutions conflict with the teachings of religious texts, the solutions are to be chiefly valued.

There is no reason why Black religion cannot or should not become more humanistic. Though religion has existed for millennia, it has not always existed in its present form. As Karen Armstrong, the author of *A History of God*, says in the September 27, 1993 issue of *Time*: "All religions change and develop. If they do not, they will become obsolete." The same might be said of people who blindly embrace religious texts.

IS IT TIME TO REEVALUATE THE ROLE OF RELIGION?

This century will be called Darwin's century. He was one of the greatest men who ever touched this globe. He has explained more of the phenomena of life than all of the religious teachers. Write the name of Charles Darwin on the one hand and the name of every theologian who ever lived on the other, and from that name has come more light to the world than from all of those. His doctrine of evolution, his doctrine of the survival of the fittest, his doctrine of the origin of species, has removed in every thinking mind the last vestige of orthodox Christianity. He has not only stated, but he has demonstrated, that the inspired writer knew nothing of this world, nothing of the origin of man, nothing of geology, nothing of astronomy, nothing of nature; that the Bible is a book written by ignorance—at the instigation of fear. Think of the men who replied to him. Only a few years ago there was no person too ignorant to successfully answer Charles Darwin; and the more ignorant he was the more cheerfully he undertook the task. He was held up to the ridicule, the scorn and contempt of the Christian world, and yet when he died, England was proud to put his dust with that of her noblest and her grandest. Charles Darwin conquered the intellectual world, and his doctrines are now accepted facts. —Robert Green Ingersoll, "Orthodoxy" (1884)

Chapter 14

September 11, 2001

"Men never do evil so completely and cheerfully as when they do it from religious conviction."

—*Blaise Pascal*

This chapter was added in response to the terrorist attacks on the United States September 11, 2001, that resulted in the deaths of more than 3,000 people and the destruction of the World Trade Center. The attack, which was carried out by Islamic extremist, focused the spotlight on Islam and roused a great amount of anti-Islamic sentiment in the United States. Fearing a backlash against American Muslims and Arabs, President George W. Bush went out of his way in speeches after the World Trade Center terrorist attack to characterize Islam as a loving and peaceful religion that had been hijacked by Islamic extremists and murderers and in many ways he was correct, but only up to a certain point because the culpability of religion in the heinous attack cannot be ruled out.

Both the Koran and the Bible speak of brotherhood, love and peace, but both also espouse a great amount of hatred, divisiveness and violence. People go out of their way in the United States to avoid discussing religion, but its underlying involvement in the acts of war against the United States is undeniable. Despite the good intentions of mainstream Muslims and Christians, there is no getting around the incendiary passages in both the Koran and the Bible there is no denying religion had a role in the September 11, 2001 terrorist attacks.

Apologists for Islam and Christianity insist on minimizing the persecution, the discrimination, the forced conversions, the massacres, the destruction of the churches, synagogues, the burning of temples and other places of worship, the destruction of great libraries including great works of art and literature that happened at the hands of religion. Unbelievers in both the Koran and the Bible are dealt with harshly. They are shown no mercy as both books contain shocking descriptions of the carnage and consequences of being a nonbeliever, which meant Christianity, Judaism, Islam or nonbelief depending upon which path one followed.

The Koran

xxii.9: "As for the unbelievers for them garments of fire shall be cut and there shall be poured over their heads boiling water whereby whatever is in their bowels and skins shall be dissolved and they will be punished with hooked iron-rods.

xlvii.4: "When you meet the unbelievers, strike off their heads; then when you have made wide slaughter among them, carefully tie up the remaining captives."

47:41: 'When you meet the unbelievers, smite their necks, then, when you have made wide slaughter among them, tie fast the bonds"

ix.5-6:" Kill those who join other gods with God wherever you may find them"

viii.12:" I will instill terror into the hearts of the Infidels, strike off their heads then, and strike off from them every fingertip."

The Bible

Exodus 22:20 "He that sacrificeth unto any god, save unto the LORD only, he shall be utterly destroyed."

Psalms 79:6: "Pour out thy wrath upon the heathen that have not known thee, and upon the kingdoms that have not called upon thy name."

Deuteronomy 13:1-5 "If there arise among you a prophet, or a dreamer of dreams, and giveth thee a sign or a wonder, And the sign or the wonder come to pass, whereof he spake unto thee, saying, Let us go after other gods, which thou hast not known, and let us serve them…And that prophet, or that dreamer of dreams, shall be put to death…So shalt thou put the evil away from the midst of thee."

Deuteronomy 13:6-10 "If thy brother, the son of thy mother, or thy son, or thy daughter, or the wife of thy bosom, or thy friend, which is as thine own soul, entice thee secretly, saying, Let us go and serve other gods, which thou hast not known, thou, nor thy fathers; Namely, of the gods of the people which are round about you, nigh unto thee, or far off from thee, from the one end of the earth even unto the other end of the earth; Thou shalt not consent unto him, nor hearken unto him; neither shall thine eye pity him, neither shalt thou spare, neither shalt thou conceal him: But thou shalt surely kill him; thine hand shall be first upon him to put him to death, and afterwards the hand of all the people. And thou shalt stone him with stones, that he die..."

Chronicles 15:10-15 "So they gathered themselves together at Jerusalem...And they entered into a covenant to seek the LORD God of their fathers with all their heart and with all their soul; That whosoever would not seek the LORD God of Israel should be put to death, whether small or great, whether man or woman. [The LORD] was found of them: and the LORD gave them rest round about."

The Bible itself gives rules for warfare (Deuteronomy 21:10-14) and commands its followers to kill people who try to turn them from God. This is but a sampling of the savagery and brutality ready for all to see in the Bible and the Koran. There are more such passages that justify the destruction and murder of people and provide the foundations for the idea of a holy war.

There are passages of peace and they must be acknowledged, but these are listed because in religions of love and peace, it is extraordinary that they exist at all. The role of religion in creating unrest throughout the world must be acknowledged as intolerance and injustice have led to rebellion and retaliation making any chances of reconciliation nearly impossible. Each day hundreds of people are dying in religious conflicts, some which have lasted so long that few remember why they are fighting and are only fueled by hatred and a tradition of fighting. In October of 1999, a group of religious leaders met in Geneva, Switzerland and issued the Geneva Spiritual Appeal. The document asks that political and religious leaders and organizations ensure that religion is not used to justify violence. Unfortunately, no one paid attention.

Chapter 15

Conclusion—They Do Protest Too Much

"Many people would rather die than think; in fact, most do."
—*Bertrand Russell*

After spending two years corresponding, talking, debating and arguing with a variety of Black atheists, agnostics and a wide range of religious skeptics, I picked up a variety of information about Blacks on the fringes of religion. In addition, I learned about the depth of Christianity and how it is practiced in the United States and in the Black community in particular. Two things stood out in my mind as I neared the end of this writing and they are that the demise of Christianity in the United States is greatly overstated and that religion has little to no impact in changing human behavior in either the white or Black communities. Although I all ready believed it to be true, I was surprised that statistics showed that the load is even more unbalanced than I thought. It appears that people, including religious people, find a way to justify what they do and want to do both before and after the fact.

Gazing at the religious terrain in the United States gives me the feeling that there are 250 million religions in this country and each individual seems to determine what is valid and what is not. It appears that there is only 10-15 percent of the Christian population who actually live by the creeds of their religion and despite protests to the contrary, it is clear that the gap between the remaining 75 percent's professed belief and actual behavior is a far cry from the exemplary Christian life style.

It seems that there is a constant push for more religion, including putting the Ten Commandments as well a prayer in public schools. Religious groups try to push their agenda through politics and numerous politicians cater to the religious community. There is a constant worry that morality in this country has slipped to the likes of Sodom and Gomorrah, but with nearly 85 percent of the country claiming Christianity it appears to be a rift among the faithful unless the remaining 15 percent are entirely to blame for the moral conditions of the country, which is unlikely.

Clearly there is an unwillingness to admit that religion has little to no effect in affecting behavior as a quick glance at statistics will show that Christians have not avoided the wages of sin no matter how strong the protest. With 85 percent of the population claiming Christianity, it seems that there are motes and beams that must be removed from a multiplicity of eyes lest the majority of the country stagger about blindly in claiming its Christianity.

After looking over the variety of belief and behavior in the Black community, it appears there is a clear and growing gap between the two. An argument can easily be made, and correctly so, that statistics can be misleading and for a variety of reasons. Although there is a clear drop in church attendance and a rise in the number of unchurched in both the Black and white communities, despite all statistics to the contrary the clear majority of American still claim they are Christians despite documented behavior in opposition to the Christian ethic.

I found that of the unchurched who identified themselves as Christians but didn't attend church services to be less than genuine. Despite the claim of it "not being necessary" to attend church to communicate with God, it seemed an excuse for non-attendance and lip-service belief especially when these same people seem to make it any other place they want to go. Even without the statistics, observation shows that church attendance is down, that fewer men attend church than women and that a large portion of the Black community does not attend church at all, especially men.

A drive through the Black community on any Sunday, with exception of Easter or Christmas will reveal just as many outside the church as there are in it. Statistics paint a clear picture that there is a marked difference between belief and behavior, especially when supplemented by the lifetime experience of growing up as a Black man, it is clear how little religion affects bad behavior. Even Gallup pollster, George Gallup admits it, saying, "While religion is highly popular in this country, survey evidence suggests that it does not change people's lives to the degree one would expect from the level of professed faith."[238]

Clearly there is a rift in thinking as 44 percent of the white population and 32 percent of the Blacks are "unchurched" leaving one to speculate how many of this "unchurched" group are actually nonbelievers pretending they are religious and how many are true nonbelievers. Regardless of the answer it is clear that people don't go to church and that those who do are not affected into any lasting behavioral changes that are significant.

Normally, the difference is not worthy of comment except when it is made a key element or differentiator among groups and individuals. When we claim to follow a higher standard that differentiates and lifts us above the rest of common humanity, then we are expected to live up to that higher standard and we will also be judged at that higher standard without the benefit of mercy. In fact, there is usually great glee associated with the downfall of the smugly pious. As people, we all tend to fall far short of the high ideals we set for ourselves which is not necessarily bad because it shows that we have aspirations, but if we have decried another's humanity in lifting up ourselves, then our demise will be that much more difficult for us and that much more entertaining for others.

The concept of Christian absolution is one of its most attractive features, but it may also promote a type of revolving door behavior, as no one expects to die immediately and thus are willing to take the risk that they can be forgiven before they die. This kind of forgiveness without accountability encourages dishonesty and promotes dangerous living by subsidizing repeated bad behavior and sanctioning self-determined forgiveness. This is just a step away from each person determining what is right or wrong, the first steps toward anarchy. Yet, there is no inward turn of the eye to look upon the body of faith as those who are "all ready" religious call for more and more religion.

Christianity and Christian education is viewed by a vast majority of Americans as being the "sure cure" to solve many of the problems of American society. However, it appears that this view of Christianity may largely be a case of "preaching to the choir" as more than 86 percent of the United States all ready claims to be Christian. Simplistic, one-dimensional thinking invites interpolation to say it is the remaining 14 percent who are the problem, but a closer examination shows that the real problem may be closer to home. That 86 percent of Americans are Christians, a figure that has actually remained fairly steady for the past 30 years suggests that there is definite disconnect between belief and behavior and there is a wealth of data that if not verifying this observation at least shows that those who blame social problems on a lack of religion or religious training, perhaps, doth protest too much.

Following the thinking that if 86 percent of the country identify themselves as Christian then it must it must follow that the other 14 percent is causing all the problems we are experiencing in this country. Of course, this is ridiculous and for a variety of reasons and foremost among them is that it shows an improper correlation. For instance, 90 percent of state and federal inmates identify themselves as Christian but to say that Christians are the root of American crime is just as ludicrous.

The fact is that there is no shortage of Christian families raising their children with Christian values and as much as some would like to believe that more religion is the cure for what ails the country, more religion isn't the answer. History shows that religion has little to no effect in curbing man's inhumanity to man. The media and general society often teach that religion is the ultimate source of ethics and morals, and that without religion's influence the world would sink into barbarous behavior and moral chaos, but a careful examination of religious history demonstrates that not only has it failed to promote good ethics and morals, but it has engaged in some of the most heinous cruelties in the history of civilization. Legislation and secular law have not stopped bad behavior, but they are more effective in regulating it because of the possibility of real and relatively immediate punishment including fines, jail time and even death, whereas the flames of Hell have little immediate effect on curbing bad behavior.

Weighing the effectiveness of religion as a deterrent, it seems that religion is more effective in turning people around after the fact. Only when people see the inside of prison, are deep in drug addiction or are about to be punished does religion seem to come to the rescue. People all tend to be sorry for their indiscretions and sins—after the fact, when they have been caught, or are sitting on the edge of death or disaster. Only when they have been caught or exposed do they seek help. It is at this point that religion does an excellent job at reintroducing these "sinners" to the community as changed people making them examples of how ones life can be turned around by God, but the number of backsliders is rarely mentioned, only the successes.

In the United States, atheists, agnostics and secular humanists receive heavy criticism for their disbelief and are accused of having no moral values or ethics, but outside of academia and select theologians, little is known about these groups by the general public, especially the Black community. Despite the overwhelming claim of Christianity and belief in God, observations reveal that belief lags far behind behavior and statistics show that despite the claims of Christianity and belief in God a majority of Christians don't abide by the Christian ethic.

In the Black community, the incidence of crime, illegal drug use, alcoholism, illegitimate births and lesser social bad behavior has remained constant despite the overwhelming degree of Christianity. There are varieties of reasons for this discrepancy in believing and behaving including living conditions, poverty and social stigmatization, but they are not the only reasons. Unfortunately, bad behavior is part of the human element and religion has never been as effective as criminal law in curbing human misbehavior.

Religion and belief in God in other industrialized nations is disappearing. Church attendance in European countries is nearly nonexistent while the belief in God is also beginning to fall away and the statistics show that the United States is a nation of Christians who wear their belief like the latest fashion—changing, rationalizing or discarding it according to how well it fits. Clearly, church attendance in the United States is falling as it is in the rest of the world. Church attendance in the Canada and England have dropped so low as to be almost nonexistent.

ON IGNORANCE

There is a vast gulf in learning and knowledge in the United States and too often it is divided along racial and class lines. It is clear to me that the problem of ignorance in the United States desperately needs to be addressed. Ignorance is a terrible thing because it exposes us to the cruelty of the world and leaves us unprotected against those who would exploit us for their own personal greed. Unfortunately, religion has contributed greatly to the problem of ignorance.

It is the 21st century and ignorance and superstition seems to have no less a hold on men and women than when thunder was thought to be the voice of the gods. Sub-standard schools, flawed role models, failure mindsets and anti-learning mentalities are just the tip of the iceberg when it comes to explaining the reason for this seemingly blatant ignorance. Ignorance in science, in history, mathematics and even religion is at an unacceptable level to bring Black people willingly into the 21st century without some kicking and screaming along the way. It is time for the Black monolith to be shattered in order to encourage free-thinking towards real solutions rather than falling back into the comfort of tribalism, smug tradition and one-dimensional thinking.

What accounts for this disrespect for the basics of reason, logic and rationality in the Black community? There are many reasons and religion cannot be discounted because of its general anti-intellectual mindset. Our world and our future are becoming increasingly dependent upon science and technology. Critical thinking skills must be learned and practiced—that's why people should strive to make a habit of being reasonable. If there is no freedom to doubt then the ability to think is useless.

While many Blacks would classify themselves as thinkers, their actions and results prove otherwise. With so many demands on our personal time rarely do we focus on the things that make life worth living, such as freedom, truth or our purpose in life. Many believe that thoughts on such subjects is the realm of philosophers, scientists and academics and therefore rarely think past the 'highlights' and 'sound bytes' provided to them by the popular media. The ability to apply critical thinking to the variety of problems confronting the world today is imperative. Critical thinking is a developed ability that is crucial to clear understanding of problems, life's complexities and general survival. All Americans tend to come up short in this vital endeavor, especially Blacks. Unfortunately, with the exception of math, critical thought is not taught in American schools until college and even then, it can be avoided.

And avoid it, we do. People today neither care about deep serious thought nor do they care about the implications that can arise from a failure to do so. Even though it is not so, for many critical thinking seems to be beyond the reach of the average person. It appears that as thinkers, most Americans have a long way to go as indicated by a 1999 Gallup poll in which 18 percent of those surveyed believed that the sun revolves around the earth.[239]

Every minute our brains are active coordinating a myriad of bodily functions including monitoring our breathing and heart rate, but that is not thinking. Thinking means to actively and consciously engage the thought process. In the ordinary world much of our thinking is unconscious, meaning we are performing rote actions, which are so standard, that little or no thought goes into decision-making. Most of our heaviest thinking is job related or driven by personal plans and endeavors. Thinking and reason are discouraged throughout the Bible which is based on faith and unwavering belief. There is no room for equivocation or second-guessing.

Although the Black community recognized early on the benefits of education it has been a love and hate relationship. Despite the scientific sophistication of our age, many people seem to have an apparently unconstrained ability to isolate their thinking. Even scientifically minded people such as chemists, engineers and doctors of medicine, seem able to cut the corners of rational thought when it comes to religion. Despite years of experience and training using the carefully reasoned procedures of verification, some of the brightest minds find a way to short circuit the process when it comes to religion.

Today's world is far more complex and complicated than it was just 20 years ago and necessarily the world depends upon technology and science to solve world problems. Technology and science help improve crops, bring better medicines and faster communications. They also bring new weapons, new ideas and new problems. Without developing the intellect the world will be left to a host of intellectual midgets who will be in charge of deciding what direction our society will take in regard to politics, nuclear weapons and genetic research.

In both the Black and white communities, the mere thought of intellectual activity is frightening and considered subversive by a surprising amount of people. Intellectuals frighten people because they have the temerity to ask why. We all were intellectuals at one time. When we were children "why" was the favorite word in our young vocabularies. We wanted to know everything. Instinctively, we knew that if the answer was not apparent the only way to find out was to ask "why."

Some say we are not supposed to know everything but I find that more of a medieval excuse than an honest assessment of the search for knowledge. Still, there is not a valid reason not to seek an answer to a question that has motivated one to seek the truth. Occasionally, it is important to veer off course and explore viewpoints different from our own. The unwillingness to honestly assess an opinion or belief that is different from ours is a form of mental in-breeding that prevents the accumulation of well-rounded knowledge and thus the gaining of wisdom. Understanding is an active process. It requires action from those who wish to be understood and those who wish to understand.

Those who do not seek to understand are by necessity branded ignorant, intolerant and superficial, as well as cowardly, depthless and dangerous. Condemnation without understanding is tyranny. Tempers are often strained when one encounters ideas that go against everything that one has been taught, however, that doesn't make that knowledge invalid, instead, it should make the individual curious or at least willing to go further into the subject to refute erroneous information, otherwise an argument based on sand is an argument that will not hold water.

It is easy to deceive ourselves, especially when we have no experience, contact or knowledge of anything other than our own closed environments, which makes us the equivalent of blind men trying to describe the tiger's stripe through our sense of touch. Not only is it impossible to do, any attempt is premeditated dishonesty and an intellectual avoidance of reality. Still, there are those who are not concerned with depth or meaning, merely living has provided them with more than they can extrapolate.

Thinking is a choice. It is also a choice that few stop to consider and are content to let others speak, think and act for them. They are fronds in the wind merely swaying with whatever direction the breeze may blow. They are not able to stop long enough to examine whether they are a force for good or for evil, if such things exist, for it would force them to examine other things as well. For the most part, they are content to leave things as they are which makes them beneficiaries who do nothing to make gains other than wait for the windfalls produced by those willing to look a little further and think a little deeper.

The Black community should especially understand that to live a life without examination whether that life has any meaning at all, is to live a life that is controlled by someone else. It is necessary to find these things out for one self or one will be forever guessing as to one's position in this world. Basically, it is understanding that all things are open to examination—all things, including religion. In fact, a religion that cannot stand to rational thought and inquiry is no religion at all; it is mere superstition, propaganda and a way to rob people who cannot think past the end of their noses.

Con Men, Card Sharps and Magic

In the Black community, it is also clear to me that superstition and gullibility thrive as an assortment of card readers, psychics, mystics and so-called prophets of God flock to areas where they know they can make a living. Visions of Daddy Grace, Father Divine and Reverend Ike immediately pop into my mind. There are plenty of others, many who are thriving at this moment, directing multi-million dollar empires promising the blessed hereafter while they enjoy the profitable "here and now." These religious con men and women regularly bilk the "willing" Black community of millions of dollars and for the most part, no one complains.

Many of these parable pushers, populist prophets and self-anointed "holy men and women" in the Black community often refer to themselves as Sister, Madame, Reverend, Bishop, Doctor, Father, Prophet, Madame Queen, Reverent Mother or Reverend Sister and most of them are not accredited by any recognized theological institution. Obviously, not all are frauds, but superstitious belief and gullibility often disarms people's natural defenses and allows them to be duped for a few minutes of feeling good. Unfortunately, dishonest preachers are stereotypical icons of the Black community and often unfairly cast a negative light upon legitimate and forthright ministers who positively affect the community.

The result of this is that these spiritual con men and women thrive on the unexplainable to exploit the ignorance of others and make fat livings by pimping the insecurities of life with appeals to emotion and feeling rather than clear thinking and science. Still, it appears that these con men and women are not always to blame as their victims are often willing accomplices who look for reasons not to accept reality and that is because superstition is alive and well in the Black community.

Viewing any late night television channel will reveal commercials by paranormal hucksters and flim-flam artists that are specifically aimed at Black audiences, which clearly indicates that there is money to be made in the paranormal business especially in the Black community. Meanwhile, these everyday criminals rake in scads of money profiting from Black gullibility and failure to think. Some how we have lost sight of there really isn't any such thing as a free lunch. Perhaps, in the world of the unscrupulous, the better saying should be 'never smarten up a chump or give a sucker an even break.

Why would any rational person fall for any of the myriad scams or institutionalized fakery? Few people want to spend the time it takes to think through an issue and most people look for reasons to avoid discomfort including accepting false information, restricted freedom and even denial of rights in return for imagined guarantees. In many cases, religion discourages looking for any deeper meaning. We have pictures from planets millions of miles away. We have cloned animals. We have harnessed the atom and yet, 52 percent of those surveyed reported a belief in astrology.[240]

Ghosts and Goblins

Spiritual warfare is a popular topic among Black protestant preachers and to hear it preached leaves one thinking that the world is filled with invisible demons and spirits who are constantly at war with one another fighting over our souls. As well meaning as this focus on the power of good and evil may seem to be, ultimately it removes responsibility from humanity by attributing good and bad behavior to outside forces. During the entire cycle of life, human choices are the defining factors. If we consciously choose to go against accepted practice, law and custom, we suffer known consequences. We also choose to change when going against the grain puts us into uncomfortable circumstances; otherwise, we keep doing what is pleasing to ourselves.

The Devil Made Me Do It

> ...and then, the devil pulled a gun on me and pushed me into the store...Flip Wilson.

The character Geraldine was comedian Flip Wilson's trademark creation. Geraldine had a weakness for spending money and it seemed that the devil was constantly after her to spend more. He was her built in alibi. In many ways, the devil is still a co-conspirator in today's sinning scenarios, while lack of character and fortitude are left waiting for determination to show up. In the Black church as witnessed by spiritual warfare, the devil exists and plays a role in the world. He has power. He can make people do things they really don't want to do. According to some preachers, one of the places the devil works the hardest is within the walls of the church. The incongruity of a powerful devil and a powerful God implies they have equal power or one would have simply vanquished the other. Certainly, no preacher or minister would ever say that Satan is a God, but the implication is certainly there.

Black stereotypes linger in both communities. That Blacks are natural athletes is a common stereotype and in the Black community, many accept it as fact. In many sectors of the Black community, it is a disgrace to lose any athletic event to a white person. Of course, this limiting stereotype also helps support the reverse view that Blacks are mentally inferior. It is the danger of "white men can't jump" in that it opens the door to reverse spin of physicality's opposite—mentality. That is why I titled this book Black and Not Baptist because the Black community is astonishingly diversified and cannot be categorized so easily.

Superstition allows people to avoid discomfort by accepting false information in return for imagined guarantees. History has shown us that so much of what we thought was the hand of God was simply the ignorance of superstition. Although we continue to learn at an even higher level, each day superstition will not die out. Meanwhile, everyday criminals rake in scads of money profiting from gullibility.

Clearly, religiosity is not always a plus for Blacks living in the United States. Comedian Dick Gregory, before he turned activist, remarked on a comedy album that the world would know if Black people were ever discovered to be living on another planet because "the next spaceship would be filled with Bibles and water melons." The biting comment was intended to show how whites viewed Blacks at that time. Inadvertently, Gregory exposes the role of religion in taming the Black community, bringing it under control.

How Much Intolerance?

The Black community has a history of being "accepting" to different points of view and people, but when it comes to atheism or agnosticism, it is not so tolerant. There are other areas of intolerance also, such as incest, homosexuality and mental illness to name three. While homosexuality uncovers short tempers, lack of understanding and general disgust but progress continues as more gay Black men and women step into the public almost daily. Most Americans still exhibit ambivalence about the overall acceptability of homosexuality in American society today, and substantial numbers of Americans continue to say that homosexual relations should be neither acceptable nor legal, but attitudes have changed. The Gallup Poll has recorded a gradual increase in adherence to the belief that homosexuality is an acceptable alternative lifestyle. Agreement with this proposition has risen from 38 percent in 1992 to 52 percent today, including the Black community. There has also been a shift in attitudes about the legality of homosexuality, with a majority of Americans—54 percent—now saying that "homosexual relations between consenting adults" should be legal, compared to 43 percent who felt this way in 1977.

Majorities of Americans now favor legislation to make it illegal to discriminate against gays and lesbians. Still, most people are still opposed to single-sex marriages and to the adoption of children by same sex couples, although majorities who feel this way have declined. Over 80 percent of Americans accept the idea of including homosexuals under the protection of equal opportunity provisions in the workplace. However, majorities of Americans, especially Blacks, remain opposed to the extension of marriage benefits to gays and lesbians.[241]

The Black community remains largely homophobic and holds a dim view of all homosexuals. However, the Black church often is forced to turn a blind-eye and keep its peace while taking a more pragmatic approach toward homosexuality because the realities of the Black church demands that some churches tone down its disapproval of gays as many of their "essential" members are homosexual and participate in a variety of church groups including the choir, music ministry and outreach programs.

NO PROTECTION FOR NONBELIEVERS

Since atheists, agnostic, humanists and freethinkers constitute no protected group such as a religious denomination, the physically or mentally disabled or any specific ethnic group or culture, many feel that is okay to disparage this group with impunity. As much as Islam is involved in the September 11 terrorist attack on the United States, all but the most imprudent have kept from making any negative remarks about Middle Eastern ethnic groups or Islam. President Bush went out of his way to say that Islam is a religion of peace and that the Arab people were not to blame for the terrorist attacks, despite street celebrations in some Middle Eastern countries.

Making bigoted statements about ethnic groups or special groups in the United States can lead to serious backlash for the speaker and for whatever organization they represent. With the exception of hate groups, nonbelievers, skeptics, humanists, atheists, agnostics are considered fair game. Former president George H. Bush said he didn't believe that atheists could even be considered American citizens. If he had said that he didn't think Eskimos should be considered Americans, the media would have hounded him into an apology and at least a trip to Alaska. Black talk show host Starr Jones made a similar comment in reference to voting for an atheist. If she said she wouldn't vote for a Latino she would be pressured into issuing an apology, her show would be boycotted, but in this kinder and gentler nation, nonbelievers are considered fair game in an open hunting season despite their humanity. Although atheists of any color are no better or worse than any one else, the blame assigned to them is enormously out of proportion to their number and influence. A case could be made for just the opposite. For instance, the vast majority of people in American prisons are overwhelmingly Christian while the number of atheists in prison is almost too small to count. Atheists also have the lowest levels of divorce in the United States. In all the horrible crimes committed in the United States against women and their children, no one points out their religious affiliation of the perpetrators unless they are other than Christian while the overwhelming majority of these crimes are indeed committed by Christians. It is barely mentioned that men and women, outside the Catholic Church, who molest children are almost always Christians. In all the social ills of the United States ranging from drug abuse and alcoholism to white-collar crime and spousal abuse, no one mentions that self-proclaimed Christians are the distinct majority. Does this mean that Christians are inherently a bad lot? Of course not, because the United States is nearly 86 percent Christian, it stands to reason that more Christians would be a part of the offending group simply because the group is larger, not more prone to bad behavior.

Since nonbelievers are not usually a visible group it is easy to potshot them because more than likely there will be no repercussions. In reality, except for their belief in one fewer God than Christians there is not much difference between nonbelievers and any other group when it comes to good or bad behavior. With nearly 86 percent of the population claiming Christianity it is readily apparent that either the remaining 14 percent of the population is responsible for all of the country's social ills or that there are many among the 86 percent who don't live up to the Christian standard.

Atheists can be mean and nasty, just like the good Christians of the South who turned their dogs on Civil Rights marchers, stoned peaceful protesters and fire bombed churches. Just like their Christian counterpart, there are nonbelievers who donate great amounts of their time and money to charities and helping people. The worst thing nonbelievers do, even surpassing hatred, lust and even murder, is to not believe in any god. That one thing apparently makes it acceptable to lay aside the "golden rule" and do whatever feels good when it comes to bashing nonbelievers. Most people are probably unaware that each day they interact with or are exposed to nonbelievers as most nonbelievers keep their thoughts to themselves for personal and prudent reasons.

DANGER IN RELIGION?

Whether religion in general and Christianity in particular have been a help or hindrance to the Black community is a continuing debate. The general feeling is that religion has had a positive impact in the Black community and there are few who would publicly challenge that mode of thinking, but there are those who think that not only has religion harmed the Black community but that it continues to harm it by promoting magic and supernatural thinking. Over the years, scholars have argued that Christianity prevented Blacks from doing more to further their own causes by encouraging submission to authority and passivity in the face of violence. Most would agree that organized religion can be an effective social agent. However, it also tends to create conflict between different groups of believers as well as nonbelievers that are based on personal interpretations. Organized religion can sometimes inspire people to be kinder, to be more charitable, and to help others, but not always.

Protestant and Catholic Christians are still killing each other in Northern Ireland. Christians carried out a genocidal campaign against Muslims in Kosovo. Islamic terrorists have murdered thousands of innocent people in order to further their goals. In the United States, Christian terrorists have attacked abortion clinics in the name of God. In addition to starting wars and inspiring fanatics to commit murder, religion can damage its believer's sense of personal responsibility by allowing them to shift their responsibility onto God or Satan.

Although most of Black Africa is free now and it seems the only thing whites left behind was religion. All though the intentions were good, the effect was not. In Africa, religion has been at the root of war and genocide while millions dwell in ignorance and poverty while being faithful in their religiosity. Tied with tribalism and superstition religion has helped devastate large portions of Africa while helping criminal rulers stay in power. It has also had a hand in the spread of the AIDS virus through its religious teachings on sexuality and its failure to teach about simple sexual protection such as condoms.

In the United States, the harmful effects of religion are not as stark, but although it is subtle—it is there. One of the most harmful effects of religion in the Black community is the negative stereotype it has created of Black people as a cowering, superstitious tribe of overly religious marks easily fooled or outsmarted. The unspoken stereotype is that of spiritual "Stepin Fetchits" who are primitive, superstitious and unintelligent.

The religiosity of the Black community constitutes a major element in the negative perception of it, despite the praise it receives. Black religious institutions are not held in the same esteem as their white counterparts. The perception of Blacks as being ignorant and uneducated is inextricable linked to outsider's views of the community as excessively religious. It is a fact that the least educated tend to have the highest levels of church attendance in both the white and Black communities and because educational opportunities are limited in the Black community, it stands to reason the Black religiosity would be even higher. With as much praise that falls upon Black religiosity comes an unspoken diminishment, which quietly moves Black religion into the backwoods of worship.

The biggest harm, however, is its perpetuation of ignorance in the Black community by discouraging inquiry and doubt. That ignorance has lead to the destruction of the community through crime, poverty and a multitude of pathologies growing out of these conditions. In some very important ways religion, Christianity, in particular, is against living. The very essence of Christianity teaches people to not become attached to things of this world because there is a better place. It is this type of thinking especially in the Black community has led to the great retribution thinking or that God will even the score in the end and it is that type of thinking that has left many people standing at the church doors while the rest of life passes them by as they wait for the blessed hereafter.

Compromising Health

Illness in the Black community is largely under reported and medical services are largely under utilized because of various things including lack of insurance, proximity and fear. Overwhelming religious faith has also led to tragedy, as people often delay needed medical attention in hopes that a miracle will occur. Often the most serious of diseases go untreated because of ignorance or fear of discovery as in AIDS related cases. Estimates say that every month between one and five children die due to the religious beliefs of their parents. Each year, 10-20 preventable deaths occur among groups like the Christian Scientists and other groups with similar ideology.

Superstition wastes time and money and of the two, time may be the most important when it comes to health issues as untried and often dangerous "cures" are taken over proven traditional medicine and many times when traditional doctors are consulted it is already too late.

Superstition and religion play a part in organ donation as most Black organ donations are withheld on religious grounds. Yet, Blacks make up more than 30 per cent of those waiting for organ transplants. Nationally, Blacks are the least likely to donate organs, but they are clearly over represented among those needing organ transplants. Religious beliefs often complicate an all ready complex matter, stopping some from donating.

Meanwhile, it is known that organs from Black donors adapt well with Black recipients, but the shortage of Black donors is dismal. Each year the life saving organs of young Black men and women are buried with them after premature deaths to murder and other social pathologies. Nationwide there are 16,000 Blacks on the waiting list for an organ transplant. Each day, four Blacks die because of the critical shortage of donors.

Other Black social problems such as mental health and incest are slipped beneath the covers and kept away from public view. Mental illness is either kept hidden or it is exploited for a government check, while stress, anxiety and depression become "weaknesses" that reflect an individual's inadequacy. It is so well hidden that white doctors often misdiagnose it and then compound the error by prescribing improper medications in wrong dosages.

According to a National Mental Health Association survey on attitudes and beliefs about depression 63 percent of Blacks believe that depression is a personal weakness and only 69 percent believe that it is an actual illness at all. Only 30 percent of the Black population said they would take drugs for depression even if prescribed by a doctor as more than 2/3 of the respondents to the survey said they believed that "prayer and faith" alone will successfully treat depression.[242] This type of thinking only exacerbates health problems in the Black community.

Incest remains hidden in the Black community even though there are significant numbers of families affected by it. It is the crime that often goes unreported because of the stigma, embarrassment and fear of reprisals from family members associated with it, but like anywhere else in the United States, incest is no stranger to the Black community. Because of the desire to keep secrets inside the community, child molesting and abuse is often not reported and the result is that thousands of Black children are irreparably scarred because of it.

In this country, a woman is sexually assaulted every two minutes, and nearly 5 percent of women report having had an incestuous experience with their father or stepfathers before reaching 18 years old. Black children are also incest victims at the same rates as whites with girls being more likely to be abused by relatives other than their fathers, such as an uncle. A random survey conducted by the Los Angeles Times found that of 2,627 women and men surveyed, 27 percent of the women and 16 percent of the men had been incestuously abused as children. [243, 244, 245, 246]

Yet, in the Black community, it is a problem that is largely suffered in silence and put under the category of "dirty laundry" not to be aired in public, but it is dirty little secret that finally came out in the national wash. In 1985, Stephen Spielberg's film of Alice Walker's *The Color Purple* was literally boycotted from winning an Academy Award partly because of the incestuous relationship it portrayed. The movie, nominated for eleven Oscars, did not win a single one after the NAACP denounced the movie saying that it portrayed Black men in a "negative" light apparently not considering the regular procession of Black men paraded across the evening news in handcuffs each night as being portrayed in a "negative light." [247] Perhaps, the movie hit too close to home.

Religion has hurt in other ways as it has soothed some people into parting with their hard earned dollars that they cannot afford to lose. There are tons of illegitimate preachers; seers, readers and everyday con artists who regularly take money from those who can least afford it. For instance, to talk on a psychic hotline people pay $3.99 per minute or $239.40 per hour to talk to these hocus-pocus hucksters and it is no mistake that the Black community is targeted for such deliberate ventures. Even those who claim the power of prayer are now being questioned.

Despite the many who find comfort in religion researchers found that the key factors that served to increase the risk of death were feelings of being abandoned or punished by God or that some patients believed that their illness was caused by the devil. "Patients who reported feeling alienated from God or who blamed the devil for their sickness, had a 19 to 28 percent increased risk of dying during the following two years.[248]

MORALITY WITHOUT GOD

Some might object that, without religion, that man would soon revert to criminal and animalistic behavior, but judging from history and what is happening today man has needed little incentive to do just that and no religion past or present has stopped it and in many cases it has been a willing accomplice. Morality and ethics grow out of common need and that common need produces civilization. A major misconception about atheists, especially in the Black community, is that they have little or no respect for life, but nothing could be further from the truth. Majorities of people have some kind of philosophy; some code of ethics that guides their lives and it is no different for atheists. In fact, many atheists adhere to rigorous life philosophies, ethical and moral systems. [249, 250]

Americans are unsure of religion's role in personal morality. The public is split about equally over whether belief in God is necessary for one to be a moral person (50 percent say such belief is not needed, 47 percent disagree). African-Americans, Southerners and older people especially women are among those who see the link between religion and morality as very important; other groups, including men, younger people and college graduates, are less likely to say that religion is a prerequisite for morality. Politically, conservatives, especially conservative Republicans place the most importance on the connection between religion and morality. Independents and liberal Democrats attach the least importance to the religion-morality link. Americans are open to the possibility that many religions lead to eternal life, but they are critical of people who do not believe in God or have no religious affiliation. Atheists get very low ratings (34 percent favorable/54 percent unfavorable) and "people who are not religious" are given better but still modest evaluations (51 percent favorable/30 percent unfavorable).[251]

The majority of atheists and agnostics adhere to well-defined codes of conduct, morals and ethics. These standards are based upon a variety of philosophies and ethical systems, including some tenets from religion. Atheists don't feel free to do as they please simply because they have no belief in a god. On the contrary, most feel inclined to be even more respectful of life in general for they believe that this life is the only chance they will have and generally practice an offshoot of the "Golden Rule" in that most adopt a "cause no pain" philosophy toward their fellow man. With the exception of disbelief, atheists are no different from religionists in that they both seek to help others, live the best life possible and to find reasonable happiness.

Thousands of years before the Bible was written, ancient society had codes of moral conduct in place. Without the God of Judaism, Christianity or Islam, people developed complex moral and ethical standards. Many researchers believe that the need for cooperation helped develop moral and ethical considerations that are still valid today. For protection, food gathering and raising family's ancient people banded together to become more effective and in effect started to civilize themselves. Universal moral concepts about lying, stealing, cheating and killing developed early on and continue to develop this day as people discovered that cooperation is beneficial. The "Prisoner's Dilemma" research vividly demonstrates how people come to cooperate simply because of their own self-interests.

> The prisoner's dilemma is a game invented at Princeton's Institute of Advanced Science in the 1950's. In the basic scenario after which it is named, two prisoners who the police know to have committed crime A, but whom they wish to convict of the more serious crime B, are held in separate cells and offered a deal:
>
> The one who testifies implicating the other in crime B will go free, while the other will receive 3 years in prison (the "sucker's payoff"). If they both testify against each other, each will receive two years. If they both remain silent, they will both be convicted of crime A and serve one year. Thus, there are two choices—usually known as to cooperate, in this scenario remain silent, or to defect, which here means to confess. And, there are four possible outcomes, depending on your partner's move: you may serve 0, 1, 2 or 3 years in prison.
>
> Cooperation either means you serve one or three years. The results of defection straddle this: you may serve 0 or 2 years. Because you do not know whether you can trust your partner (there is no opportunity to communicate when deciding your move), most rational players will choose to defect in order to maximize the upside (0 years) and minimize the downside (only 2 years instead of 3). Yet, the outcome consistently is better for two cooperating players than for two defecting players.[252]

The Prisoner's Dilemma demonstrates the importance of cooperation, as motivation is clear as non-cooperation often results in negative consequences for one party or the other and sometimes both. This spirit of cooperation has been the civilizing influence behind man's progress, and has been co-opted by various religions over the centuries, although most are only cooperative to their own or to those they can convert, despite what is written.

Concerns

"Giving all praise and glory to God" is a phrase common to the beginning of many prayers and it is a phrase that marks the Black community's subservience to the supernatural. It is a self-effacing, self-belittling phrase that makes no pretension of having any consideration of the self. It is groveling for a pat on the head by the loving master. It totally dismisses one's hard work, worry and even suffering as secondary. In essence, it gives credit to someone else.

It concerns me as a member of the Black community that it seems to rely on Jesus and God to deliver it from the problems it encounters in the real world. This thinking leads people to substitute a fantasy life for the life that is taking place in the here and now. Most religious people seem to be interested in life and it's meaning, but religious dogma seeks to transcend life and look for meaning to substitute for reality. Because of that, many people are just as interested in avoiding having to live life as it is because of its intensity and unpredictability.

It would be impossible to deny the good the Black church has done. The humanity it offered during inhumane times, the hope it provided during hopeless conditions and the buffer it provided during buffeting times is undeniable. The Black church provided leadership and a voice to the outside world and continues to do so. It fed the hungry, clothed the naked and tendered solace to the dying. It has also built multi-million dollar edifices to God, but has not built hospitals, shelters or daycare centers of similar opulence or splendor. Of the things the Black community needs it would seem like another church would be far down the list. This is not to criticize the work the Black church does, but it is criticism of how it spends its money.

There are multi-million dollar campuses and religious megaplexes featured in Ebony Magazine, but where are similar shelters for the homeless? Where is the medical insurance for the indigent, money for prescriptions for those who can't afford them, medical clinics, rehabilitation centers, food centers, shelters for abused women and children, high quality schools or homes for the elderly? It concerns me that we can build multi-million dollar structures to God and we cannot build hospitals or even a clinic, that we cannot build a classroom much less a school. It bothers me that we can overlook the abused women and children in the community when we can build edifices to God that sit empty most of the week.

It concerns me how much faith we have in Jesus and how little we have in ourselves when it comes to changing our lives. It concerns me how much faith we have in the Holy Ghost when we need doctors, financial advisors and business leaders; how much faith we have in the various preachers, priests and apostles rather than in books, education and ourselves. I am concerned that people give their money to the church when they can't keep the electricity on or the water flowing.

I am concerned that despite all the good thoughts and ideas that spring from the church that there seems to be small correlation between those rules and acceptable behavior. I am concerned that the people most affected by the sneezes of this country catch cold in the form of crime, illegitimate births, venereal disease, drug abuse and alcoholism. I am concerned that Jesus has not stemmed the rates of infidelity, adultery and violence but has made some people rich and famous while doing little for those who helped them get rich. I am concerned that only when we are no longer able to sin, because of age, infirmity or incarceration does God seem to make a difference.

I am concerned that the community continually turns to the clergy for ideas while the greater populace consults with business leaders, scientists, teachers and politicians. I am concerned that the reliance on Jesus and God to get things done leaves the community in the position of trying to catch up in the race for stability and success, while other groups jump ahead by doing things for themselves. Black theologians have zeroed in on Liberation theology, which seems to place Blacks and the disfranchised into a permanent loser category suffering righteously here on earth waiting for the retribution of God, which seems to be a modified "pie in the sky" philosophy. This thinking promotes a God of power. The God who "makes a way out of no way." A God who personally intercedes in the way of the world to change it. This same God has led to an over reliance on the supernatural to "fix" or change things.

I am bothered by the millions of Blacks who spend money going to healers and herbalists rather than going to a doctor. The number of Blacks who believe that the Bible is the literal word of God and don't believe in evolution frightens me. I am even more shocked by the number of Blacks who have never read the Bible and yet claim it holds all the answers. Religion encourages people to dispense with thinking and carefully reasoned procedures of verification to accept on faith. Even educated Black professionals trained in problem solving and scientific thinking somehow manage to skip past religion when it comes to prolonged and thoughtful examination. Despite living in an age of unbridled technological triumph and scientific sophistication, large numbers of people possess the uncanny ability to compartmentalize their thinking and skirt reason and rationale. Even trained scientific professionals seem to be able to jump over hurdles of rational thought when it comes to religion.

Calling Religion to Task

Throughout the history of mankind, religion has been a mixed blessing often dividing the world into "true believers and infidels" thereby providing the groundwork for division, hatred and warfare. The people who make these distinctions have murdered, tortured and exterminated including members of the same faith if those people fell on the outside of those who called themselves true believers.

In the incendiary aftermath of that terrorist attack, the glowing embers and coals of simmering hatred have landed on human kindling to fan the flames of religious bigotry. Those who planned the attack are sure that God has granted them a great victory, while many here wonder why God turned his back and allowed such a terrible thing to happen, but the real truth of the matter is that God had nothing to do with the events of September 11.

The terrorist attacks were the work of people, just as the lapse in US security is partially a result of people ignoring world events and taking their freedom for granted. Naturally, there are those who are quick to condemn Islam because of this dastardly attack, but Islam is not the problem anymore than Christianity is the problem in Northern Ireland or Judaism in the Middle East. The problem is people.

Religious Wars

The disaster of September 11 was a combination of audacity, lax security, warped religion, lengthy planning, smug arrogance and underestimation. It was a man-made event developed, planned and exploited by men. The valiant efforts of the New York Police Departments and Fire Departments and others were the actions of those dutiful, dedicated and caring people. No matter how it is clothed, the intentional slaughter of non-combatants is murder. In sufficient quantities, it is genocide. The atrocities committed in the name of God are enough to embarrass even the most blood thirsty of vampires. Too often the actions of misguided men, fringe fanatics and vision starved zealots are interpreted as acts at the behest of God when they are nothing more than what they seem—the horrendous acts of savage men.

A fragile peace settled on Bosnia after U.N. troops broke up the fighting there between Serbian Orthodox Christians, Muslims and Roman Catholics who had been at each other's throats for decades. U.N. Troops are also helping to keep a shaky peace in Cypress where Christian Greeks and Turkish Muslims continue to fight. Hindus, Muslims and Sikhs in India have been fighting for years and show no signs of quitting. Muslims and Christians in Indonesia have made a shambles of the land where 20 percent of the population has died by starvation, disease or murder.

Even the prospect of a nuclear war has done nothing to quell the violence between Hindus and Muslims in Kashmir. In Kurdistan, Christians and Muslims continue to bomb each other while Jews and Muslims can find no peace in the Middle East. This religiously fueled unrest has reached into Africa where Yoruba, Christian and Muslims are locked in a complex religious and ethnic conflict as the once Muslim dictatorship begins to fall. Religious conflict has wracked the Sudan where slavery is still practiced while Christian and Muslims make war. Other sites of religious strife include Tibet, Sri Lanka, Serbia, the Philippines, Pakistan, Northern Ireland, Thailand and Bangladesh.

> *"The surest way to work up a crusade in favor of some good cause is to promise people they will have a chance of maltreating someone. To be able to destroy with good conscience, to be able to behave badly and call your bad behavior "righteous indignation"* —*this is the height of psychological luxury, the most delicious of moral treats.*
>
> —*Aldous Huxley*

The concept of a Holy war is nothing new to religion and although Islam is in the spotlight now, other religions have a long history of intolerance and fanatical fundamentalism including Judaism and Christianity. Christianity had The Inquisition, The Crusades, witch trials and played a major role in American slavery. For all the good that religion has done, most of it is outweighed by the tonnage of carnage committed in its name by—people. That is the key. Once it becomes clear that religion is the façade for the bristling ambitions and fanaticism of misguided people, then, some sense can be made of the horrific crime against mankind that occurred September 11.

Although hijacked by a variety of religious extremists, religion still plays a role in the troubles of the world. There are fringe groups in both Islam and Christianity and that is to be expected, but not tolerated by those religions. The Ku Klux Klan is an example of a religious extremist group in the United States and although there are others, it is probably the best known among the general populace. Now, since the September 11 terrorist attack and destruction of the World Trade Center, Al-Qaeda has become just as well known. Religion has been used throughout history to justify the unjustifiable. It has been used to breed hatred, fuel contempt, encourage sexism, support racism and encourage violence in the name of God. The pages of world history, demonstrate that overt tyranny and bloodshed fill the greatest part of religious history. The Bible actually sanctions the killing of heretics and over the years became a basic church doctrine during the rule of the Roman Emperor Constantine in the 4th century and continues to this day with bloodshed in the name of the Christian religion. Part of the fault lies with the sacred texts of these various religions which were written during a time when the world was different and warring tribalism was the best of civilization, but literal interpretation of ancient texts in today's complex and scientific age is not only incorrect but irresponsible.

A "holy war" is the same as being "pretty ugly", it is an oxymoron used as a fancy suit to dress up a pig of human behavior that under any circumstances would be viewed as primitive, animalistic and bloodthirsty. This high sounding term is nothing more than men granting themselves a license to do all of the despicable things that men can do without feeling any guilt, because they are acting in the cause of God. Perhaps, lunatics, fanatics and the mentally unstable buy into this thinking but there is no such thing as a Holy war just as there is no such thing as educational television.

Still, there is enough in the Bible to justify a "Holy war," which is a paradox considering the general view of Christianity as a peaceful religion, but a careful reading of the Old Testament reveals the God of Moses to be a God of war. Throughout history, men have justified war and cruelty in the name of God. The Crusades and other holy wars were fought to fulfill Biblical prophecies, and the reign of terror known as the Inquisition. Killing for religious reasons has been a widely accepted church doctrine for nearly two-thirds of Christian history. Similar atrocities have been the general rule throughout the history of most other religions as well. The Islamic religion has its own long history of holy wars fought to establish their beliefs through force. Even today, Islamic holy wars and terrorist acts are a regular feature of news broadcasts around the world. The Inquisition and the Crusades are just two examples of "Holy wars" that were barely disguised attempts at colonialism and plain old theft. Islam also had its wars of conquest and invoked the term "Holy war" to cover its tracks also.

There is nothing Holy about war at all and that is why men and women of reason and rationale go out of their ways to avoid it, but for those who are inadequate of the world and its many complexities, it is the perfect rallying call for those mindless throngs who seek answers elsewhere rather than to peer too deeply into reality. This type of fundamentalism, whether Christian or Islamic, reflects a basic weakness in dealing with the real world and moderninity. There is little difference between the Christian fundamentalist and the Islamic fundamentalist or for that matter any fundamentalist—most are seeking not a return to fundamentals, but a return to when the world lived in ignorance and fear of the unknown.

On God

It is very difficult to speak of religion to anyone and it is that way with many subjects. The only difference is that religion is discussed under the cloak of divinity and absoluteness is invoked without regard to any sense of thought, logic or reasoning by making it seem that what we do not understand must be the work of God. However, with each day that passes new disclosures show that we have been wrong in our mental meandering concerning the unknown. A definite claim can be made that what is unknown will remain unknown until it becomes known and each day that passes diminishes the amount that is unknown, regardless of the existence of God. In fact, after the Biblical crucifixion of Jesus, the active God of the Bible seems to have disappeared from the world and is no longer visible destroying cities, rolling back seas or stopping the sun like he is described as doing in the Old Testament. Emily Dickinson said, "They say God is everywhere, and yet we always think of Him as somewhat of a recluse."

Despite the enormity of tragedies that often afflict mankind, it is difficult to make a case for divine providence. The tragedy for man is just that—a tragedy for man. Only when mankind is involved does it become a tragedy. Long before man appeared on this earth nature ruled the planet. It has only been with the appearance of man that we have come in conflict with nature. Nature is always nature. It would be nature if man were here or not and occurrences of catastrophic events which have been happening since the beginning of time have no tragedy in them without man—they are only nature.

It is natural for man to doubt what he cannot see simply as a defense mechanism. We are afraid of the unknown. We want reassurances. Religions provide this in the form of a benign, loving and caring God. Still, for many this innocuous father figure does not give comfort. Instead, it opens the doors for questions that are difficult to answer and thus, we have atheists. It appears that atheism is man's natural state while religion is a human construct that is exclusively linked to proximity. Religious choice is largely a matter of where one is born and the belief's of ones parents. Anyone born in former East Germany over the past 30 years is likely to be an atheist or nonbeliever, whereas, those born in Rome during the same period are likely to be Christian, just as anyone born during the same time in Egypt is likely to be Muslim. Clearly, the religion of the mother or father is also likely to be the religion of the son or daughter.

Chapter 16

Alternatives and Options

Religion is impervious to logic.

—Paul Kurtz

Universalist Unitarians

> *Unitarian Universalism—Unitarian Universalism is a liberal religion— that is, a religion that keeps an open mind to the religious questions people have struggled with in all times and places. We believe that personal experience, conscience and reason should be the final authorities in religion, and that in the end religious authority lies not in a book or person or institution, but in ourselves. We are a "non-creedal" religion: we do not ask anyone to ascribe to a creed.*
>
> *—Excerpts from "We Are Unitarian Universalists"* [253]

Universalist Unitarians hold a special spot in this writing because of the decidedly different view held by members of these societies and the high participation of Blacks. In many ways, the Unitarian Universalist Church is the traditional church stripped of its mystery and ceremony while keeping its promise of good deeds, community service and solid living without the vengeance or guilt associated with many traditional religions. Too many, this is what makes it attractive—

a religion with only an "up" side. According to the Unitarian Universalist Association, Unitarian Universalists make up less than 1 million adherents on the religious landscape with the majority of American adherents located in Massachusetts, New York and California. Although they are barely a blip on the religious radar, the overall impact of the small denomination has been felt through out the United States because of its dedication to human and civil rights which are two of its touchstones. It is a growing religion that attracts many because of its non-denominational and non-creedal approach.

In addition, The Unitarian Universalist Association elected its first Black president in the denomination's 40-year history two years ago, electing the Rev. William G. Sinkford who succeeds the Rev. John A. Buehrens, who served two four-year terms. Sinkford is not only the first Black UUA president, but he also is the first Black to head any predominately white religious denomination.[254]

A Unitarian Universalist is one of a community of religious persons whose beliefs and ethics are freely chosen and constantly evolving throughout their lives. In general, Unitarian Universalists believe in the oneness or reality of God and think of God as a unity rather than a trinity. They honor the ethical leadership of Jesus without considering him their final religious authority. From a belief standpoint, they rely upon their own reason and personal understanding, while they seek the guidance and inspiration of the great pioneers of religious insight of many cultures and various traditions.

Unitarian Universalists believe in the worth of all human beings and recognize their responsibility to help create a just and peaceful social order for all peoples. They believe that significant meaning and value can be discovered in life on earth without necessarily affirming a life after death. They believe in the principles of freedom, trusting that a free society provides maximum opportunity for all persons to find and enjoy the good life. They have organized churches as free religious communities in which they can unite for the celebration of life, for sharing values, for service, and for comfort-without being required to accept a dogmatic creed. The majorities of Unitarian Universalists do not believe in or question the existence of a deity or deities and often describe themselves as agnostics, atheists, humanists, free thinkers or skeptics. About one in four identifies themselves to be Christian.[255, 256]

Unitarian Universalists share the following beliefs—that:[257]

Each person, because of her/his humanity inherently has dignity and worth.

Each person seek his/her unique spiritual path, based upon their personal life experience, the use of reason and meditation, the findings of science and her/his fundamental beliefs concerning deity, humanity, and the rest of the universe.

The prime function of a clergyperson and congregation is to help the individual members to grow spiritually.

All the great religions of the world, and their sacred texts, have worth.

There should be no barrier to membership, such as compulsory adherence to a creed.

Their lives, their congregations and association are governed by the concepts of democracy, religious freedom and religious tolerance.

In spite of their relatively small numbers, Unitarian Universalists have played important roles in American history, as many of the framers of the constitution were Unitarians. Unitarians have also played major roles in the battle for equal rights directing much of their effort towards achieving equality for everyone regardless of race, gender, sexual orientation or religious orientation. Within a single congregation, there will be some individuals who are unsure of the existence of God(s) and Goddess(es). Others believe in no deity, a single deity or many deities. They hold various views on life after death, including complete annihilation of the person, some form of afterlife removed from earth, or reincarnation. They are free to have beliefs that parallel those of conservative Christians; but few do so. They have adopted what is positive from other religions of the world and left behind the elements that are divisive, mean-spirited and cruel. In addition, nearly 50 percent of Unitarian Universalists ministers are female, which is by far more than any other religion in the United States. [258]

In many ways humanists, agnostics and atheists are very similar in that they all nourish freethought and a stated respect for the individual to live a full and fruitful life on this earth without a religious creed or dogma. It is this aspect that attracts many to the doors of Unitarian Universalist societies. It is the Church without the strict dogma that has turned many way away from religion altogether and it is for these reasons that I have included them along with freethinkers, agnostics, skeptics and nonbelievers.

HUMANISM

> *"...Humanism has at its core the belief that the welfare of humanity—rather than divinity—is of central importance..."*

Humanism is a distinct alternative to traditional religion in that it is a system of good conduct and practical living that does not rely upon gods or other supernatural forces to solve problems or provide guidance for conduct. It is a philosophical stance that promotes individuals as the master of their fate, using education, reason and critical intelligence to solve human problems. Accordingly, moral behavior is strictly up to the individual, as humanists believe that it is possible to form ethical choice on rational intelligence, moral growth and development without the need for religion or the supernatural.

Humanists believe that life has meaning on its own without the need for a supernatural afterlife to find fulfillment in living. Rather, humanists believe that the "good life" can be achieved in the here and now, on earth, through positive thinking, enlightened self-interest and the sharing of ideas. Key to the humanist philosophy is the reliance on the methodology of science as the most reliable source of information about what is factual or true about the universe. In line with that philosophy, humanists emphasize the importance of education, reason and critical intelligence for solving human problems and understanding the world around them. The defining thought behind humanism is that it seeks to free men, not to limit them.

What Is Secular Humanism? [259]

Secular Humanism is a term, which has come into use in the last thirty years to describe a worldview with the following elements and principles:

A conviction that dogmas, ideologies and traditions, whether religious, political or social, must be weighed and tested by each individual and not simply accepted on faith.

Commitment to the use of critical reason, factual evidence, and scientific methods of inquiry, rather than faith and mysticism, in seeking solutions to human problems and answers to important human questions.

A primary concern with fulfillment, growth, and creativity for both the individual and humankind in general.

A constant search for objective truth, with the understanding that new knowledge and experience constantly alter our imperfect perception of it.

A concern for this life and a commitment to making it meaningful through better understanding of ourselves, our history, our intellectual and artistic achievements, and the outlooks of those who differ from us.

A search for viable individual, social and political principles of ethical conduct, judging them on their ability to enhance human well-being and individual responsibility.

A conviction that with reason, an open marketplace of ideas, good will, and tolerance, progress can be made in building a better world for ourselves and our children.

AFRICAN AMERICANS FOR HUMANISM

> *African Americans for Humanism (AAH) is engaged in developing humanism in the African American community. We exist for those who are unchurched or free from religion and who are looking for a rational and ethical approach to life. Our organization believes that the solving of problems and attainment of happiness are rooted in reason, free inquiry, and critical thinking. We do not embrace ESP, astrology, numerology, or any other paranormal belief. We strive to deal with the problems of the world by fully developing our minds and properly analyzing ethical ideas.*

African Americans for Humanism (AAH) grew in response to the large numbers of Blacks who follow fundamentalist religions or who are unchurched and unaware of the humanism in the Black community. It seeks to develop wisdom and good conduct through living in the Black community by using rational and scientific methods of inquiry.[260] Founded by Norm Allen Jr., African Americans for Humanism disseminates the secular humanist message in the Black community, and promotes reason and understanding as paths to betterment for African Americans.

Allen is the Executive Director of the African Americans for Humanism organization (http://www.secularhumanism.org/aah/index.htm) and author of *African American Humanism: An Anthology*. Mr. Allen's latest book, *The Black Humanist Experience: An Alternative to Religion* is a compilation of African American humanists talking about why they left traditional religion behind and embraced humanism. He is also the editor of the *African American Humanist Newsletter*. Based in Buffalo, New York, the *African American Humanist Newsletter* publishes articles relating to humanist activities, the separation of church and state and a variety of essays and articles relating to humanism and free thought.

As well as publishing its own newsletter, AAH presents the humanist viewpoint to the African-American media.[261] AAH strongly opposes racism and challenges long held beliefs, which have consistently kept African Americans at a disadvantage socially, politically, and economically. Mr. Allen believes that AAH can help fight racism through humanistic education and by utilizing a strong humanist heritage, African Americans will have a better understanding of their problems and the potential solutions.

> *The need for critical thinking skills and a humanistic outlook in our world is great. This is no less true in the Black community than in others. Many*

African Americans have been engulfed by religious irrationality, conned by self-serving "faith healers", and swayed by dogmatic revisionist historians. Many others, however, have escaped the oppression of such delusions, and live happy and upstanding lives free of superstition. African Americans for Humanism (AAH) exists to bring these secular humanists together, to provide a forum for communication, and to facilitate coordinated action. In an irrational world, those who stand for reason must stand together.

—Norm Allen Jr.

Humanism and Atheism

Are humanists atheists? Most would probably describe themselves as being atheist or agnostic in the strict sense of the words. Their stance of disbelief is based on their philosophy that there is insufficient evidence to claim that God has in any fashion intervened in human history or revealed himself to a chosen few. Although atheism stresses intellect, humanist believe it is not enough as life involves passion and the search for meaning, which humanist believe can be adequately supplied by life as it is without resorting to supernatural explanations of mysteries. For humanists it is not enough to reject faith and religion but insists that humanists must engage in finding new channels of meaning and purpose in the present to make humanism a positive alternative to atheism. Humanism stresses the positive aspects of life and living and seeks ways to improve life in the present tense through the use of the intellect, reason and logic.

Appendix:

History of Black Nonbelief and Skepticism, etc.

"The Bible is a wonderful source of inspiration for those who don't understand it."

—*George Santayana*

Searching history for Black nonbelievers and freethinkers is like trying to find a lump of coal in the dark. Since only 4-12 percent of the population is identified as nonbelievers, it is easy to see why the search would be difficult. Nonbelievers and freethinkers represent a distinct and often unpopular minority. In the United States, Black nonbelievers represent a minority within a minority that is not inclined to make its presence known in an even more hostile Black community. The history of religion in the Black community fills tome upon tome, but there is little or no mention of nonbelief or freethought as an alternate life style. In most cases, nonbelief and freethought is spoken of as an aberration.

Considerable information exists concerning white nonbelievers and freethinkers, but in comparison, the amount of data about Black nonbelief is so small as to be almost nonexistent. Therefore, this writing is hardly exhaustive of the subject, it merely scratches the surface as much of Black oral history has been neglected and along with it, much of the tradition of skepticism that has long been part of the lives of Black men and women. An undercurrent of freethought has long flowed through the Black community but has remained hidden under a cloak of respectability, pretense and denial of such proportions, that nonbelievers and freethinkers in the Black community often pretend to be religious to avoid difficulty.

Despite the end of slavery in 1865 with the enactment of the Emancipation Proclamation, Black people in America continued to suffer its effects well into the 20th century. Slavery was replaced with Jim Crow laws and Blacks still suffered overt and often violent racism. It was the start of the great migration of Blacks from Ku Klux Klan saturated hearts of Dixie to the industrialized Mecca's of northern cities like New York, Chicago and Philadelphia.

Upon arriving in the North, things were quite different than most had imagined and in many ways worse than it had been in the South. This led to a resurgence of religion for some but for many it started a search for more concrete answers and communism and socialism became attractive alternatives for those looking for acknowledgement and action.

Although there were hints of nonbelief as far back as the beginning of slavery, it wasn't until what came to be known as the Harlem Renaissance that the undercurrent of nonbelief and freethought finally burst to the surface. Because of its large Black population, New York City became the focal point of an Black resurgence which produced a wealth young radical activists and freethinkers like Hubert H. Harrison, J. A. Rogers, George S. Schuyler, John G. Jackson, Asa Phillip Randolph and Chandler Owen among others and over the years that unexpressed undercurrent found its way to the surface in the voices and the pens of social activists, iconoclasts and intellectuals all over the world.

Although information during this period is rich and full, information concerning the identification of this mixture of agnostics, atheists, freethinkers and skeptics is difficult to document. Although all of the men and women listed wrote or spoke about their personal beliefs in the various articles and books they authored, in many cases their true beliefs are gathered through inference. Another problem with doing this kind of research is that many "Black" historians have seen fit to overlook or even misidentify the "religious" orientation of these notable men and women.

The following list was compiled from variety of researchers and sources. Much of the information has been taken directly from named sources or paraphrased for conciseness. The list reflects a variety of freethinkers, skeptics and nonbelievers from the community of African descent. The size of the entry has no bearing on importance. These brief biographies are in no way meant to be all inclusive nor totally reflective of an individual's entire life, rather, they are intended as brief markers along the river of thought concerning nonbelief and freethought in the Black community and the people who have contributed to that steady flow.

Atheists, Freethinkers, Nonbelievers, Skeptics, Etc.

Kelly Abbey—A New York "atheist and proud of it." "I lived across the street from a church and made many trips there, but I eventually made up my own mind about religion."[262]

Niitse Akufo Awnku Ado-Dwanka—Ado-Dwanka is a rationalist and a nuclear physicist with a Ph.D. from Cambridge.[263]

David Allen—David Allen is a writer from the Washington, D.C. area and a member of the African Americans for Humanism Advisory Board.[264]

Norm R. Allen Jr—As Executive Director of African-Americans for Humanism, Allen spreads the secular humanist message in the Black community, and promotes reason and understanding as paths to betterment for African Americans. Allen is the author of "African American Humanism: An Anthology." "...I learned that Christianity has about as much originality as a mimeograph machine. I eventually broke free of religion, and I have been much happier and more confident as a result. And today, I use my "God-given" talent to bash the supposed God every chance I get." [265]

James Andrews—Andrews is a professor of mathematics at Florida State University and is a member of the African Americans for Humanism Advisory board.[266]

Freda Amakye Ansah—She is a member of the Rational Centre in Accra, Ghana and an outspoken critic of female circumcision and the early marriage of African women.[267]

Amenhotep III—Believed to have lived in the fourth century, Amenhotep III is one of the oldest individuals listed as a heretic.[268]

Brenda Anthony—Rappers, Brenda Anthony and Tracy Slocum are the hip-hop duo known as Razen Kane. "We're humanists, we're artists, we're positive, and we're proud freethinkers. We're tired of being stepped on by these God-loving, God fearing record companies. We notice all of the rappers screaming, 'Lord, Lord,' while their killing is paying off." [269]

Saundra Brown Asante—Saundra is a Unitarian Universalist. She is a health educator a self-described "recovering Seventh Day Adventist from Washington, D.C.

Richard B. Boddie—Although his father, grandfather and great grandfather (Charles Emerson Boddie, Jacob Benjamin Boddie and Cooley E. Boddie) were all Baptist ministers, dating back to African slavery in America, Richard Benjamin (aka Dick) Boddie has always been a free thinker, then a skeptic and since the early 1980s, a renowned Libertarian activist. Once an anti-war student radical, Boddie was active in the student takeover and closing of Syracuse University on May 5, 1970, the day after the Kent State University massacre. Now living in Southern California, Boddie who received his Bachelors Degree in Political Science from Bucknell University (Pennsylvania) in 1961, also holds a law degree from Syracuse. A Libertarian/Objectivist freethinker "and a religious agnostic at best, or at least", Boddie's career has spanned bank management; the law; third party neutral dispute and conflict resolution; radio and television; corporate/business marketing and sales; being an Ombudsman; an adjunct college professor; lecturer; writer; professional motivational speaker; teacher/trainer; law school director of admissions; author and political candidate. He is also a former AAU Decathlon Champion, who was the Libertarian Party U.S. Senate Candidate in California in 1992 and 1994, after having sought the nomination to be their U.S. Presidential Candidate for 1992. Boddie most recently was a candidate for the U.S. House of Representatives in the 46th District of California. He continues to be a dynamic and entertaining speaker and motivator, and advocate of individual liberty, individual achievement and the free market. And although not actually a religious "believer", he is indeed an enthusiastic "secular evangelist".

Egbert Ethelred Brown—(1875-1956) A Universalist Unitarian, Brown founded the Harlem Community Church. In 1928, Brown changed the name of the church to the Hubert Harrison Memorial Church in honor of the late orator and writer. The name of the church was again changed in 1937 to The Harlem Unitarian Church. He was a founder and the first president of the Montego Bay Literary and Debating Society in Jamaica, and helped organize the Negro Progressive Association and the Liberal Association in Kingston. He founded the Jamaica Progressive League and was chairman of the British Jamaican Benevolent Association and vice-president of the Federation of Jamaican Organizations. In 1936, Brown became first Secretary of the Jamaica Progressive League. [270, 271]

Herb Brown—Civil rights and human rights activist and member of the Central Ohio Chapter of American Atheists.[272]

Sterling A. Brown—(1901-1989) A poet and humanist, Brown was another writer of the Harlem Renaissance whose "fundamental assertion of a humanistic vision is rooted in the democratic principles of the U.S. Constitution".[273]

Josef ben-Jochannan—Dr. Yosef ben-Jochannan a scholar of Black-African history. He has studied at Cambridge University and the University of Barcelona and is multilingual. Originally a graduate in civil engineering, he developed skills in history, philosophy, law, and earned his doctorate degree in cultural anthropology. Dr. Yosef ben-Jochannan was adjunct professor at Cornell University. He has written and published over forty-nine books and papers, revealing much of the information unearthed while he was in Egypt. Two of his better-known works include, "Black Man of the Nile and His Family" and "Africa: Mother of Major Western Religions". Over five decades have passed and Dr. ben-Jochannan, a preeminent scholar and Egyptologist, remains focused on Nile Valley Civilization. He is a 390° Mason of The Craft. "I say the Black [sic] man has called upon Jesus Christ for so many years here in America, and now he starts calling on Mohammed and there are many who are calling on Moses, and at no time within this period has the Black [sic] man's situation changed, nor has the Black [sic] man any freedom. It is obvious that someone didn't hear his call or isn't interested in that call—either Jesus, Moses, or Mohammed." [274, 275]

James Baldwin—(1922-1987) One of America's greatest writers, activist and humanist, James Baldwin was a prolific writer producing such pieces as his first major novel, "Go Tell It On The Mountain." Baldwin produced plays like "Blues for mister Charlie" and wrote a screenplay on the life of Malcolm X, which later became a blueprint for Spike Lee's movie, Malcolm X. Baldwin's "Giovanni's Room" is considered by many a precursor to the gay liberation movement although he steadfastly refused to painted as a gay writer.[276, 277]

Chauncey Bell—(1901-1993) Bell went from a porter in a cleaning plant to a wealthy businessman and ardent atheist. He attended Fisk University through high school and graduated from the University of Chicago. Born of mixed parents, Bell said, "...my degree didn't mean a thing because I was officially Negro. All I could get was a job as a porter." However, Bell learned from his job as porter and used his knowledge to start his own business and become very wealthy. He studied paleontology, geology and biology and was a life member of Chicago's world famous Field Museum. "That Bible story is absolutely foolish. Anybody who knows anything about the history of this world knows that the basis of not only Christian religion, but every other religion is foolishness—utter nonsense." [278]

William Waring Cuney—(1906-1976) Cuney is a lesser-known writer of the Harlem Renaissance. He and Langston Hughes were both attended Lincoln University at the same time and became friends. His poem "No Images" has remained popular over the years and has been recorded by numerous artists, including Lou Rawls.[279] His first collection of poems, Puzzles, wasn't published until 1960. His second collection, Storefront Church, wasn't published until 1973.[280]

Frank Crosswaith—(1892-1965) A political activist and journalist, Frank Rudolph Crosswaithe was a socialist who was part of the labor movement and headed the Negro Labor League with headquarters in Harlem.[281, 282]

John Henrik Clarke—(1915-1998) As a writer and educator Clarke often challenged Black people to question their religious indoctrination. He was a prolific writer and his writings include "Rebellion in Rhyme", "American Negro Short Stories", "Harlem U.S.A.", "Harlem: A Community in Transition", "Malcolm X—The Man and His Times", and "Marcus Garvey and the Vision of Africa". He wrote the introduction to John G. Jackson's "Introduction to African Civilizations".[283, 284]

Deborah Clark—She is the former Director of the Virginia Beach Chapter of American Atheists. She later moved on to hold the same position for the Washington, DC chapter.[285]

Eldridge Leroy Cleaver (1935-1998)—Cleaver was a writer, political activist, and former minister of information for the Black Panther Party. He ran as the Peace and Freedom Party candidate for the 1968 presidential elections. He also worked with Bobby Seale and Huey P. Newton.[286] He later established himself as a gifted essayist, humanist and cultural critic with the publication of "Soul on Ice", a collection of prison writings that earned him the Martin Luther King Memorial Prize in 1970. Prior to his death, Cleaver became a born-again Christian.[287]

Eugene Charrington—Former president of the now defunct Harlem Atheists Association.[288]

Rene Depestre—An activist and poet, Depestre was affiliated with Haiti's' radical left. He edited a revolutionary journal and his Marxists views eventually led to his imprisonment. His poetry is widely available in communist countries. His most popular books include, "A Rainbow for the Christian West" and "Vegetations of Splendor." "Making revolution is the foremost historical evidence, and the foremost cultural value which involves us in a new postulate of reason: I make revolution, therefore I am, and therefore 'WE' are."[289, 290]

Ssekitooleko Deogratias—Deogratias heads The Uganda Humanist Association (UHASSO). The group's motto is 'Toward a Free, Humanitarian, and Scientific World.[291]

Frederick Douglass—(1818-1895) An Abolitionist, freethinker and former slave, Douglass became the world's foremost orator against slavery and a lifelong crusader for reform. Douglass was an orator, intellectual and humanist. In 1847, he became editor of the North Star, an abolitionist newspaper. During the Civil War, Douglass helped organize two Black regiments in Massachusetts. After the war was over, he worked in the South to promote civil rights for African Americans. He later secured important positions as marshal of Washington, D.C. and minister to Haiti. Frederick Douglass was a freethinker who knew that getting Black people to become Christians was one of the ways white slave owners had kept Blacks under control. Douglass was a good friend of America's most famous 19th century freethinker, Robert G. Ingersoll. In a Fourth of July speech, Douglass said, "…But the church of this country is not only indifferent to the wrongs of the slave; it actually takes sides with the oppressors. It has made itself the bulwark of American slavery, and the shield of American slave-hunters." [292, 293]

Cheikh Anta Diop—(1923-1986) Senegalese historian and humanist, he is noted for his study of the crucial role played by Black Egyptian peoples. His book "The African Origin of Civilization: Myth or Reality" created a major stir. His other published works include, "The Cultural Unity of Black Africa" and "Precolonial

Black Africa". An avid political activist, he served as Secretary-General of the Rassemblement Democratique Africain (RDA) and helped establish the first Pan-African Student Congress in Paris in 1951. He also participated in the First World Congress of Black Writers and Artists held in Paris in 1956.[294] His first major work, "The African Origin of Civilization: Myth or Reality" (1955) is still disturbing the white historians. The book refutes the myth of Egypt as a white nation and shows its southern African origins.[295] His dissertation to the Sorbonne in 1951, based on the premise that Egypt of the pharaohs was an African civilization—was rejected. Regardless, this dissertation was published by Presence Africaine under the title Nations Negres et Culture in 1955 and won him international acclaim. In 1960, he published "The Cultural Unity of Black Africa" and "Precolonial Black Africa".[296]

Emanuel dos Santos—A Trinidadian, dos Santos edited the freethought magazine, "Progress." [297]

W. A. Domingo—W.A. Domingo was a Socialist Party member. He briefly edited Marcus Garvey's newspaper, The Negro World. Subsequently, he helped found the pro-independence Jamaican Progressive League in New York City in 1936. Some historians credit W. A. Domingo with first stating the "New Negro" philosophy.[298, 299]

Angela Yvonne Davis—At an early age Davis joined Advance, a Marxist-Leninist youth group with ties to the Communist Party. She served on the board of the National Alliance Against Racism and Political Repression, an organization she helped found with Charlene Mitchell. In the Fall of 1995, she was appointed to the University of California at Santa Cruz Presidential Chair and became a consultant to the PhD program there. Davis has written several books on gender and class issues, and is a major figure in the orthodox Communist Party. [300]

Frank Marshall Davis—(1923-1987) Frank Marshall Davis was a significant figure during the 1930s and 1940s when his works were popular during the Harlem Renaissance. A poet and journalist, Davis published four collections of poetry including "Black Man's Verse", "I Am the American Negro", "Through Sepia Eyes" and "47th Street Poems". He also was known for his journalistic innovation and served as editor for the Chicago Evening Bulletin, the Chicago Whip, the Chicago Star and the Atlanta World. Much of Davis's life remained shrouded in mystery until the Black Arts Movement during the 1960's and 1970's stirred a renewed interest in his work.[301, 302]

W.E.B. DuBois—(1868-1963) Critic, editor, scholar, author and civil rights leader, Dr. William Edward Burghardt DuBois is one of the most influential Blacks of the twentieth century. DuBois' "The Souls of Black Folk" was selected to be among the "100 Humanist Events That Changed the World" over the past 1,000 years by the editor of Free Inquiry Magazine. [303] One of the founders of the National Association for the Advancement of Colored (NAACP) in 1909, DuBois served as that organization's director of publications and editor of "Crisis" magazine until 1934. A noted anti-cleric, in 1944, DuBois returned from Atlanta University to become head of the NAACP'S special research department, a post he held until 1948. Dr. DuBois emigrated to Africa in 1961 and became editor-in-chief of the Encyclopedia Africana, an enormous publishing venture which had been planned by Kwame Nkrumah. DuBois died in Ghana in 1963 at the age of 95. His numerous books include "The Suppression of the Slave Trade", "The Philadelphia Negro" and "The Souls of Black Folk." [304]

David Eaton—A Universalist Unitarian minister, Eaton was initially refused entrance to seminary, but in 1969 he was called to serve All Souls Church in Washington, DC, a congregation that was 90 percent white. At that time, there were 15 African American clergy and 199 women in the Universalist Unitarian denomination. A David Eaton Scholarship for $2500.00 per year has been established for African American woman in or preparing for seminary dedicated to creating an anti-racist, multi-cultural religious organization and country.[305]

Charles W. Faulkner—Dr. Faulkner is a behavioral counselor and syndicated newspaper columnist in Washington, D.C. who has published more than 1400 articles. He is also a member of the African Americans for Humanism Advisory Board. Dr. Faulkner served as a college instructor for twenty years. He also has a nightclub show, as a Stage Hypnotist and has presented the show all over the country. In addition, Dr. Faulkner has appeared on radio and television nearly one hundred times to discuss to discuss human behavior, especially hypnotherapy. Specializing in motivational seminars and educational consultation, Faulkner says he was "Inclined toward humanism since early high school, although regular church attendee for my early years [in sync with my religious doctrinaire family]. I never completely bought the idea of a Supreme Being, although I, at first, did not question it openly. Initially, I considered myself an agnostic." "I attempted to incorporate logic into religion. It didn't work. Every time that I asked for 'evidence', I was sternly told to be more studious in my study of the Bible and pray more. Humanism and its fearless logic can open the door to freethinking and freedom for all people, especially African-Americans."

Dr. Faulkner is working a book concerning the humanist approach to personal problem resolution.[306, 307]

James Forman—Civil Rights activist and self-proclaimed atheist, James Forman, was the former executive secretary of the Student Nonviolent Coordinating Committee (SNCC). He also served as president of the Unemployment and Poverty Action Council (UPAC). Foreman has also written several books including "Sammy Young Jr.", "The Political Thought of James Forman" and "The Makings of Black Revolutionaries" in which he devotes an entire chapter to his atheism. In 1994, he was presented with the African American Humanist of the Year award in Orlando, Florida at the Free Inquiry Convention.

Frantz Fanon—(1925-1961) A psychoanalyst and philosopher was a leading theoretician of Black consciousness and identity, nationalism and its failings. His best known work is "Peau noire, masques blancs" (Black Skin, White Masks) which had a major influence on civil rights, anti-colonial, and Black consciousness movements around the world. In "Masks" Fanon argued that white colonialism imposed an existentially false and degrading existence upon its Black victims to the extent that it demanded their conformity to its distorted values.[308, 309]

James Farmer—James Farmer was an educator, humanist, administrator, and one of the founders of the Congress of Racial Equality-CORE. In 1998, President Bill Clinton awarded him the Congressional Medal of Freedom, the nation's highest civilian award. He also attended Divinity School but later decided to work in another area.[310]

Rothchild Francis—He was an editor on a freethought newspaper in the Virgin Islands.[311]

Gregory Gross—Gross has been a member of the Central Ohio Chapter of American Atheists. He is an accomplished musician and writer for the American Atheist magazine.[312]

Ken Hamblin—Known as the "Black Avenger, Hamblin hosts a regular conservative radio talk show out of Denver, CO.[313]

Leonard Harris—Leonard Harris is a Professor of Philosophy at Purdue University. He received the Alain L. Locke Award in recognition for pioneering efforts and outstanding contributions to research in Africana. Books he has written or edited include "Critical Pragmatism of Alain Locke" and "The Philosophy of Alain Locke".[314]

Alex Palmer Haley—(1925-1992) American biographer, scriptwriter and author who became famous with the publication of the novel "Roots", which traces his ancestry back to Africa. In 1977, Roots won the National Book Award and a special Pulitzer Prize. The United States Senate passed a resolution paying tribute to Haley, comparing "Roots" to "Uncle Tom's Cabin" by Harriet Beecher Stowe in the 1850s. ABC Broadcasting adapted the book to television for a mini-series that attracted a record setting 130 million viewers. Haley's first success as a writer came in 1965 when he wrote "The Autobiography of Malcolm X". Haley wasn't without his critics. Harold Courlander filed a suit charging that Roots plagiarized his novel "The African". Courlander received a $650,000 settlement in 1978 after several passages in Roots were found to be almost verbatim from "The African".[315]

Lorraine Hansberry—(1921-1965) Hansberry became the first African-American and the fifth woman to win the New York Drama Critics' Award for her landmark play, "A Raisin in the Sun." A civil rights activist, Hansberry died of cancer at 34. Her lesbianism remained hidden long after her death until scholars brought it to light in the 1980s. [316, 317, 318]

Hubert H. Harrison—(1883-1927) Harrison was considered one of the foremost intellects of his time. He was an accomplished speaker and made a name for himself as a soapbox orator. He was self-educated and was considered by many to be an intellectual genius. His ability to read Hebrew, Greek, Latin and Arabic aided in his studies of the Bible. An ardent atheist and against superstition, Harrison held that any Black man who accepted Christianity needed to have his head examined. In his rejection of Christianity Harrison said he refused "to worship a lily-white God and a Jim Crow Jesus". Harrison was a respected lawyer in his early twenties. At 24, he was writing reviews for the New York Times, New York Sun and Tribune.[319, 320, 321, 322, 323]

Walter Everette Hawkins—(1915-) Hawkins edited "The Poet's Corner" of The Messenger. He published his own poetry in the African Times and Orient Review of London. His writings included "Negro Poets and Their Poems," and "Chords and Dischords." His letter to the Truth Seeker Magazine which was often hostile toward Blacks, won the magazine's contest for the best letter on the topic: "Why I Became an Atheist." under his pen name Gaultheria Quinoas.[324, 325]

Langston Hughes—(1902-1967) His life and work helped shape the artistic contributions of the Harlem Renaissance of the 1920s. In 1924, Hughes first book of poetry, "The Weary Blues", was published. Hughes is particularly known for his insightful, colorful portrayals of Black life in America from the twenties through the sixties. He wrote novels, short stories and plays, as well as poetry, and is also known for his engagement with the world of jazz and the influence it had on his writing."[326, 327]

Dr. Willis Nathaniel Huggins—A Pan-Africanize and collaborator with John G. Jackson specializing in African history. Before teaming up with Jackson to produce historic research, Huggins was Jackson and John Henrik Clarke's mentor.[328]

Gladman C. Humbles—He was the first Black firefighter in Paducah, Kentucky and the first Black president of the International Firefighter's Union. He has received two awards for outstanding leadership as the president of the Paducah NAACP.[329]

Zora Neale Hurston—(1901-1960) She was the author of seven full length novels and over one hundred other publications including short stories, plays and articles, Hurston went unrecognized by the literary community and died impoverished. Her work was "rediscovered" In the 1970's and has generated much interest. Here writings include, "Jonah's Gourd Vine", "Mules and Men", "Tell My Horse" and "Their Eyes Were Watching God" of which the latter two have stirred much interest because of their reference to Voudon or Voodoo. The name "Tell My Horse" came from a phrase used in Voodoo ceremonies where the person becomes possessed by a spirit and is ridden like a horse by the spirit.[330, 331, 332]

Leo Igwe—Leo Igwe is the Executive Secretary of the Nigerian Humanist Movement, Development Policy Centre of Nigeria.[333]

Patrick Inniss—Inniss is a columnist with The Secular Humanist Press. He also edits the newsletter of the Humanists of Washington and is a member of the African Americans for Humanism Advisory Board.[334]

John G. Jackson—(1907-1993) John Glover Jackson was a noted educator, lecturer, author and historian. He said he had been an atheist since he could think. He wrote for the Truth Seeker Magazine and was a writer and associate of the Rationalist Press Association in London. He also lectured at the "Ingersoll Forum" of the American Association for the Advancement of Atheism from 1930 to 1955. He co-authored "A Guide to the Study of African History" with his mentor Dr. Willis Nathaniel Huggins, in 1934. In 1937, he and Dr. Huggins authored "Introduction to African Civilizations." Jackson also authored "Ethiopia and the Origin of Civilization." In 1974, he completed "Introduction to African Civilizations". Jackson taught and lectured for the Black Studies Department of Rutgers University from 1971 until 1973. From 1973 to 1977, he was a Visiting Professor at the University of New York and later held the same position at the Northeast Illinois University until 1980. He also wrote "Pagan Origins of the Christ Myth", "Man, God and Civilization," and "Christianity Before Christ" and which he completed in 1985 all of which brought continued recognition and controversy.[335]

Ishmael Jaffree—Ishmael Jaffree is responsible for the law forbidding school prayer. An Alabama attorney, Jaffree filed the case after his children were required to take part in school prayer. It was a landmark case and in 1985, the Supreme Court agreed with Jaffree saying, "States have no greater power to restrain the individual freedoms protected by the First Amendment than does the Congress of the United States." Jaffree is a frequent contributor to the AAH Newsletter and is a member of the African Americans for Humanism Advisory Board.[336]

William R. Jones—Universalist Unitarian and author of "Is God a White Racist?", Dr. William R. Jones is an internationally recognized scholar in the areas of Multiculturalism, Liberation Theology, and Oppression. Due in large part to programs developed by Dr. Jones, FSU has become a national leader in the production of African American doctorates across the disciplines. Dr. Jones has been the recipient of myriad humanitarian, teaching, and scholarly awards. Among them are the Martin Luther King, Jr. Distinguished Service Award (1986) and the American Humanist Association Humanist Pioneer of the Year (1992). He is currently at work on two books outlining "the Jones Analytical Method" and "the Jones Oppression Grid: The Mis-Religion of the Negro and Oppression: The Good That People Do." [337]

Bill T. Jones—A 1994 recipient of a Macarthur Fellowship, he was co-founder of the American Dance Asylum in 1973, before forming the Bill T. Jones/Arnie

Zane Company in 1982. He choreographed and performed internationally as a soloist and with his late partner, Arnie Zane. He has created dances for modern and ballet companies including Alvin Ailey American Dance Theater, Boston Ballet, Lyon Opera Ballet, Berkshire Ballet, Berlin Opera Ballet, Diversions Dance Co., and others.[338]

James Weldon Johnson—Johnson is best known as the author of the Black national anthem "Lift Every Voice and Sing", but he was a versatile man whose career included being an educator, novelist, diplomat, publisher, poet and lawyer. He was the first Black admitted to the Florida Bar and in 1906 at the urging of Booker T. Washington, President Theodore Roosevelt appointed him U.S. Consul to Venezuela and later he held the same position in Nicaragua. During his stint as U.S. Consul, Johnson wrote "The Autobiography of an Ex-Coloured Man." After leaving government service, Johnson took a position with the newly formed NAACP and in 1920; he became general secretary of that organization. It was during his service with the NAACP that his first book of poetry "Fifty Years and Other Poems" appeared. He followed that with "The Book of American Negro Poetry in 1922 and then he established his literary reputation when he published "God's Trombones" in 1927. Johnson was killed in a train-car-train crash in 1938 as he traveled to his summer home in Maine. In his autobiography, "Along the Way", he confessed that religion meant nothing to him. He could prove neither the existence nor the nonexistence of God, so he concluded that he was an agnostic.[339]

Makeda Judkins—She is the president of the National Association of Mental Stressed African American Families and a member of the African Americans for Humanism Advisory Council.[340]

Alfred Kisubi—Kisubi is Assistant Professor of Human Services at the University of Wisconsin-Oshkosh. He writes a syndicated column called "The Africans: 'Our' and 'Their' Perspective in this Global Village."[341]

Nu Otto Kwame II—He considers himself a rationalist and has given land for the Rationalist Centre of Ghana. Kwame is also chief of the village where the donated land for the Rationalist Centre will be located. A former accountant, as chief of the village he serves as a combination of social worker, counselor, priest, and medicine man who must deal with the problems of his six thousand villagers in ways set down by long-established tradition.[342]

Alton Lemon—Alton Lemon is the best know for the "Lemon Test." The Lemon Test is the Supreme Court standard for judging separation of church and state. The Lemon Test, named after plaintiff Alton Lemon, is a three-pronged test first employed by the Supreme Court in Lemon v. Kurtzman (1971). Over the last 25 years, it has been used by the Supreme Court and many lower courts in deciding church-state separation cases. The Lemon Test states that a law is in violation of the constitutional separation of church and state, unless it meets all of these three criteria: 1. It must have a secular legislative purpose 2. Its principal or primary effect must be one that neither advances nor inhibits religion 3. It must not foster excessive entanglement with religion. Lemon served as President and Vice President of the Philadelphia Ethical Society and is a member of the American Civil Liberties Union (ACLU). During the sixties Lemon was an advisor for the U.S. Department of Housing and Urban Development and he was once the Program Director the North City Congress Police-Community Relations Program in Philadelphia.[343]

Alaine Leroy Locke—(1885-1954) Locke was an intellectual, educator and editor of "The New Negro", the anthology credited with defining the Harlem Renaissance. Locke graduated Harvard University, where he was elected to Phi Beta Kappa and received a B.A. in philosophy magna cum laude in 1907. He was also a Rhodes scholar. Locke edited an issue of the Survey Graphic subtitled, Harlem: Mecca of the New Negro, which included poetry, fiction, and essays by W. E. B. DuBois, James Weldon Johnson, Langston Hughes, Countee Cullen, Jean Toomer, and Anne Spencer who were considered the best and the brightest Black America had yet produced.[344]

Mike McBryde—McBryde is a freelance writer and artist from Pittsburgh and is a member of the African American for Humanism Advisory Board.[345]

Claude McKay—(1890-1948) McKay was a poet and humanist.[346] His popular poem "If We Must Die" helped to initiate the Harlem Renaissance of the 1920s. Between 1922 and 1934, he lived in Great Britain, Russia, Germany, France, Spain, and Morocco. His writings include four volumes of poems, many essays and his autobiography, "A Long Way from Home". McKay joined the Catholic shortly before his death.[347, 348, 349]

Thelma "Butterfly" McQueen—(1911-1995) McQueen, was best known for depicting Prissy in the movie "Gone with the Wind." She gained her unusual name after dancing in a butterfly ballet as a child in a production of "A Midsummer Night's Dream." She quit movie acting in 1947 to avoid further typecasting, although she returned as a maid on the TV show "Beulah" in 1950-1953. She appeared occasionally on Broadway and returned to films in 1974, playing Clarice in "Amazing Grace" and Ma Kennywick in "Mosquito Coast" in 1986 with Harrison Ford. That same year she appeared in a PBS version of "The Adventures of Huckleberry Finn."[350]

Emmanuel Kofi Mensah—Is the founder of Action for Humanism in Nigeria. He is the editor of the humanist newsletter, "Sunrays", and is on the Advisory Board of African Americans for Humanism.[351]

Richard B. Moore—He was a Black socialists' and Caribbean militant. In 1960, he published "The Name 'Negro': Its Origin and Evil Use" which was is a comprehensive study of the use and definition of the word, "Negro," connecting its origins too the beginning of the African slave trade. Moore shows how the name, "Negro," was used to separate people of African descent and confirm their supposed inferiority.[352]

Monica G. Moorehead—She was the 2001, presidential nominee of the Workers World Party. Moorehead is a former schoolteacher and has been a. militant unionist and communist political organizer, since the 1970s. She was a Contributing Editor for Workers World newspaper, during the 1990s and is Co-Author of, Feminism and Marxism in the 90's.[353]

Ayida S. Mthembu—Mthembu is Assistant Dean of Student Affairs at Massachusetts Institute of Technology and a member of the African American for Humanism Advisory Board. She was selected as the 1997 winner of the YMCA Black Achiever Award at MIT. As part of the program, the winners agree to commit at least 40 hours with youths in the Black Achievers Community Service Program.[354]

Edgar Marese-Smith—He was the president of the National Secularist branch in Trinidad during the 1890s.[355]

Mark D. Morrison-Reed—The Rev. Mark D. Morrison-Reed's groundbreaking book, Black Pioneers in a White Denomination, opens eyes about the history of racial injustice in the Universalist Unitarian denomination.[356]

Huey P. Newton—(1942-1989) A political activist and humanist, Newton and Bobby Seale co-founded the Black Panther Party, with Seale as chairman and

Newton as Minister of Defense. Newton was sent to prison in 1967 for manslaughter after a confrontation with Oakland police left a policeman dead. He later fled to Cuba, returning in the late 1970s to face murder and assault charges stemming from an early 1970s incident.[357] The California Court of Appeals reversed his conviction in 1971. He was charged with shooting a prostitute, but after two hung juries, the charges were dropped. Newton earned a PhD from the University of California in 1980 but he continued to have problems with the law and he was charged with embezzling state and federal funds from an educational and nutritional program he headed in 1985 and in 1987, he was convicted of illegal possession of guns. In 1989, he was fatally shot by a low-level drug dealer.[358]

Charles Nichols—Nichols is the former chairman of the Metropolitan Airports Commission in Minneapolis and a member of the Minnesota Atheists Organization.[359]

Kwame Nkrumah—(1909—1972) Known as the Father of African Nationalism, Nkrumah was an African hero. He became an international symbol of freedom as the leader of the first Black African country to break away from colonial rule. The first head of an independent Ghana he was voted Ghana's "Man of the Millennium".[360]

Tony Iyke Nweke—President, Humanist Friendship Centre (IHEU), in Ghana.[361]

Domonic I Ogbonna—A Nigerian humanist, Ogbonna helps the Nigerian Humanist Movement strive to make humanism relevant to ordinary Africans. The group started a newsletter, Humanist Concern. The first issue took a strong stand against female genital mutilation (FGM—sometimes euphemistically called "female circumcision"). The Nigerian Humanist Movement has also produced an educational pamphlet against FGM.[362]

Chijioke Ogwurike—The author of "Concept of Law in English-Speaking Africa" and addressed the Fourth International Humanist and Ethical World Congress held in Paris, 1966.[363]

Jesse Owens—(1913-1980) A Universalist Unitarian, son of a sharecropper and grandson of a slave achieved what no Olympian before him had accomplished. He won four gold medals at the 1936 Olympics. His stunning victories and achievement of four gold medals at the 1936 Olympic games in Berlin has made him the best remembered of all Olympic athletes.[364]

Chandler Owen—(1923-1967) Owen along with A. Phillip Randolph founded The Messenger Magazine in 1917. Both Owen and Randolph were arrested and charged with treason because of their association with the Socialist Party. They were released after no evidence could be found. Owen eventually broke with the Socialist Party to become the editor of the Chicago Bee. He later opened a successful public relations company and remained active in mainstream politics writing speeches for Wendell Wilkie and Thomas Dewey. He also wrote speeches for Dwight D. Eisenhower and Lyndon B. Johnson who both went on to become President of the United States.[365]

Nkeonye Otakpor—Otakpor is senior lecturer in philosophy at the University Benin, Nigeria, and a member of the Executive Board of the Nigerian Philosophical Association.[366]

George Padmore—(1901-1967) A leading activist of Pan-Africanism and Black liberation, Padmore joined the Communist Party in the 1920s. In 1931, he wrote "The Life and Struggles of Negro Toilers". Eventually, he broke away from the Communists and later established the International African Service Bureau, a network that coordinated voluminous correspondence between African and Caribbean nationalists, trade unionists, editors and intellectuals. Padmore's small journal, the International African Opinion, became an invaluable source of information and analysis for Black radicals. Padmore was the mentor and influential theoretician to an entire generation of Black leadership, including Jomo Kenyatta of Kenya and the charismatic Pan-Africanist Kwame Nkrumah of Ghana.[367]

Lucy E. Parsons—(1888-1942) She was an activist during the labor movement of the late 1800s and early 1900s. The daughter of a former slave, Lucy Eldine Parsons became a noted agitator for workers rights. Parsons, a life long atheist, preached revolution as the way to obtain justice for the poor. She came to prominence in Chicago during the famous Haymarket Riot of 1886 where the Chicago police described her as "more dangerous than a thousand rioters. She was one of the first African American women to write against lynching and other racial attacks in the South. She was also involved with labor unions and spoke at a "Religion of Humanity" conference, where she said: "Socialism is the 100-cents-on-a-dollar religion…We have heard enough about a paradise behind the moon. We want something now. We are tired of hearing about the golden streets of the hereafter. What we want is good paved and drained streets in this world.[368]

Nell Irvin Painter—Painter is an Edwards Professor of History at Princeton University and has written extensively about the Black experience in America during the 19th century. Her writings include, "In Sojourner Truth: A Life, A Symbol". Painter received her Ph.D. in American History from Harvard University and studied at the Center for African Studies at the University of Ghana. Her other books include "Exodusters: Black Migration to Kansas after Reconstruction" and "The Narrative of Hosea Hudson: His Life as a Negro Communist in the South".[369]

Anthony Pinn—Dr. Pinn is associate professor at Minnesota's Macalester College religious studies department, teaching courses on African American religion, history of Black religious thought and Black theology. He is the author of several acclaimed books, including "Why Lord? Suffering and Evil in Black Theology" and "Varieties of African American Religious Experience". He is currently researching religion in the African Diaspora and social protest thought in the AME church. His expertise is in Humanism within African American Communities, Liberation Theology, African American religious history and African American intellectual history.[370]

Wendall Potter—A staunch atheist from Detroit, who after years of searching finally accepted his atheism and later wrote an article about it in the Secular Nation, 1995.[371]

Ptah-Hotep—Believed to have lived during the second or third century he was described as an ancient Egyptian moralist.[372]

John Ragland—John is a frequent contributor to the AAH Magazine. He is a former member of the Central Ohio Chapter of American Atheists, including broadcasting the American Atheist Television Forum. In 1985, he was made part of the hierarchy at the American Atheist.[373]

Asa Phillip Randolph—(1923-1979) Randolph organized the Brotherhood of Sleeping Car Porters and eventually became vice-president of the AFL-CIO. He was a key figure in the "March on Washington" protesting the entry of the United States into World War II. Randolph also played a major role in the "March on Washington for Jobs and Freedom" that attracted nearly 400,000 people. Speakers along with Randolph included Dr. Martin Luther King Jr. King who was the final speaker that day and delivered his famous "I Have a Dream" speech. Randolph along with Chandler Owen founded The Messenger Magazine in 1917. Billed as a Journal of Scientific Radicalism, the magazine exhibited the strong atheistic values of the young men. "Our aim is to appeal to reason, to lift our pens above the cringing demagogy of the times, and above the cheap peanut politics of the old reactionary Negro leaders. Patriotism has no appeal to us; justice has. Party has no weight with us; principle has. Loyalty is meaningless; it depends on what one is loyal to. Prayer is not one of our remedies; it depends on what one is praying for. We consider prayer as nothing more than a fervent wish; consequently the merit and worth of a prayer depend upon what the fervent wish is." The A. Philip Randolph Institute was established in 1966 and funded by the AFL-CIO. In 1970, he was selected as Humanist of the Year.[374, 375, 376]

J. Saunders Redding—(1906-1988) Redding was one of the most prominent African-American authors, critics, and educators of the twentieth century. He was the first Black member of an Ivy League faculty, the first Black to serve as a Brown fellow, and the first Black to have his portrait hung in Sayles Hall at Brown University. Redding's books include "To Make a Poet Black, an analysis of African-American poetry" and his 1942 autobiography "No Day of Triumph". As a visiting professor at Brown in 1949, Redding became the first African American to teach at an Ivy League school. His course on Blacks in American literature was the first such course given at a Northern college. After serving as a professor of English at Hampton Institute in Virginia for twenty years, he ended his career as the first African-American professor at Cornell's college of arts and sciences.[377]

Paul Robeson—(1898-1976) Robeson was an athlete, singer, actor, and advocate for the civil rights. He rose to prominence in a time when segregation was legal in the United States. He won a four-year scholarship to Rutgers University and was twice named to the All-American football team. He received the Phi Beta Kappa key in his junior year and graduated as Valedictorian. At Columbia Law School (1919-1923), Robeson met and married Eslanda Cordoza Goode, who was to become the first Black woman to head a pathology laboratory. A noted freethinker, Robeson graduated from Columbia Law School, the third Black man to do so, but he left the practice of law to use his artistic talents in theater and music. He starred in eleven films. Although Robeson was intrigued with communism and was an outspoken critic of the outdated religious practices, he was a member of the AME church most of his life.[378]

Joel A. Rogers—(1883-1966) Joel Augustus Rogers was one of the most prolific and prominent members of The Messenger group and was well known as a scholar and intellectual even though he never finished high school. He was widely recognized as a historian, anthropologist and journalist. Rogers was the first Black war correspondent and during the Ethiopian-Italian War in 1935, Rogers was a correspondent for the Pittsburgh Courier. He was also known for his books. His best known books include "Natures Knows No Color line," "Africa's Gift to America," "World's Great Men of Color" (two volumes) and "Sex and Race" (three volumes. He visited more than sixty countries during his lifetime and spoke Spanish, German, Portuguese and French.[379]

Jacques Roumain—(1907-1944) Roumain was one of the most important figures in Haitian literature. He was an activist, communist, diplomat, and co-founder of the Bureau of Ethnology in 1941. He was a focal point of Haitian intellectual life and resistance in the occupation and post-occupation period. He is most famous for his novel, "The Masters of the Dew".[380]

George Schuyler—(1895-1977) George S. Schuyler became a member of the Messenger in 1923 and eventually became its managing editor. He also contributed articles to popular magazines including Opportunity, Crisis, Modern Quarterly, Nation, American Mercury and American Opinion. Schuyler was always skeptical of the Black church and in 1932, he wrote "On the horizon loom a growing number of iconoclasts and Atheists, young Black [sic] men and women who can read, think, and ask questions, and who impertinently demand to know why Negroes should revere a God who permits them to be lynched, Jim-crowed and disfranchised." In 1928 noted atheist E. Haldeman-Julius published Schuyler's "Racial Intermarriage in the United States" and later published Schuyler's "The Black Man's Burden—Religion." [381]

Arthur A. Schomburg—(1874-1938) A noted historian and bibliographer, Schomberg collected thousands of works on Black culture over his life time and his personal collection was purchased by the Carnegie Corporation and given to the New York Public Library. In 1973, the collection became known as the Schomburg Collection of Negro Literature and History, the name was later changed to the Schomburg Center for Research in Black Culture. Schomburg was also a journalist, editor, lecturer and New York Public Library curator. He co-founded the Negro Society for Historical Research in 1911.[382]

Amy Scott—She was the first African American to join a Universalist Unitarian church (Philadelphia). [383]

Bobby Seale—A revolutionary humanist, Seale together with Huey P. Newton, founded the Black Panther Party for Self Defense in October 1966. With their original Ten Point Program, Seale and Newton called for full employment; decent housing; true history education; an end to economic exploitation; preventive medical health care; fairness in the courts and constitutional democratic civil-human rights for all peoples. Today, Bobby Seale is also Community Liaison with Temple University's Department of African American Studies Africology. He is the author of several books including "A Lonely Rage" and "Seize the Time" which is his best-known work.[384]

Léopold Sédar Senghor—He was among the first African statesmen who led their countries to independence and was a major proponent of a moderate "African socialism". [385]

Tai Solarin—(1922-1994) The Nigerian nationalist and humanist is not well known in the West but he is probably the most famous and controversial atheist and secular humanist in African history. He was an outspoken social critic, educator and received his Ph.D. from the University of London.[386]

Wole Soyinka—Nobel Prize winning playwright, poet and novelist, Soyinka published over 40 works in a career spanning 5 decades. He received his Doctorate from Leeds University and was a dramatist for London's Royal Court Theater. He taught at various universities including Ibada, Lagos and Ife. He won the Nobel Prize for literature in 1986, the first African to win the award. [387, 388]

Luke Stanton—(1960-1993) A Trinidadian humanist, Stanton was a member of AASH. He owned a New York City hairdressing salon. Stanton spent a lifetime trying to overcome his early Catholic upbringing.[389]

Hope N. Tawiah—Is the chairman of the Rational Centre of Ghana whose motto is "Down with Superstition" and is also a member of the African Americans for Humanism Advisory Board.[390]

Thandeke—She is a Universalist Unitarian Theologian. She works with various Unitarian Universalists societies on subjects relating to race.[391]

Ngugi wa Thiong'o—Kenyan humanist, activist and writer. His works include "Weep Not Child", "The River Between" and "A Grain of Wheat".[392]

Melvin B. Tolson—(1898-1966) Poet, activist and educator, Tolson taught at Langston University in Langston, Oklahoma where he also served three terms, from 1954 to 1960, as the town Mayor. Tolson published his first collection, "Rendezvous with America" in 1944. In 1947, he was invited to compose a centennial ode for the African republic of Liberia. "Libretto" sketches a history of the founding of Liberia. He became Professor of English and drama at Langston University in 1947, the same year in which he was appointed poet laureate of Liberia. These appointments climaxed a career that had already included publication of his "Dark Symphony" and "Rendezvous with America". The Tolson Collection of Black Literature and Art, part of the Langston University Libraries holdings, is one of the most extensive collections of its kind in the country. [393, 394]

Charles Ufomadu—Ufomadu is a member of the Bigard Memorial Seminary, Imo State, Nigeria and a member of the African Americans for Humanism Advisory Board. [395]

Franz Vanderpuye—A journalist and former Rational Centre member, is a leading African scholar who writes articles on traditions and religious practices among Ghanaians. Vanderpuye does a humanist program that appears on the Ghanaian Broadcasting Corporation's national television station. He is also a member of the African Americans for Humanism (AAH) Advisory Board.[396]

Alice Walker—Best known for her book "The Color Purple", Walker is a naturalist and activist. The book won the Pulitzer and the American Book Award for 1982-3. "The Color Purple" later became a popular Steven Spielberg movie. Through her novels, short stories, poems and essays, she is outspoken about racism, sexism and other subjects.[397]

Corey G. Washington—Dr. Washington is an Assistant Professor of Philosophy at the University of Washington Washington's work is concerned with questions on the border of philosophy and linguistics. Among his publications are "The Identity Theory of Quotations" in The Journal of Philosophy in 1992, "Use and Mention" in The Encyclopedia of Philosophy.[398]

David M. Washington—Is a freelance artist from Chicago and a member of the African Americans for Humanism Advisory board[399]

Brianna Waters—She founded the Atheist Student Association at the University of Maryland along with Ali Aliabadi.[400]

Dorothy West—(1907-1998) A writer and humanist, West founded the "Challenge", a journal dedicated to creative writing and issues of social and political activism. In 1937, Richard Wright joined her, and they collaborated to form the "New Challenge," a successor to her earlier effort.[401]

Daniel Hale Williams—(1856-1931) Universalist Unitarian, Daniel Hale Williams was a successful African-American physician who was the first doctor to perform a successful heart surgery.[402] He opened and operated his own hospital, "Provident Hospital and Medical Hospital" in Chicago in 1891. With only twelve beds, Provident Hospital was named the first official Black-owned hospital in the United States. Not only was it the first Black-owned hospital, but Williams also provided a staff of both African-American and white doctors. He also opened and maintained a nurses' training school. In 1913, Daniel Hale Williams was the only Black man to be a member of a 100-member group called the American College of Surgeons. He founded and became the first vice-president of the National Medical Association. In 1970, the National Medical Association introduced a bill to Congress to issue a commemorative stamp in his honor. The home that Daniel Hale Williams lived in while he was growing up was made a National Historic Landmark on May 15, 1975.[403]

Annie B. Willis—Willis was director of the Universalist Unitarian Neighborhood House and principal of the Jordan school, a Universalist institution which emphasized character building and self-esteem for African American children.[404]

Kwasi Wiredu—A professor of philosophy at the University of South Florida and former head of the Department of Philosophy at the University of Ghana. He is author of "Philosophy and an African Culture".[405]

Carter G. Woodson—(1875-1950) Humanist, historian and founder of Negro History Week, which has now grown into Black History Month, Woodson dedicated his life to researching and preserving the saga of the African-American experience. In 1915, Woodson founded the Association for the Study of Negro Life and History, now the Association for the Study of Afro-American Life and History Inc. The association was created to promote and preserve African-American history and culture. He is well known for his book "The Miseducation of the Negro."[406]

Celia Parker Woolley—A Universalist Unitarian, she founded the Frederick Douglass Center in South Chicago.[407]

Dr. Bobby E. Wright—(1934-1989) A psychologist, he encouraged freedom from religion among Black folk. Wright was an instructor and psychologist for the Chicago Public School System. He earned a doctorate degree in clinical psychology from the University of Chicago. He was a consultant for the Alcohol/Drug Abuse Mental Health Administration of the Department of Health, Education, and Welfare (HEW), a former president of the National Black Psychologists Association and was a member of the Association for Black Psychologists and the National Alliance for Black School Educators. Wright was also the director of Garfield Park Comprehensive Community Mental Health Center in Chicago. Wright coined the term "mentacide" which he defined as the "deliberate and systematic destruction of a group's minds with the ultimate objective being the extirpation of the group."[408]

Judge Bruce Wright—Retired New York State Supreme Court Justice Bruce "Cut Them Loose Bruce" Wright is well know in the New York State for his candor and commitment. Wright was elected to the Supreme Court in 1982 and went on to serve with distinction until he retired at the mandatory age of 76. "The church is superstition to me. I'm a lawyer, and I look for evidence: haven't seen a Holy Ghost, haven't seen a God or anything of that sort…I have no religion. I am what probably could be called an atheist. Wright picked up the moniker "Cut Them Loose Bruce" because of his policy of setting low bail when he thought it was appropriate, a practice that often came under criticism from his foes. Wright published his thoughts on the American system of justice in Black Robes, White Justice" in 1993, an in depth look into a justice system that Wright asserts is fundamentally unfair to Black Americans.[409]

Richard Nathaniel Wright—(1908-1960) Widely known for his two major works "Native Son" and "Black Boy", many considered Wright to be a literary genius. "Native Son" was national bestseller and was the first book by an African American author to be a Book-of-the Month Club selection. In 1932, Wright joined the communist party because of his disillusionment with the state of race relations in the United States. He quit the party in 1944 but after World War II, he became the subject of FBI monitoring and in 1947 Wright moved to France in frustration with the continued racism he suffered in the United States. Along with author George Plimpton and others, Wright helped found the Paris Review.[410]

Vern Young—Atheist and member of the Minnesota Atheists Organization is a voluntary worker contributing large portions of his time to work for the Courage Center.[411]

Whitney Young—A Unitarian Universalist, Young became the Executive Director of the National Urban League. His mother was a commissioned Postmistress (the first Black to hold that position in the United States). When his death was announced in 1967, the United States Congress passed a joint resolution saying: "His life and his accomplishments reflect much credit upon the entire human race. President Nixon gave the eulogy. It was the first time a President of the United States had ever spoken at the gravesite of a Black person.[412]

AND THE LIST GOES ON

I have only brushed the surface with these short biographies. There is so much more to know about these men and women. For an in depth overview of the African American atheists, agnostics, freethinkers, humanists, skeptics and Unitarian Universalists see "Who's Who In Hell," by Warren Allen Smith, which lists thousands of nonbelievers, skeptics, humanists and freethinkers throughout the world.

About the Author

My interest in this aspect religion is part of the natural inquisitiveness and curiosity that led me into a journalism career. It is also because I was born and baptized Catholic, attended Catholic school and received daily lessons from my battered blue Baltimore Catechism book. Religion has been a part of my life since I was born and I have been examining it since I learned to think. As a member of the Black community, I have participated in religion for more than 30 years and I have investigated or belonged to a variety of religious denominations. I have no formal religious training other what I have read or experienced. I have read extensively and studied a wide range of religious topics ranging from the history of the Bible and Catholicism to books about the gods of ancient Egypt and the writings of Pope John Paul II.

Endnotes

INTRODUCTION

1. The Distinguished Annie Clark Tanner Lecture, 16th-annual Families Alive Conference, Weber State University, May 8, 1997, Dr. Maya Angelou

2. Religion In The News, Church, Lies, and Polling Data, Andrew Walsh, Fall 1998, Vol. 1, No. 2, http://www.trincoll.edu/depts/csrpl/RIN percent20Vol.1No.2/Church_lies_polling.htm

3. Barna Research Online, Reported Giving to Local Churches, 1999, http://216.87.179.136/cgi-bin/PageCategory.asp?CategoryID=36

CHAPTER 1: RACE AND RELIGION

4. Phrase borrowed Emerge magazine article

Introduction: Nonbelief and Skepticism In The Black Community

5. "That Nigger's Crazy," Richard Pryor, Reprise, 1974

6. George S. Schuyler, "Black American Begins to Doubt." American Mercury, 1932, American Atheists, "No More Ham", http://www.atheists.org/Atheism/roots/ham/

7. The Gallup Organization, March 28, 2000, Unchurched America Has Changed Little in 20 Years, Michael Lindsay, http://www.gallup.com/poll/releases/pr000328b.asp

Chapter 2: The Black Church

8. The Mis-Education of the Negro, p.35, Carter G. Woodson, 1933

9. The Gallup Organization, March 28, 2000, Unchurched America Has Changed Little in 20 Years, Michael Lindsay, http://www.gallup.com/poll/releases/pr000328b.asp

10. Religious Tolerance.Org, Religious Beliefs in the United States, General religious beliefs, http://www.religioustolerance.org/chr_poll.htm

11. Lies, Fraud, Atrocities The Truth shall Set You Free, The God Biz by James A. Haught, http://relfrauds.www4.50megs.com/evangelists/godbiz.html

12. Skeptic, Vol. 8, No. 1, 2000, p. 15, The changing Religious Landscape

13. Religion in the News, Fall 1998, Vol. 1., No. 2, Church, Lies, and Polling Data, Andrew Walsh, http://www.trincoll.edu/depts/csrp1/RIN percent 20Vol.1No.2/Church_lies.htm

14. Congregational Life Centre Web Site, GIA Millennium Study, Taylor Nelson Sofres Intersearch, 1999, http://www.congregationallife.com/articles/survey.htm

15. New Research Casts More Doubt On Church Attendance Figures, May 23, 1998, http://www.atheists.org/flash.line/church1.htm

16. Thomas C. Reeves, "The Empty Church: Does Organized Religion Matter Anymore?" Simon & Schuster: New York, NY (1998), Page. 64." Cited in http://www.adherents.com/Na_169.html

17. Http://www.rci.rutgers.edu/-religion/jseminar/miller1.html, the Jesus Seminar and its critics, Robert J. Miller, 1997

18. The Gallup Poll Organization, The Age Factor in Religious Attitudes and Behavior, Christa Ehmann, 1999, http://www.gallup.com/poll/releases/pr990714b.asp

19. University of Michigan, Institute for Social Research, Church attendance drops, 2000, http://www.umich.edu/~newsinfo/Releases/2000/Jan00/r011100.html

20. Ibid, pg. 26

21. Ibid, pg. 5

22. Barna Research Online, One Out of Three Adults is Now Unchurched, http://216.87.179.136/cgi-bin/PagePressRelease.asp?PressReleaseID=18&Reference=D

23. Researcher Predicts Mounting Challenges to Christian Church, April 16, 2001, http://www.barna.org/CGI-BIN/PagePressRelease.asp?PressReleaseID=88&Reference=B

24. USA Today, Amen to a church-free life, Cathy Lynn Grossman, Thursday, March 7, 2002

25. Barna Research Online, African Americans, 1997, http://216.87.179.136/cgi-bin/PageCategory.asp?CategoryID=1

26. Barna Research Online, Church Attendance Drops Again: Boomers Cut Church from Regular Schedule, February 28, 1996

27. The Gerontologist, Religious Participation Among Elderly Blacks, R. J. Taylor, 26:630-636

28. Churched and Unchurched Black Americans, Hart M. Nelsen and Conrad L. Kanagy

29. Barna Research Online, Church Attendance, Average Church Service Size, 1999, http://216.87.179.136/cgi-bin/PageCategory.asp?CategoryID=10

30. Six in Ten Americans Read Bible at Least Occasionally, Alec Gallup and Wendy W. Simmons, http://www.gallup.com/poll/releases/pr001020.asp

31. Contemporary African American Religion: What Have We Learned From the NSBA?, Christopher Ellison, http://www.isr,umich.edu/rcgd/prba/persp/win97/comtemporary.html

32. Pass It On: Outreach to Minority Communities, Charyn D. Sutton, Big Brothers/Big Sisters of America, 1992

33. Barna Research Online, Women Are the Backbone of the Christian Congregations in America, 2000, http://216.87.179.136/cgi-bin/PagePressRelease.asp?PressReleaseID=47&Reference=E

34. http://www.positiveatheism.org/hist/marjoe.htm

35. The Religion Racket, Dr. Norman H. Wells, http://www.gospelweb.net/racket22.htm

36. Contemporary religion is new entertainment, Scott Bridges, http://www.usc.edu/student-affairs/dt/V135/N54/01-contem.54v.html

37. Learning from Lyle Schaller: Social Aspects of Congregations, Daniel V.A. Olson, http://www.religion-online.org/cgi-bin/relsearchd.dll/showarticle?item_id=323

38. Church Attendance, Barna Research Group, http://www.barna.org/cgi-bin/PageCategory.asp?CategoryID=10

CHAPTER 3: UNDERSTANDING BLACK RELIGION

39. Two Sermons Preached to a Congregation of Black Slaves, at Parish Church of S.P. in the Province of Maryland (London, 1782).

40. Reasoning from the Scriptures Ministries, Black Theology, Black Power, and the Black Experience, Ron Rhodes, http://home.earthlink.net/~ronrhodes/BlackTheology.html

41. Bible, Race & Slavery, November 25, 1998, http://atheism.about.com/library/weekly/aa112598.htm

42. Orishas and Santeria, http://www.batadrums.com/background/orishas.htm

43. African Religions, The religion of the Yoruba people, http://members.aol.com/ishorst/love/Yoruba.htmlin

44. Candomble, http://www.geocities.com/Area51/Chamber/5015/candomble.htm

45. What is Santería?, http://www.seanet.com/~efunmoyiwa/santeria.html

Endnotes 237

46. Origins of Voodoo, http://archive.nandotimes.com/prof/caribe/origins.html

47. General Background, http://www.religioustolerance.org/voodoo.htm

48. Arab American Institute, Time Magazine, p. 72, October 1, 2001.

CHAPTER 4: BLACK BELIEF

49. Barna Research Online, African Americans, 1996, http://216.87.179.136/cgi-bin/PageCategory.asp?CategoryID=1

50. Barna Research Online, Existing Stereotypes about African-Americans Are Way Off the Mark-and Impede Reconciliation, 2000, http://216.87.179.136/cgi-bin/PagePressRelease.asp?PressReleaseID=42&Reference=B

51. Religious Beliefs In The United States, http://www.religioustolerance.org/chr_poll.htm

52. Barna Research Online, Existing Stereotypes about African-Americans Are Way Off the Mark-and Impede Reconciliation, 2000, http://216.87.179.136/cgi-bin/PagePressRelease.asp?PressReleaseID=42&Reference=B

53. Barna Research Online, African Americans, 1996, http://216.87.179.136/cgi-bin/PageCategory.asp?CategoryID=1

54. Barna Research Online, Existing Stereotypes about African-Americans Are Way Off the Mark-and Impede Reconciliation, 2000, http://216.87.179.136/cgi-bin/PagePressRelease.asp?PressReleaseID=42&Reference=B

55. Annual Study Reveals America Is Spiritually Stagnant, March 5, 2001, http://www.barna.org/CGI-BIN/PagePressRelease.asp?PressReleaseID=84&Reference=B

56. The Gallup Organization, Americans Remain Very Religious, but Not Necessarily in Conventional Ways, Frank Newport, 1999, http://www.gallup.com/poll/releases/pr991224.asp

57. International Social survey Program (ISSP), 1991 & 1993. Quoted in George Bishop, "What Americans really believe," Free Inquiry, 1999-Summer, Pages 38 to 42.

58. The Gallup Organization, Americans Remain Very Religious, but Not Necessarily in Conventional Ways, December 24, 1999, http://www.gallup.com/poll/releases/pr991224.asp

59. Barna Research Online, African Americans, 1996, http://216.87.179.136/cgi-bin/PageCategory.asp?CategoryID=1

60. Barna Research Online, The Bible, 1993, http://216.87.179.136/cgi-bin/PageCategory.asp?CategoryID=7

61. The Gallup Organization, Six in Ten Americans Read Bible at Least Occasionally, Alec Gallup and Wendy W. Simmons, 2000, http://www.gallup.com/poll/releases/pr001020.asp

62. The Washington Post National Weekly Edition, The Church of Public Opinion, Richard Morin, November 6-12, 1995,

63. "Answers to frequently asked questions," at: http://www.barna.org/PageStats.htm

64. Barna Research Online, Women Are the Backbone of the Christian Congregations in America, 2000, http://216.87.179.136/cgi-bin/PagePressRelease.asp?PressReleaseID=47&Reference=E

65. The Gallup Organization, Six in Ten Americans Read Bible at Least Occasionally, Alec Gallup and Wendy W. Simmons, 2000, http://www.gallup.com/poll/releases/pr001020.asp

66. Religious Beliefs Vary Widely By Denomination, June 25, 2000, http://www.barna.org/CGI-BIN/PagePressRelease.asp?PressReleaseID=92&Reference=B

CHAPTER 5: SLEEPING WITH EXTRATERRESTRIALS

67. ABC News.com, The Power of Belief, John Stossel, 2000, http://abcnews.go.com/ona...pecials/stossel990603_belief_trans.html

68. The Gallup Organization Beliefs Poll Newsletter Archive, It Was A Very Bad Year: Belief In Hell And The Devil On The Rise: But Heaven Reigns Supreme, Leslie McAneny, 1995, http://psych.butler.edu/bwoodruf/courses/clarifybelief/Gallup/beliefspoll.html

69. Believing in Magic: The Psychology of Superstition, Stuart A. Vyse, Oxford Press, 1997, New York, p. 95

70. Americans' Belief in Psychic and Paranormal Phenomena Is up Over Last Decade, Frank Newport and Maura Strausberg June 8, 2001, http://www.gallup.com/poll/releases/pr010608.asp

71. Psychic History: Lessons of the Past: A Pathway to the Future, Jennifer Banever, http://www.haunt.net/study/history.html

72. Do you believe that phone psychics can predict your future?, The Web Poll, http://www.4allfree.com/cgi/wpres.id?thefunnypage

73. Americans' Belief in Psychic and Paranormal Phenomena Is up Over Last Decade, Frank Newport and Maura Strausberg, http://www.gallup.com/poll/releases/pr010608.asp

74. Americans' Belief in Psychic and Paranormal Phenomena Is up Over Last Decade, Frank Newport and Maura Strausberg, http://www.gallup.com/poll/releases/pr010608.asp

75. Psychic History: Lessons of the Past: A Pathway to the Future, Jennifer Banever, Hope, 1998, http://haunt.net/study/history.html

76. Dial A Psychic, Reginald V. Finley, http://www.infidelguy.com/index.htm

77. Psychic Friends, Intellectual Enemies, Patrick Inniss, http://home.sprynet.com/~inniss/aahpsych.htm

78. What is Humanism?, Dr. Charles W. Faulkner, African-Americans for Humanism, 1992

79. The Daily Revolution, Miss Cleo Unmasked, Richard Daverman, http://dailyrevolution.org/allgood/010608.html

80. Missouri's Attorney General Accuses Company That Promotes TV Psychic of Consumer Fraud, Paul Sloca Associated Press, July 25, 2001, http://ap.tbo.com/ap/breaking/MGAEI2Z1LPC.html

81. The Facts About Faith Healing, George Nava True II, Discover, August, 1984, http://www.netasia.net/users/truehealth/Psychic percent20 Surgery.htm

82. Archives of Internal Medicine, August 13, 2001

83. Ibid

84. The Faithhealers, James Randi, Prometheus Books, Buffalo, NY, 1989, p 35

85. Some Thoughts on Faith Healing, Stephen Barrett, M.D., Quack Watch, http://quackwatch.com/01/QuackeryRelated Topics/faith.html

86. The New Faith in Medicine, T. McNichol, USA Today, April 7, 1996, pp. 4

87. Child Fatalities From Religion-motivated Medical Neglect, Seth M. Asser and Rita Swan, Pediatrics Vol. 101 No. 4, April 1998, http://www.rickross.com/reference/general/general90.html

88. Get this from hardcopy

89. Rose Louis, Faith Healing, Baltimore, Penguin Books, 1971

90. Healing: A Doctor in Search of a Miracle, William Nolen, Random House, Inc., New York, 1974

91. The Faith Healers, James Randi, Prometheus Books, 1987

92. Freethought Today, Adventures in Faith Healing, Matthew Barry, March 1998, http://www.ffrf.org/fttoday/march98/barry.html

93. Abusing Science: The Case Against Creationism, Philip Kitcher, The MIT Press, Cambridge, Massachusetts, 1992

94. When Religion Becomes Evil, Charles Kimball, HarperSanFrancisco, 2002, p. 29, 72

95. Religious Tolerance.Org, Religious Beliefs in the United States, General religious beliefs, http://www.religioustolerance.org/chr_poll.htm

96. The Gallup Organization, Substantial Numbers of Americans Continue to Doubt Evolution as Explanation for Origin of Humans, Deborah Jordan Brooks, March 5, 2001, http://www.gallup.com/poll/releases/pr010305.asp

97. What Americans Really Believe, George Bishop, Free Inquiry magazine, Volume 19, Number 3, http://www.secularhumanism.org/library/fi/bishop_19_3.html

CHAPTER 6: GLOBAL RELIGIOUS ESTIMATES

98. Global Evangelization Movement, Pointing the way to the least evangelized, North America: Decline & Fall of World Religions, 1900-2025, Justin D. Long, http://www.gem-werc.org/mmrc/mmrc9805.htm

99. Ontario Consultants on Religious Tolerance, Latest update: 2001-JAN-29, B.A. Robinson, Number of adherents of world religions, http://www.religioustolerance.org/worldrel.htm

100. Encyclopedia Britannica, Worldwide Adherents of All Religions by Six Continental Areas, Mid-1997, http://www.britannica.com/bcom/eb/article/single_table/0,5716,126024,00.html

101. Adherents of All Religions by Six Continental Areas Mid-1999, 2000 Encyclopedia Britannica Book of the Year

102. The National Black Catholic Congress, http://nbcongress.org/facts/count2.htm

CHAPTER 7: RELIGION IN THE UNITED STATES

103. Barna Research Online, Christianity Has a Strong Positive Image Despite Fewer Active Participants, February 5, 1996, http://216.87.179.136/cgi-bin/PagePressRelease.asp?PressReleaseID=34&Reference=E

104. Religious Tolerance.Org, Response of Christians and others towards Atheism, http://www.religioustolerance.org/atheist.htm

105. Charting the unchurched in America, by Cathy Lynn Grossman, USA TODAY

106. Contributing: Anthony DeBarros, http://www.usatoday.com/life/2002/2002-03-07-no-religion.htm

107. Stated Willingness to Vote for a Candidate from Various Backgrounds, The Gallup Organization, March 29, 1999. http://www.gallup.com/poll/releases/pr990329.asp

108. Would You Vote for an Atheist?, http://www.Blackwebportal.com/RobPollTest.cfm?&showresults=Atheist

109. Education and Religion, Bruce Sacerote and Edward L. Glaeser, Working Paper 8080, http://www.nber.org/papers/w8080

110. Education and Religion, Bruce Sacerote and Edward L. Glaeser, Working Paper 8080, http://www.nber.org/papers/w8080

111. The Culture of Disbelief: How American Law and Politics Trivialize Religious Devotion. By Stephen L. Carter. Basic Books. 328 pp

112. For Goodness' Sake: Why So Many Want Religion to Play a Greater Role in American Life, 2001 Public Agenda, p. 14

CHAPTER 8: ACTIONS SPEAK LOUDER THAN WORDS

113. The Washington Post National Weekly Edition, The Church of Public Opinion, Richard Morin, November 6-12, 1995

114. The Gathering Darkness: America In The 21st. Century, Scott Bidstrup, http://www.bidstrup.com/america.htm

115. The Gathering Darkness: America In The 21st. Century, Scott Bidstrup, http://www.bidstrup.com/america.htm

116. The Freethought Zone, Morality and Religion, http://freethought.freeservers.com/reason/morals.html

117. The World's Most Dangerous Places, Robert Young Pelton, HarperResource, 2000, pp. 932-33

118. US News Online, Was it good for us?, May 5, 1997, David Whitman, http://www.usnews.com/usnews/issue/970519/19sex.htm

119. Majority of Americans Say Roe v. Wade Decision Should Stand, January 22, 2001, Joseph Carroll, http://www.gallup.com/poll/releases/pr010122.asp

120. http://www.concentric.net/~tycho4/RelCrime.htm

121. Crisis Pregnancy Ministry, Abortion and the African American Community, Peggy Lehner, 2001, http://www.family.org/pregnancy/general/A0017534.html

122. Culture of Life Foundation & Institute, Abortion and the African-American Community, http://www.christianity.com/partner/Article_Display_Page/0,PTID4211|CHID102753|CIID367285,00.html

123. Reproductive Freedom-In Defense of Our Greatest Civil Right, Judy D. Simmons, Emerge, June, 1991

124. Ibid

125. U.S. Bureau of the Census, cited in Douglas Besharov, "Poverty, Welfare Dependency and the Underclass," UCLA, 1993.

126. Source: "Sexuality, Contraception, and the Media." American Academy of Pediatrics Committee on Public Education. 1/2001 http://www.aap.org/policy/re0038.html

127. Source: Centers for Disease Control and Prevention. New CDC Report Tracks Trends in Teen Births from 1940—2000. September 25, 2001

128. Nonmarital Childbearing in the United States, 1940-99. NVSR Vol. 48, No. 16. 39. pp. (PHS) 2001-1120.

129. Barbara DaFoe Whitehead, "Dan Quayle was Right," The Atlantic Monthly, April 1993.

130. Andrew J. Cherlin, Marriage, Divorce, Remarriage, rev. and enl. ed., (Cambridge, Mass.: Harvard University Press, 1992), 98-99.

131. "After the Starting Line: Blacks and Women in an Uphill Pace," Reynolds Forley, Demography 25, no. 4 (November 1988): 487, Figure 6.

132. Dennis A. Ahlburg and Carol J. DeVita, "New Realities of the American Family," Population Bulletin 47, no. 2 (August 1992) 8.

133. Andrew J. Cherlin, Marriage, Divorce, Remarriage, rev. and enl. ed., (Cambridge, Mass.: Harvard University Press, 1992), 110 .

134. Christopher Jencks, "Is the American Underclass Growing," 86, Table 14. In Jencks and Peterson, eds., Urban Underclass, (Washington, D.C.: Brookings Institution, 1991).

135. Barna Research Online, Christians Are More Likely to Experience Divorce Than Are Non-Christians, December 21, 1999, http://www.barna.org/cgi-bin/PagePressRelease.asp?PressReleaseID=39&Reference=B

136. Dennis A. Ahlburg and Carol J. DeVita, "New Realities of the American Family," Population Bulletin 47, no. 2 (August 1992): 15.

137. Ameristat, Racial, Ethnic Diversity in Female-Headed Households, 1998, http://www.ameristat.org/racethnic/femhead.htm

138. (U.S. Bureau of the Census, 1971, 1991a, 1991b).

139. National Opinion Research Center, http://www.norc.uchicago.edu/

140. Infidelity: America's Dark Secret, http://broadcast.webpoint.com/wphl/infpo.htm, Who cheats?

141. Mitchell Files Case History, Statistics on Cheating Spouses, 2001, http://shop.store.yahoo.com/eaglesnestpub/statoncheats.html

142. Prevalence, Incidence and Consequences of Violence Against Women Survey, National Institute of Justice and Centers for Disease Control and Prevention, 1998.

143. Commonwealth Fund Survey of the Health of Adolescent Girls, 1998

144. TeenHealth, Date Rape, http://www.teenhealthissues.org/rape.htm

145. Rape, Abuse & Incest National Network, RAINN Statistics, http://www.rainn.org/statistics.html

146. Promise: Facts About Prostitution, http://www.sirius.com/~promise/facts.html

147. Casting Stones: Prostitution and Liberation in Asia and the United States, Susan Brock and Nakashima and Thistlethwaite, Fortress Press. 1996.

148. Priscilla Alexander, Prostitution: A Difficult Issue For Feminists, (in Frederique Delacoste and Priscilla Alexander, Sex Work: Writings by Women in the Sex Industry, San Francisco: Cleis Press, 1987.) www.bayswan.org/stats.html

149. Danger for prostitutes increasing, most starting younger, Beacon Journal, 21 September 1997

150. US Dept of Labor, Prostitution of Children, 1996

151. Kathlyn Gay, Child Labor: A Global Crisis, 1998, citing Joan J. Johnson, Teen Prostitution, 1992

152. UNICEF, State of the World's Children, 1997

153. From an Affair of the Mind by Laurie Hall.

154. Report of the Attorney General's Task Force on Family Violence, U.S. Department of Justice, Washington, D.C., 112.

155. Practical Outcomes Replace Biblical Principles As the Moral Standard http://www.barna.org/cgi-bin/PagePressRelease.asp?PressReleaseID=97&Reference=F, September 10, 2001

156. Effect of Pornography on Women and Children, U.S. Senate Judiciary Committee, Subcommittee on Juvenile Justice, 98th Congress, 2nd Session, 1984, 227.

157. The War Against Pornography," Newsweek, 18 March 1985, 60

158. Source: Harder, James. "Porn 500." InsightMag.com.

159. USA Today, 9-5-97 & UPI News, November 19, 1997

160. Sex and Music: Has it Gone too far?, Lerrone Bennett Jr., Ebony, October, 2002, p. 146

161. Memmott, Mark. "Sex Trade may lure 325,000 U.S. Kids; Report: Abused children, runaways typical victims." USA TODAY. 9/10/01

162. Wall Street Meets Pornography, New York Times, October 23, 2000

163. Source: Elias, Marilyn. "Cybersex follows Mars, Venus patterns." USA Today. 2/26/02

164. Christianity Today, 2001

165. Christianity Today, 2000

166. "Zogby/Focus Survey Reveals Shocking Internet Sex Statistics." Legal Facts: Family Research Council. Vol. 2. No. 20. 3/30/00

167. Zogby/Focus Survey Reveals Shocking Internet Sex Statistics, Family Research Council, Vol., 2, No. 20, March 30, 2000.

168. Source: Koerner, Brendan I. "A lust for profits." U.S. News online, http://www.usnew.com/usnews/issue/000327/eporn.htm. 3/27/00

169. The NetValue Report on Minors Online…" Business Wire. (taken from study by NetValue, Internet activity measurement service) December 19,2000

170. Survey Shows Widespread Enthusiasm for High Technology." NPR Online http://www.npr.org/programs/specials/poll/technology

171. Source: The Harm of Pornography, Cincinnati, OH: National Coalition for the Protection of Children and Families, 1998.

172. Source: Parker, Kathleen. "It's common sense to restrict Internet usage in libraries." The Orlando Sentinel online. 3/19/00

173. Source: "Schools grapple with Internet filters." COMTEX Newswire. Biloxi, Miss. 3/2/00

174. (MSNBC). http://www.effectiveoptimizations.com/statistics.htm

175. Eric Retzlaff, Pornography's Grip Tightens by Way of the Internet, National Catholic Register, June, 2000

176. (eMarketer.com)

177. Network Magazine, February 1, 2001

178. Source: Dushman, Candi. "'Stop pretending.'" World Magazine, 8/5/00

179. The Truth About California's Adult Industry, 1999, The US adult entertainment industry trade association, The Free Speech Coalition

180. Ammerman, R. and Hersen, M. (1991). Case Studies in Family Violence. New York: Plenum Press.

181. Domestic Violence and African American Women in Rural Communities, Sharon E. Williams

182. Battered Women's Shelter, Peace Begins at Home, Battered Women's Statistics for the United States, http://www.rfcram.com/bwsstatistics.htm

183. "The overlap between child maltreatment and woman battering." J.L. Edleson, Violence Against Women, February, 1999

184. Violence by Intimates: Analysis of Data on Crimes by Current or Former Spouses, Boyfriends, and Girlfriends, U.S. Department of Justice, March, 1998

185. Uniform Crime Reports of the U.S. 1996, Federal Bureau of Investigation, 1996, Domestic Violence, National Statistics, http://www.ndvh.org/dvInfo.html

186. 1999 National Household Survey on Drug Abuse, http://www.health.org/govstudy/bkd376/index.htm#TopOfPage

187. University of Michigan, Monitoring the Future Project, http://monitoringthefuture.org/

188. Partnership for a Drug-Free America, Review the Partnership's research studies into the attitudes of Americans towards drug abuse in the Partnership Attitude Tracking Studies (PATS), 2000, http://www.drugfreeamerica.org/research/default.asp

189. Public Agenda Online, Illegal Drugs, The Issue at a Glance, www.publicagenda.org/issues/overview.cfm?issue_type=iilegal_drugs

190. National Household Survey on Drug Abuse: Population Estimates 1998, Any Illicit Drug Use—Race/Ethnicity, http://www.samhsa.gov/oas/NHSDA/Pe1998/TOC.htm

191. ASAP Family: Drug & Alcohol Statistics, 1999, Public Agenda Online, http://www.publicagenda.org/issues/overview.cfm?issue_type=alcohol

192. Public Agenda Online, Alcohol Abuse, The Issue at a Glance, www.publicagenda.org/issues/overview.cfm?issue_type=alcohol

193. The Gallup Organization, More Than a Third of Americans Report Drinking Has Caused Family Problems, Frank Newport, November, 1999, www.gallup.com/poll/pr991103.asp

194. "Number of deaths and age-adjusted death rates per 100,000 population for categories of alcohol-related (A-R) mortality, United States, 1979-96," National Institute on Alcohol Abuse and Alcoholism, http://silk.nih.gov/sil.niaaa1/database/armort01.txt

195. Voas and Tippetts "Ethnicity and Alcohol-Related Fatalities: 1990 to 1994" http://www.madd.org/stats/0,1056,1773,00.html

196. NHTSA Traffic Tech#152 IIHS Status Report Volume 32, No. 3 "Drinking and Driving in the US: The National Roadside Survey" March 1997

197. Sex and Music: Has it Gone too far?, Lerrone Bennett Jr., Ebony, October, 2002, p. 146

198. Centers for Disease Control and Prevention. Tobacco use among middle and high school students—United States, 1999. MMWR 2000; 49: 49-53

199. U.S. Department of Health and Human Services. Tobacco Use Among U.S. Racial/Ethnic Minority Groups—African Americans, American Indians and Alaska Natives, Asian Americans and Pacific Islanders, and Hispanics: A Report of the Surgeon General. Atlanta: U.S. Department of Health and Human Services, Centers for Disease Control and Prevention, 1998

200. Centers for Disease Control and Prevention, Chronic Disease in Minority Populations. Atlanta: CDC, 1994: 2-16

201. Smoking Attributable Mortality and Years of Potential Life Lost," Morbidity and Mortality Weekly Report (Atlanta, GA: Centers for Disease Control, 1997), May 23, 1997, Vol. 46, No. 20, p. 449.

202. Centers for Disease Control and Prevention. Cigarette smoking among adults—United States, 1997. MMWR 1999; 48: 993-6.

203. Centers for Disease Control and Prevention. At-A-Glance. Tobacco Use Among U.S. Racial/Ethnic Minority Groups—African Americans, American Indians and Alaska Natives, Asian Americans and Pacific Islanders, and Hispanics, Atlanta: CDC, 1998

204. Centers for Disease Control and Prevention, Office on Smoking and Health, Unpublished data, 1995

205. American Cancer Society, Inc.. Cancer Facts and Figures 2000. Atlanta: ACS, 2000.

206. Ebony, October, 2002, p48.

207. International Gaming

208. LaFluer World Gambling Almanac*

209. Casino Gambling, National Gambling Impact Study Commission, Final Report, Problem and Pathological Gambling, http://www.casino-gambling-reports.com/GamblingStudy/ProblemGambling/page10.htm

210. Gemini Research, Research on Gambling, http://www.geminiresearch.com/

211. Public Agenda Online, Gambling, The Issue at a Glance, www.publicagenda.org/issues/overview.cfm?issue_type=gambling

212. The Detroit News, $195 billion lost to tax cheaters, Melissa Preddy, April 11, 1999 http://detnews.com/1999/biz/9904/11/04110037.htm

213. ibid

214. Cheating and Plagiarism in the Internet Era: A Wake Call, Ann Lanthrop and Kathleen Foss

215. The Harris Poll #58, October 4, 2000, Huge Differences Between Values Of Young Adults And Older Adults, By Humphrey Taylor

216. Guilty of shoplifting, Ryder is lost for words, Sharon Waxman, November 8 2002, http://www.smh.com.au/articles/2002/11/07/1036308427668.html

217. Taking Retail to New Heights", Jon Schallert, Who's Shoplifting from Your Store? Part 2, http://www.retail-usa.com/articles/who_is_shoplifting.html

218. TaxFree Inc.(corporate tax evasion), Tim Dickinson, Mother Jones Interactive, 2000, http://www.findarticles.com/cf_dls/m1329/2_25/60019942/p1/article.jhtml

219. In the Eighties, Savings and Loan Scandal, http://www.inthe80s.com/sandl.shtml

220. Everyone Pays the Cost, Business First, Thomas Pack, 12/20/2002, http://louisville.bizjournals.com/louisville/stories/2002/12/23/focus2.html

221. Health Care Fraud: National and Local Perspective on a Growing Trend, http://www.fbi.gov/contact/fo/norfolk/hcf.htm.

222. Practical Outcomes Replace Biblical Principles As the Moral Standard, September 10, 2001, http://www.barna.org/cgi-bin/PagePressRelease.asp?PressReleaseID=97&Reference=D

CHAPTER 9: NO ONE IS IMMUNE

223. The Mis-Education of the Negro, p.44, Carter G. Woodson, 1933

224. The Lyons Den, James A. Haught, Secular Humanist Bulletin, Summer 1998, http://www.escape.ca/~dkost/lyonsden.htm

225. Voodoo Science: The Road from Foolishness to Fraud"

226. Salon.com, Oh God You Devil, Stephen Bender, http://www.salon.com/people/feature/2000/11/21/tilton/index2.html,

227. Oh God, You Devil, Stephen Bender, Salon.Com, http://www.salon.com/people/feature/2000/11/21/tilton/index2.html

228. The Prophet Of Profit?, Liberty Online, Stephen Phillips, http://www.libertymagazine.org/issues/97-07/prophet.html

229. Lies, Fraud, Atrocities The Truth shall Set You Free, The God Biz by James A. Haught, http://relfrauds.www4.50megs.com/evangelists/godbiz.html

230. Resurrection: Black Television Network Gives Forum To Discredited Sleazoid Evangelists, American Atheist, Flashline, December 13, 2000, http://www.atheists.org/flash.line/church28.htm

231. http://www.thelinkup.com/stats.html

232. Probe Ministries, Adultery in the Church, November 14,1998, http://www.probe.org/docs/c-adultery2.html

233. Models Of Flock Disappointment From American Church History: Parallels With The Duping Of The Y2K Flocks, Americanwasteland.com, January 5, 2000, D. Marty Lasley, http://www.americanwasteland.com/y2kmodels.html

234. Kenneth Woodward, "Sex, Morality and the Protestant Minister," Newsweek (28 July 1997), 62

235. Probe Ministries, Adultery in the Church, November 14,1998, http://www.probe.org/docs/c-adultery2.html

236. http://www.thelinkup.com/stats.html

237. Clergy Sexual Abuse, Connecticut Sexual Assault Crisis Services, Inc. Newsletter, July, 1996, Frances Park, http://www.advocateweb.org/cease/csa.htm

CHAPTER 15: CONCLUSION—THEY DO PROTEST TOO MUCH

238. The Washington Post National Weekly Edition, The Church of Public Opinion, Richard Morin, November 6-12, 1995

239. The Gallup Poll Organization, New Poll Guages Americans' General Knowledge Levels, Steve Crabtree, 1999, http://www.gallup.com/poll/releases/pr990706b.asp

240. Ibid

241. American Attitudes Toward Homosexuality Continue to Become More Tolerant, Frank Newport, June 4, 2001, http://www.gallup.com/poll/releases/pr010604.asp

242. African American Attitudes Towards Depression, http://www.intelihealth.com/IH/ihtIH/WSIHW000/8596/8836.html

243. National Crime Victimization Survey, Bureau of Justice Statistics, U.S. Department of Justice, 1977

244. The Secret Trauma, Diana Russell, Basic Books, 1986

245. "The Long-Term Effects of Incestuous Abuse: A Comparison of African American and White American Victims," Diana Russell, et al. Lasting

Effects of Child Sexual Abuse, ed. By Gail E. Wyatt, Sage Publications, 1988

246. By Silence Betrayed, John Crewsdon, Little Brown, 1988

247. Washington Post.Com, Most Oscar Nominations by Film, http://www.washingtonpost.com/wp-srv/style/movies/oscars/filmnoms.htm

248. Ibid

249. The Meaning of Life, Adrian Barnett 1997, http://www.abarnett.demon.co.uk/atheism/life.html,

250. The Case Against Religion: by Albert Ellis, Ph.D., Psychotherapy http://www.matriarch.com/case.htm

251. http://people-press.org/reports/display.php3?ReportID=150

252. The Prisoners Dilemma, The Ethical Spectacle, September 1995, http://www.spectacle.org/995/pd.html

Chapter 16: Alternatives and Options

253. Pamphlet #3047, Copyright Unitarian Universalist Association, 1995 5/22/95

254. Unitarians Elect First Black Leader, Associated Press, 2001, http://www.beliefnet.com/story/82/story_8263_1.html

255. What is a Unitarian Universalist?, Christopher Gist Raible, http://www.eecs.umich/~don/philosophy/whatis.html

256. Unitarian Universalist Association, http://uua

257. Ibid

258. Ibid

259. Council for Secular Humanism, What is Secular Humanism, Fritz Stevens, Edward Tabash, Tom Hill, Mary Ellen Sikes, and Tom Flynn, http://www.secularhumanism.org/intro/what.html

260. Council for Secular Humanism, African Americans for Humanism Home Page, http://www.secularhumanism.org/aah/

261. African American for Humanism, International Humanist News, Norm Allen Jr., http://www.iheu.org/IHN/v5-3&4/norm_r_allen_jr.htm Atheists, Freethinkers, Nonbelievers, Skeptics, Etc.

262. From Norm Allen, Executive Director of African Americans for Humanism

263. Free Inquiry, (Volume 14 No 3)

264. AAH Examiner, Personal Paths To Humanism, Summer, 1993—Volume 3, Number 2

265. African Americans for Humanism, Fall, 1994—Volume 4, Number 3, http://www.secularhumanism.org/library/aah/index.htm

266. Ibid

267. AAH Examiner, Summer, 1999—Volume 9, Number 2, http://www.secularhumanism.org/library/aah/mensah_9_2.htm

268. Who's Who In Hell, Warren Allen Smith, Barricade Books, 2000, pp. 27

269. Freethought In Modern Music, Heather Lucio, http://www.rthoughtsrfree.org/aof/newsltrs/1996_aof/030196af.htm, Atheists and Other Freethinkers, March 1996

270. Through Many Toils: The Ministry of E. E. Brown 2-21-99 Judith Quarles, 1875 in Jamaica. http://www.dmcom.net/uuso/sermons/s990221.html

271. New York Public Library Digital Collections, Brown (Egbert Ethelred) Papers, 1908-1964, http://digilib.nypl.org:80/dynaweb/ead/nypl/scm-geebr/@Generic__BookView

272. American Atheist, Atheists of a Different Color, February, 1987

273. Tidwell, John Edgar, guest editor. "Oh, Didn't He Ramble: Sterling A. Brown (1901-1989)," special section of Black American Literature Forum, 23.1 (1989): 89-112, http://www.georgetown.edu/bassr/heath/syllabuild/iguide/browns.html

274. Biographical Sketch of Dr. Yosef A.A. ben-Jochannan, Yosef A.A. ben-Jochannan Virtual Museum, http://www.nbufront.org/html/Masters-Museums/DocBen/BioInfo.html

275. BBB Interviews Dr. Yosef ben-Jochannan, Black Boots Bulletin 5, 4 (Winter 1977)

276. Free Inquiry, Fall, 2000, James A. Haught, James Baldwin, http://www.wvinter.net/~haught/baldwin.html

277. Biography, James Baldwin, http://www.uic.edu/depts/quic/history/james_baldwin.html

278. American Atheist, Atheists of a Different Color, February, 1987, pp. 41

279. The Black Renaissance in Washington, William Waring Cuney, http://www.dclibrary.org/blkren/bios/cuneyww.html

280. Ibid.

281. Records of the Brotherhood of Sleeping Car Porters, Grace P. Campbell, 1925-1968, http://www.lexis-nexis.com/cispubs/guides/african_american/bscp/bscp3.htm

282. Africana, The Encyclopedia of the African and African American Experience, Kwame Anthony Appiah and Henry Louis Gates, Jr. Editors, Basic Civitas Books, 1999, p. 531

283. Afrikan.net, John Henrik Clarke's Autobiographical Obituary http://www.mumia.org/wwwboard/messages/1346.html

284. USAfrica Online, John Henrik Clarke: The Knowledge Revolutionary, Kwaku Person-Lynn, 1998, http://www.usafricaonline.com/JohnHenrik-Clarke.html, 1998

285. American Atheist, Atheists of a Different Color, February, 1987, pp. 23

286. Campus Times, May 8, 1998, Araceli Esparza, http://www.ulv.edu/~ctimes/980508/cleaver.htm

287. Africanca.com, Eldridge Leroy Cleaver, http://www.africana.com/tt_713.htm

288. From Norm Allen, Executive Director of African Americans for Humanism

289. Who's Who in Hell, Warren Allen Smith, Barricade Books, 2000, pp. 286

290. Gale Literary Databases, Gale Group, http://galenet.com/servlet/GLD/hits?c=1&secondary=false&origSearch=true&u=CA&u=CLC&u=DLB&t=KW&s=1&r=d&o=DataType&n=10&I=d&locID=dall44684&NA=Rene+Depestre

291. Who's Who in Hell, Warren Allen Smith, Barricade Books, 2000, pp. 285

292. James M. Gregory's, Frederick Douglass, the Orator (New York, 1893), 103-06. http://douglass.speech.nwu.edu/doug_a10.htm,

293. Camp Quest, Famous U.S. Freethinkers and Humanists Of History, Fred Edwords, 1999 http://www.edwinkagin.com/campquest/files/famous-freethinkers.htm

294. Cheikh Anta Diop A Brief Biography Of An African Champion, http://www.cwo.com/~lucumi/diop2.html

295. John Henrik Clarke Virtual Museum, Cheikh Anta Diop and the New Light on African History by John Henrik Clarke (1974), http://www.nbufront.org/html/MastersMuseums/JHClarke/Contemporaries/CheikhAntaDiop.html

296. Http//www.cwo.com/~lucumi/runoko.html Cheikh Anta Diop Posted By Runoko Rashidi, A Brief Biography of Cheikh Anta Diop http://home3.inet.tele.dk/mcamara/antadiop.html

297. Who's Who in Hell, Warren Allen Smith, Barricade Books, 2000, pp. 305

298. Remembering George Padmore, Black Revolutionary, Manning Marable, http://www.raceandhistory.com/Historians/george_padmore.htm

299. Social Contributions of The Harlem Renaissance, Henry Rhodes, 1918, http://www.yale.edu/ynhti/curriculum/units/1978/2/78.02.08.x.html

300. Legal Defense Collection, http://digilib.nypl.org:80/dynaweb/ead/nypl/scmdavisa/@Generic__BookView

301. Notable Kansans of African Descent, Kansas State Historical Society, 1997, http://www.kshs.org/people/afampeop.htm#d

302. Davis, Frank Marshall (Arkansas City). Livin' the Blues: Memoirs of a Black Journalist and Poet. Edited by John Edgar Tidwell, University of Wisconsin Press, 114 N Murray, Madison, WI 53715-1199

303. Free Inquiry Magazine, Volume 20, Number 2, http://www.secularhumanism.org/library/fi/100_humanist_20.2.htm

304. http://classiclit.about.com/arts/classiclit/gi/dynamic/offsite.htm?site=http percent3A percent2F percent2Fwww.triadntr.net percent2F percent7E rdavis percent2Fdubois.htm

305. The Journey Toward Wholeness October 18, 1998 The Rev. Jane Dwinell, http://www.uua.org/news/hatecrime/jdwinell.html

306. Who's Who in Hell, Warren Allen Smith, Barricade Books, 2000, pp. 364

307. What is Humanism?, Dr. Charles W. Faulkner, African-Americans for Humanism, 1992

308. Frantz Fanon: an Introduction Benjamin Graves '98, Brown University http://landow.stg.brown.edu/post/poldiscourse/fanon/fanon1.html

309. Books and Writers, Frantz Fanon, http://www.kirjasto.sci.fi/fanon.htm

310. CORE—Online, http://www.core-online.org/History/james_farmer.htm

311. American Atheist, Atheists of A Different Color, February, 1987

312. American Atheist, Atheists of a Different Color, February, 1987, pp. 36

313. American Atheist, Atheists of A Different Color: A Minority's Minority, R. Murray-O'Hair, February, 1987

314. http://www.leonardharris.com/vitae.htm

315. The African American Almanac, 7th ed., Gale, 1997, Photo credit © Gale Group Inc. 2000. http://www.galegroup.com/freresrc/blkhstry/haley-ale.htm

316. History, Playwright Lorraine Hansberry, David Bianco, August, 1999, http://icq.planetout.com/pno/news/history/archive/08161999.html

317. Voices from the Gaps, Women Writers of Color, Lorraine Hansberry, http://voices.cla.umn.edu/authors/LorraineHansberry.html

318. To Be Young, Gifted and Black by Lorraine Hansberry, Robert Nemiroff (Mass Market Paperback—July 1987

319. American Atheists, The Black Atheists of the Harlem Renaissance: 1917-1928, John G. Jackson, 1984, http://www.atheists.org/Atheism/roots/harlem/

320. Yale-New Haven Teachers Institute, The Social Contributions of The Harlem Renaissance, Henry Rhodes, 1978, http://www.yale.edu/ynhti/curriculum/units/1978/2/78.02.08.x.html

321. American Atheists, Hubert Henry Harrison: The Black Socrates, John G. Jackson, 1987, http://www.atheists.org/Atheism/roots/harrison/

322. World's great men of color, J.A. Rogers, Macmillan, New York, 1972

323. AAH Examiner, Hubert Henry Harrison: Great African American Freethinker, http://www. Seculrrhumanism.org/library/aah/inniss-4-4.html

324. American Atheist, The Black Atheists of the Harlem Renaissance (1917-1928), John G. Jackson, 1984, http://www.atheists.org/Atheism/roots/harlem/

325. American Atheist, Atheists of A Different Color, February, 1987

326. Famous Dead Non-theists, Copyright 1995-2000, http://www.visi.com/~markg/atheists.html, http://www.visi.com/~markg/atheists.html

327. Who's Who In Hell, Warren Allen Smith, Barricade Books, 2000, pp. 537

328. Dr. Willis Nathaniel Huggins, http://www.cwo.com/~lucumi/jackson.html

329. Fall, Personal Paths To Humanism, AHH Examiner, 1993—Volume 3, Number 3, Fall, 1993—Volume 3, Number 3

330. http://www-hsc.usc.edu/~gallaher/hurston/hurston.html

331. Africana.com, Zora Neale Hurston, Lisa Clayton Robinson, 1999, http://216.46.224.11/Articles/tt_436.htm

332. Zora Neale Hurston (1891-1960) http://www.library.csi.cuny.edu/dept/history/lavender/386/zhurston.html

333. Secular Humanist Bulletin, Volume 16, Number 2., http://secularhumanism.org/library/shb/igwe_16_2.htm

334. Who's Who in Hell, Warren Allen Smith, Barricade Books, 2000, pp. 572

335. American Atheist, Atheists of A Different Color, February, 1987, pp. 29

336. Touro College Jacob D. Fuchsberg Law Center, 1997, http://www.touro-law.edu/patch/Wallace/,

337. Black Studies Program, Florida State University, http://www.fsu.edu/~blk-study/Bio/jones.html

338. Bill T. Jones dance Company, http://www.geocities.com/Broadway/Balcony/3252/

339. Modern American Poetry, James Weldon Johnson's Life and Career, Herman Beavers, http://www.english.uiuc.edu/maps/poets/g_l/johnson/life.htm

340. Council for Secular Humanism, African Americans For Humanism (AAH) Advisory Board, http://www.secularhumanism.org/aah/advisors.html

341. Frontier Report, Vol. 2 (10): 2, April, 1993, School of Education and Human Services, University of Wisconsin-Oshkosh. Ph.D. http://www.coehs.uwosh.edu/hspl/vita/kisubivita2.html

342. Free Inquiry, (Volume 14 No 3)

343. http://www.secularhumanism.org/library/shb/cherry_12_3.html, http://cns-web.bu.edu/pub/dorman/lemon_v_kurtzman.html

344. Africana.com, Lisa Clayton Robinson, http://www.africana.com/tt_164.htm

345. Council for Secular Humanism, African Americans For Humanism Advisory Board, http://www.secularhumanism.org/aah/advisors.html

346. The Academy of American Poets—Poetry Exhibits: Claude McKay, http://www.poets.org/lit/poet/cmckay.htm

347. The American Academy of Poets, Poetry Exhibits, http://www.poets.org/poets/poets.cfm?prmID=26

348. Commonweal, Home At Last : The pilgrimage of Claude McKay, David Goldweber, Sept 10, 1999, http://www.findarticles.com/cf_0/m1252/1999_Sept_10/55820350/p1/article.jhtml

349. "McKay, Claude," Microsoft® Encarta® Online Encyclopedia 2000 http://encarta.msn.com © 1997-2000 Microsoft Corporation

350. Freethought Today January/February 1996, Butterfly McQueen Remembered, http://www.ffrf.org/fttoday/jan_feb96/butterfly.html

351. AAH Examiner, Summer, 1999—Volume 9, Number 2, http://www.secularhumanism.org/library/aah/mensah_9_2.htm

352. Richard B. Moore, Caribbean Militant in Harlem, edited by W. Burghardt Turner and Joyce Moore, Indiana University Press, 1992

353. Presidency 2000: Monica G. Moorehead of New Jersey Workers World Party Presidential Nominee, http://www.politics1.com/wwp2k.htm

354. MIT News Office, December 17, 1997, Ayida Mthembu wins Black Achiever Award, Alice C. Waugh, http://web.mit.edu/newsoffice/tt/1997/dec17/mthembu.html

355. Who's Who In Hell, Warren Allen Smith, Barricade Books, 2000, pp. 715

356. Ministerial Settlement Homepage Ministry Homepage, Unitarian Universalist Associationhttp://www.uua.org/ministry/settlement/berry180.html

357. The Revolution & The Movement, HUEY P. NEWTON, http://www.angelfire.com/va/casanegro/index.html

358. Huey P. Newton, The African American Almanac, 7th ed., Gale, 1997. http://www.galegroup.com/freresrc/blkhstry/newtonhu.htm

359. Minnesota Atheists, Positive Atheism in Action, http://www.mnatheists.org/pr02.htm

360. Kwame Nkrumah's Vision of Africa, BBC World Service, Thursday 14 September, 2000, http://www.bbc.co.uk/worldservice/people/highlights/000914_nkrumah.shtml

361. http://www.atheistalliance.org/directory/nigeria.htm

362. Secular Humanist Bulletin, Volume 16, Number 2., http://secularhumanism.org/library/shb/igwe_16_2.htm

363. Who's Who In Hell, Warren Allen Smith, Barricade Books, 2000, pp. 1084

364. The Jesse Owens Foundation, http://www.jesse-owens.org/about1.html

365. American Atheist, February 1987, Atheists of a Different Color, p. 26

366. African-American Humanism: An Anthology, Norm R. Allen, Jr., ed., Prometheus, Buffalo, NY, 1991, p. 279

367. Remembering George Padmore, Black Revolutionary, Manning Marable, http://www.raceandhistory.com/Historians/george_padmore.htm

368. Lucy Parsons (1853-1942): The Life of an Anarchist Labor Organizer, Joe Lowndes, Free Society, vol. 2, no. 4, 1995, http://www.tigerden.com/~berios/parsonsl-bio.html

369. Nell Painter: Making it as a Woman of Color in the Academy, http://www.diversityweb.org/Digest/F97/painter.html

370. Council for Secular Humanism's Speaker's Bureau, http://www.secularhumanism.org/speakers/index.htm

371. Who's Who In Hell, Warren Allen Smith, Barricade Books, 2000, pp. 880

372. Who's Who In Hell, Warren Allen Smith, Barricade Books, 2000, pp. 889

373. American Atheist, Atheists of a Different Color, February, 1987, pp. 33

374. A. Phillip Randolph Institute, Biographical Notes on A. Phillip Randolph, 1889—1979, http://www.aprihq.org/

375. In Search of A. Phillip Randolph, Juan Williams, http://www.pbs.org/weta/apr/juanwms.html

376. The Humanist, July-August, 1997

377. Brown Alumni Magazine, Volume 101, Number 2/November—December, 2000, http://www.brown.edu/Administration/Brown_Alumni_Magazine/01/11-00/features/history.html

378. Paul Robeson Centennial Celebration Web Site, http://www.mind.net/rvuuf/pages/robeson.htm

379. The Global African Community, The Life & Legacy of Joel Augustus Rogers: Chronicler of a Glorious African Past, Runoko Rashidi, 1998

380. Jacques Roumain: A Brief Biography from Nicholls, 1979, p. 160 ff.

381. Policy Review Online, Justice to George S. Schuyler, Mark Gauvreau Judge, August, 2000, http://www.policyreview.com/aug00/judge.html

382. The African American Almanac, 7th ed., Gale, 1997, http://www.galegroup.com/freresrc/blkhstry/bio/schomburga.htm

383. Who's Who In Hell, Warren Allen Smith, Barricade Books, 2000, pp. 984

384. Speaking Across America, L.M. Johnson, Reach Cinema Speakers, http://www.bobbyseale.com/bio.htm

385. Britanica.Com, http://search.britannica.com/search?query=l percentE9 opold+s percentE9dar+senghor

386. African-American Humanism: An Anthology, Norm R. Allen, Jr., ed., Prometheus, Buffalo, NY, 1991, p. 195, Tai Solarin, His Life, Ideas, and

Accomplishments, International Humanist News, http://www.iheu.org/IHN/v5-3&4/norm_r_allen_jr.htm (1995)

387. Freedom Forum.org, http://www.freedomforum.org/templates/document.asp?documentID=4828

388. New York State University Writers Institute, The Writer, 1999, Wole Soyinka,1999, http://www.albany.edu/writers-inst/soyinka.html

389. Who's Who In Hell, Warren Allen Smith, Barricade Books, 2000, pp. 1043

390. Council for Secular Humanism, African Americans For Humanism Advisory Board, http://www.secularhumanism.org/aah/advisors.html

391. Who's Who In Hell, Warren Allen Smith, Barricade Books, 2000, pp. 1084

392. Who's Who In Hell, Warren Allen Smith, Barricade Books, 2000, pp. 802

393. Modern American Poetry, Melvin B. Tolson (1898-1966), http://www.english.uiuc.edu/maps/poets/s_z/tolson/tolson.htm

394. Langston University: A History, by Zella J. Black Patterson. Norman: University of Oklahoma Press, 1979

395. Ibid

396. Ibid

397. Green Lap, Brown Embrace, Blue Body: The Ecospirituality Of Alice Walker, Pamela A. Smith, Cross Currents, April, 2000, http://www.aril.org/smith2.htm

398. The Craig Washington Debate: Does God Exist?, William Lane Craig and Corey G. Washington, 1995, http://www.infidels.org/library/modern/corey_washington/craig-washington

399. Council for Secular Humanism, African Americans For Humanism Advisory Board, http://www.secularhumanism.org/aah/advisors.html

400. International Humanist News December 1996 The Madman's Speech by Tim Madigan, Secular Humanist Bulletin, Volume 12, Number 4.

401. Voices from the Gaps, Women Writers of Color, http://voices.cla.umn.edu/authors/DorothyWest.html

402. African American Almanac, 1997, pp. 1078-1079

403. Elizabeth Cogdell-Sessoms, "A Decision Maker," http://198.87.162.139/HTMLpages/dhwilliamsMD.html

404. Unitarian, Universalist, and Unitarian Universalist Leaders, http://www.uua.org/info/photos.html, Who's Who In Hell, Warren Allen Smith, Barricade Books, 2000, pp. 1183

405. Who's Who in Hell, Warren Allen Smith, Barricade Books, 2000, pp. 1192

406. Lorraine Blackwell, Black History: Virginia Profiles, http://www.gateway-va.com/pages/bhistory/1997/wood.htm

407. Who's Who In Hell, Warren Allen Smith, Barricade Books, 2000, pp. 1200

408. American Atheist, Atheists of a Different Color, February, 1987, pp. 32

409. African American Humanism: An Anthology, edited by Norm Allen Jr., Prometheus Books, 1991, p. 158—170

410. Instant Knowledge.Com, Richard Wright, http://www.instantknowledge.com/KnowledgeNotes/Knotes/BlackBoy/BlackBoy.html

411. Minnesota Atheists, Positive Atheism in Action, http://www.mnatheists.org/pr02.htm

412. August 15, 2000 by Elena Davidson http://www.uua.org/families/1999/exploring.html

0-595-28789-1

Printed in the United States
1310700004B/51